T0384282

WHAT I
BELIEVE

WHAT I BELIEVE

HUMANIST IDEAS AND PHILOSOPHIES TO LIVE BY

EDITED BY
ANDREW COPSON

PIATKUS

PIATKUS

First published in Great Britain in 2024 by Piatkus

1 3 5 7 9 10 8 6 4 2

A CIP catalogue record for this book
is available from the British Library.

ISBN: 978-0-34943-842-9

Typeset in Caslon by M Rules
Printed and bound in Great Britain by Clays Ltd, Elcograf S.p.A.

Papers used by Piatkus are from well-managed forests
and other responsible sources.

Piatkus
An imprint of
Little, Brown Book Group
Carmelite House
50 Victoria Embankment
London EC4Y 0DZ

An Hachette UK Company
www.hachette.co.uk

www.littlebrown.co.uk

Contents

Love, respect and empathy

Freedom, equality and justice

Introduction

What I Believe takes its title from two separate essays, one by the philosopher Bertrand Russell, written in 1925, and one by the novelist E. M. Forster, written in 1938. These two humanist writer-activists set out their approach to life – their fundamental world view – in a way that was intended to be accessible to all. The concept proved popular, and publishers George Allen & Unwin emulated it in *I Believe*, a collection of essays published in 1940 that stayed in print continuously for more than twenty-five years. The nineteen contributors to *I Believe* were almost all humanists, and included Russell and Forster themselves, along with the author H. G. Wells, the scientist J. B. S. Haldane, the politician Harold Laski, the sexologist Havelock Ellis and the evolutionary biologist Julian Huxley.

In 1966, with *I Believe* out of print, George Allen & Unwin published a new volume, *What I Believe*. Unlike the original *I Believe*, the eighteen contributors included at least half a dozen Christians and a number of contributors whose views blurred the lines between a humanist and a religious world view. In his introduction to the 1966 collection, George Unwin said that the inclusion of Christians and the increased fuzziness of world views on display simply reflected the times. Compared with what he called the 'giants' of the 1940 collection and their 'forthright' humanism, he said that the humanists of 1966 were more inward-looking, while Christians had become more outward-looking. Perhaps. But his decision was also part of a general pushback in many establishment circles against the humanist view of things, and in favour of a more conservative and Christian one.

The BBC had led the way in this pushback, commissioning a series of radio broadcasts in the mid-1940s, also published as *What I Believe* in 1948, in which only three of the twelve contributors were humanists. In the eight decades since, public broadcasting has given humanists barely a dozen unmediated opportunities to directly describe their beliefs to the listening public as such, whereas it has given religious thinkers the chance to speak directly about theirs on at least a daily basis: a ratio of about three thousand to one over the years.

When I started the podcast *What I Believe*, it was inspired by the original twentieth-century humanists' expressions of their world views, and the continuing decades-long exclusion of humanists from popular opportunities like the BBC's *Thought for the Day*. Between 2020 and 2024, I interviewed more than sixty humanists in an effort to understand more about the values, convictions and opinions by which they live today.

The appeal of well-known people talking about their personal philosophies is obvious. It gives us a glimpse into the minds of people whom we already admire or have an interest in, and offers us an opportunity to know them better. Often, their ideas may be more organised than our own as a result of their work or experience, but even if not, we certainly will learn something from them – and the more self-reflective of us will have personal responses, seeing things from a different perspective, and perhaps even changing our own minds.

You don't have to agree with them to be fascinated by what they believe.

For me, the appeal of interviewing humanists in particular was twofold. First, people in the UK today are much more in tune with the humanist approach than they were in the early twentieth century. Opinion polls and surveys show that humanist beliefs are now very widespread – that this life is the only one we know we have; that science and reason can explain the universe; that morality and meaning are human creations, not divine gifts. Although many people's world views are still fuzzy, with a range of different beliefs and values, many aspects of the humanist approach have become common sense. But there are still not many opportunities for people to encounter explicitly humanist ideas, framed as such. Messages I received from listeners to the podcast often said what a refreshing experience it had been to hear views they shared explained at length, sometimes for the first time in their lives.

My second motivation was my desire to explore the diversity of humanist thought today. The original two essays of Russell and Forster nearly a century ago were different in their emphasis, but fundamentally similar. In the last twenty years of working for the humanist movement, I've been struck by the diversity of thought and opinion expressed by humanists. They have a wide range of motivations and fascinations, and I wanted to capture something of that.

The contributors who appear in this volume are all humanists, with the vast majority being members of Humanists UK, and so of course they have many ideas in common: a desire to know the world and seek out truth; a respect for both human creativity and human reason; a humanitarianism that seeks to reach across all boundaries and borders; an appreciation of human diversity, not just as the necessary consequence of human freedom (another common value), but as something beautiful and fascinating in itself. But the routes by which they arrived at their beliefs are diverse, the worlds in which they practise their professions have shaped their values and beliefs in particular ways, and they do have different priorities from each other. They differed on questions around how to understand the balance of freedom and equality, of reason and emotion, of universal ethics and moral relativism, and of personal responsibility and serendipity in the shaping of our destinies.

Three main headlines emerged for me as I reread the conversations. Some interviewees dwelled in particular on curiosity, a love of truth and knowledge; others on their fascination with and love for human beings; others on social values like justice and fairness. In every single case these concerns overlapped and were interrelated, but to give some structure to this book they form the three section headings for this collection.

Some interviewees spoke directly, laying out their thoughts as opinions. Others spoke in anecdotes that illustrated their values by example, or recounted formative experiences as stories. Some interviewees knew exactly what they believed. For others, talking about their ideas was roundabout, and their world views emerged for the listener as much from their digressions as anything else. I've kept the edited excerpts in this anthology as transcripts because of the value of reading people as they think out loud, and have edited them only as far as was necessary to make sense of spoken words on the page. The original discussions were longer than the podcasts and the edited versions in this book are even shorter again. Over fifty hours of discussion had to be filleted down to around 80,000 words – far less than half of what was originally broadcast – and so I have tried to select the parts of each conversation that were most distinctive. Particularly painful has been the fact that fewer than half of the episodes would even fit in this book at all. (But, as a result, a whole mass of fascinating material still awaits you in the podcasts, so do take a listen!)

I am enormously grateful to have had the opportunity to speak with the many humanists who gave their time to contribute to the *What I Believe* podcast. Some of them I knew well, others I was speaking with for the first time, but from all of them I gained valuable insights and reflections that have stayed with me. The humanist view of life is progressive and dynamic. All ideas, values and beliefs are open to question and revision. There is no immemorial tradition or unquestioned authority. Instead, there is a millennia-old conversation to which all are invited, and from which we all can learn. I hope this collection contributes to your own engagement in this fulfilling enterprise.

Andrew Copson
Leicestershire, February 2024

Thanks

I'm grateful to Sophie Castle for her tireless dedication in producing the original podcast and for her assiduous work on transcription (although any errors that remain are undoubtedly my own), and to Tim Monaghan for the donation of a catchy podcast jingle. I am also grateful to Alan Palmer, whose funding for the *What I Believe* project allowed this book to come together.

REASON, SCIENCE
AND TRUTH

Jim Al-Khalili on reality and storytelling

March, 2021

> Jim Al-Khalili is a professor of quantum physics and Distinguished Chair at the University of Surrey. He is a science communicator known for his popular science books, TV documentaries, and radio programmes, mostly for the BBC.

You study a bit of science that I think most people would see as mind-bendingly weird, because it's so divorced from our daily experience. How do you manage to jump out of our normal everyday way of thinking about things and into the quantum world?

I don't think I or other people who work in these more obscure theoretical areas of fundamental physics struggle to jump from one world to the other, from being buried in equations and Greek symbols and the fuzzy uncertainty of atoms to suddenly being in the real world. It's like any other job. It's something we enjoy. The nice thing about working in an area like quantum mechanics is that it really does (or should) push you to think about the meaning of reality itself. What is there? Is there an objective truth and objective reality out there that we as scientists are trying to reach? With quantum mechanics, of course, it's all that business of 'Just by the act of observing an electron, you alter its behaviour – does this mean that all possible universes exist? Are there an infinite number of mes?' That's one version of what

3

quantum mechanics tells us. So, it does really overlap with a lot of deep philosophical ideas, more so than a lot of other areas of science.

How has your work in quantum mechanics affected your view of things in normal everyday life?

Like in any area of fundamental physics, we are careful not to say, 'I believe this', 'the world is like this', but I do feel that the mathematical equations that I work with need a narrative to go along with them. How do they connect to the real world? Do they describe reality as it really is? Is there a reality out there? There's no room for metaphysics. I still think some of the work I do is spiritual in the broadest sense of the word. Spiritual in that it's uplifting. It's inspiring. I find it sort of magical sometimes, but it is describing a concrete, absolute truth that's out there. I may be along the wrong tracks; maybe quantum mechanics is wrong, and we need a better theory. But what we're trying to do is approximate the best we can to a physical reality that is out there. Then I think, in everyday life, I imagine that there is a physical reality out there. I have very little time for the more sort of postmodern ideas of relative truths – 'My truth is as good as yours', that sort of thing. Well, no – there's an absolute truth out there. There are other ways of trying to get to it, but for me, science and the scientific method are the most reliable ways of getting to that truth that's there.

Some of the wannabe relativists that you're rejecting there, they actually love quantum anything, and they'll use the word 'quantum' liberally.

Part of my view is a reaction against that, because quantum has been used and abused. It's partly the fault of physicists back in the sixties

4

and seventies, who were all high on LSD, and they'd think, *Quantum mechanics is quantum, man. Suddenly, telepathy and paranormal activity can all be explained. Quantum is weird, those things are weird, therefore it must be connected.* I think now we're sort of backtracking and being much more hard-nosed about it. No! That isn't what quantum mechanics is about. So my view is a reaction against any vagueness.

I did say something the other day about objectivity. I was posting about something that Richard Dawkins said, that the truths of science have been and always will be true. I tweeted that I don't always agree with him, but on this, I do. Of course, there were loads of others who came forward to say science is a social construct. Well, I don't do the usual thing that others do on Twitter, which is take a side and stick with it 100 per cent. You know what I'm like. I'm conciliatory. But I think when Richard talks about science, he means scientific knowledge or absolute truths about reality that we can reach by science. That is not a social construct. The scientific method, of course, *is* a social construct, because we've invented it. We human beings have invented it. It could have been constructed by aliens as well. AI could come up with a scientific method. But at the moment, it's constructed by humans. So I said, 'So everyone's right.' You know? Hurrah. There wasn't much of a response after that. So there were probably people who may have been spoiling for an argument, which didn't work out well, and left [them] a little deflated . . .

You've described science as a human enterprise, as something you admire. Is that important to you: the idea of science as a human quest?

It is. If there are aliens living on some distant planets, in a distant galaxy, they will also be wanting to discover truths about the universe and the laws of physics, which will be no different for them than for us. They may well hit upon exactly the sorts of approaches we've adopted in science, what we call the scientific method. But, as it stands, the scientific method is something that we humans have developed, and I think it's so useful to us that we really should be extending it to other walks of life as well. The ideas of valuing evidence and data over opinion; examining your own biases, which are quite a natural part of human nature; being prepared to admit when you're wrong; changing your mind in the light of new evidence – these are the sort of things that we find so difficult in everyday life, yet scientists are trained to do them. And I think we should try and get more people using the scientific method, not to do science, but simply to cope with all the information that we have bombarding us every day of our lives at the moment.

Do you believe that for our private lives, to make us better people and better able to cope with things, or for public life?

I think both are important. Certainly, as individuals, we should be examining our own biases, trying to be as objective as possible in the views that we have, but it certainly applies to public life as well. To some extent, since the pandemic, we're now seeing politicians saying, 'Well, we're not sure. Given the evidence that we have, we think this is the approach we should take.' Brilliant. If only our politicians had said that before – because in the past, certainly in public life and in politics, expressing uncertainty or doubts was a weakness. In science, it's the opposite. It's a strength. It is showing that you are open-minded towards new evidence that would mean you have to alter your view. I think we are seeing that because of the heavy reliance by society and politicians on the evidence related to the pandemic. We're understanding how science works and how that has to then be reflected in government policy.

You think science is a universal pursuit, something that can be conducted across cultures, and you've famously written about science in the Arab Golden Age. What drew you to that time and place?

Well, part of it is my own heritage. I was born in Baghdad. I grew up in Iraq, although it was a very sort of Western English home I grew up in, with my mother being English. I went to school there until I was sixteen. There were a lot of scientific achievements during the medieval period, when the Islamic Empire was new, and certainly during particular very powerful and stable dynasties, when there was a lot of scholarship and knowledge. These are stories that I learned about at school. I think even there, in the Islamic world, and the Arab world in particular, they aren't known well enough. The narrative about how science developed really is that the ancient Greeks were very clever, then nothing happened, because Europe went to sleep for a thousand years, and then suddenly you have Vesalius and Copernicus and Galileo, and you get the Renaissance and the Scientific Revolution. So part of my motivation was to say that science is a continuum, advancing our knowledge about how the world works. Yes, it might get repeated, or we might go down cul-de-sacs and then come back and realise that we were wrong, but by and large it progresses, as we can learn from the experiences of past empires and scholars.

That period, the Golden Age of what was called Arabic science because all the texts were written in Arabic language, was rich with wonderful discoveries and wonderful scholarship across all areas of science. I just felt that it was a story that wasn't told.

So part of it was that it's just a fascinating story. Part of my motivation was also to shout it back at the Islamic world and say, 'Here are your own ancestors, who were rational, who were logical thinkers, who knew that if you wanted to learn how the world works, you didn't just get it from a holy book, you went off and did experiments and you talked and understood what other people were thinking about. They were doing real science back then.' To some extent, that had been – and still is, sadly – forgotten in many parts of this world. It was just a reminder that if you can take pride in your own ancestors' achievements from a thousand years ago, how can you possibly start moving backwards? Why not advance from there?

And I enjoyed the storytelling. Unlike a lot of scientists, I was always interested in the history of how scientific ideas developed and what would lead someone to come up with a new concept or theory about the world, or devise a new experiment, or make an observation that tells them something different. How did it come to them? And within the time that they lived? How was that possible? I find those stories bring the scientific concepts alive. I know a lot of scientists who are interested in quantum mechanics but not in Erwin Schrödinger. They might ask 'Why? Why care about the personality or the person who invented it?' But I want to find out about what sort of person Erwin Schrödinger was. What was his personality like? For me, it's the people who are developing our scientific knowledge that bring that knowledge alive.

I find them inspiring. I remember, as an undergraduate student studying physics, for a year I just basically gobbled up all the biographies of the great physicists of the early twentieth century. Niels Bohr, Werner Heisenberg, Paul Dirac: all the people that, as a physicist, I knew very well, but I knew them through their contributions to science. Seeing an equation named after a famous scientist didn't really do much for me. It's interesting in terms of solving a mathematical puzzle. But to find out about the person and what they were thinking? That just got me excited. Not that I wanted to do what they were doing, but somehow I think there is something inspirational about these heroes. There's no difference – sporting heroes, movie stars, pop stars. It's just people you aspire to become, people you admire.

You're a professor of public engagement in science. So what are the extra values on top of the values of being a scientist that are important for public engagement and communication?

I think I'm coming around to the idea that trying to explain the scientific method is as important, if not more important, than explaining the science itself. Yes, it's good to have a scientifically literate society to some extent, so that we know the difference between vaccines and antibiotics, and so that we know that vaccines can't carry chips, or that 5G networks can't spread coronavirus. People need to have some level of understanding of science, even if they don't know what happens if you fall into a black hole. But more importantly, people need to understand how science works, and why evidence about the world – scientific evidence, in particular – can be believed and can be trusted. It's not just, 'This scientist is an expert in vaccines, and they're telling me I should have the vaccine, therefore I should, because they've spent years studying it.' It's 'What is the clinical trial? Why should we trust clinical trials?' My father had the Covid vaccine. He said, 'I'm eighty-nine. I'm having the jab first. I'm the guinea pig.' And I said, 'No, there were forty thousand people who were guinea pigs; that's called clinical trials. We now know it works!'

So at one level, science communication is about inspiring

people and getting science embedded into popular culture, talking about scientific ideas, because it's fun, because it's inspiring in the same way as talking about music and politics and art and sports. That's one level. The other is that there is that method, the way we *do* science, the way we learn about the world. I think there's a valuable lesson in the reproducibility of results, the gathering of reliable evidence, putting uncertainty on what you know, being prepared to change your mind, falsifiability, the Karl Popper ideas. All those ideas that we use to do science, we could actually apply much more generally in everyday life to have a much more rational view of the world.

***

I don't tend to like confrontation. It's not that I shy away from it because I'm afraid I'm going to lose an argument, in a cowardly sort of way. It just doesn't appeal to me. The polarisation of views is just never something that I bought into. Even growing up as a kid, I was always quite happy to listen to the other side. It wasn't about point-scoring or winning an argument for me. It was about trying to find out what was right, where the truth was. If the other side had a truth, then so be it. Maybe I just have less cognitive dissonance than average. I don't know. Maybe it's partly my scientific training, being able to admit that, actually, you've got a point, I've changed my mind. I back down. I don't have a problem doing that. I know a lot of people, if painted into a corner, will just come out fighting regardless, and they'll never back down. I just find that senseless.

Susan Blackmore on being wrong and taking drugs

August, 2022

> Susan Blackmore is a psychologist, lecturer, and writer researching consciousness, memes, and anomalous experiences, and Visiting Professor at the University of Plymouth. She is best known for her popular science book *The Meme Machine* and textbook *Consciousness: An Introduction*.

I can tell you lots of things I don't believe, rather than being able to tell you what I *do* believe. That's because I've been finding things that don't work, and moving on into the great wide world of more things that might work if this one doesn't.

Let's start with that, then. If that's your approach, where do you think that came from? Is that scientific training?

Well, it's partly that, but mostly from very early on, as you know, when I had a dramatic out-of-body experience. I was convinced that this was proof of life after death, souls and spirits, telepathy and clairvoyance – you name it – all paranormal phenomena. It took me several years of research and a PhD in parapsychology to find that, as far as I can tell, there's no such thing. Each time I found that something doesn't work ... it was, 'Oh, maybe this next idea works ... well, what's around the next corner? Maybe if clairvoyance doesn't work, maybe telepathy does ... if telepathy doesn't work, maybe tarot cards work' – you know, on and on and on, until I got to the point of thinking, *Well, maybe none of these is true.* So that was a very powerful lesson in the scientific method. I wouldn't have called it that then. But it was a lesson in having a theory that you really, really care about and invest yourself in: 'I'm the one who believes in psychic phenomena, and I'm going to prove to the world, to all those close-minded scientists who don't believe in it, that they're wrong.' And then *I was* wrong. That was tough. It's fine, and it's fantastic to look back on and think, *that was really good training.* To take your theories, to work as hard as you can to see if they're right, and then, when they're wrong, to realise, 'Oh, actually, the world opens up to all the more possibilities.' And so you move on. And in my case, you find out you're wrong, lots of times, but you kind of get used to it.

That's a very positive way of looking at it: being happy to find out you're wrong, and then moving on to other things.

Well, I'd much rather be right!

I was going to ask, did you want to be right? Presumably, you wanted to be right?

I very, very, very, very, very, very much wanted it to be right, yes.

Why was that? Why do you think you had so much invested in wanting it to be right?

Now, of all the millions of questions people ask again and again, nobody's asked me that one. Very interesting. I would say there were two reasons why I so desperately wanted to be right. One was the out-of-body experience, and some other experiences of 'oneness', and expansion into the universe - these seemed more real than real. And we have reasons now to understand *why* they seem more real than real, because of how the brain manages reality discrimination, and because during those experiences there's nothing else, and you're totally invested in this thing. But the fact that it feels and looks real in every way, it seems more real than ordinary life – that was one driving emotional reason. And the other reason for wanting to be right was – I kind of demonstrated it a moment ago – 'I'm going to prove to all those scientists that they're wrong. I'm going to be right about this amazing theory I've got about memory and ESP [extra sensory perception] being out in the Akashic record.' And blah, blah, blah, you know: my crazy theory. And, 'I'll show them.'

Was it an important part of your identity during the time you were doing it?

Yes. Not only that, but I dressed in the hippy gear, and I ran the Oxford University Society for Psychical Research. And we invited mediums and spiritualists, and psychical researchers, and ghostbusters, and other people to come and give us talks and demonstrations. And we did Ouija boards, and we went looking for haunted houses around the colleges. That's who I was.

What has your time researching these things left you with in terms of beliefs about the people who do believe in them?

There's no one answer to that. There are a few really awful frauds. I came across very, very few, but those were horrible – exploiting people for their own ends. Then there are the soppy, soft people, for whom you can tell that it's so important to their life to believe in God, or the next life, or that their wife is in heaven, and they're going to meet her again, and I don't want to argue with them. Then there are the types who 'know' they are right – for example, in the Society for Psychical Research, or in parapsychology in general. Some of them are so committed to their views that they don't want to listen to any alternatives, and it's really, really annoying. What upset me most though was when mediums, psychics or spiritualists would say, 'If you had an open mind, then you would believe X.' That made me so angry, because having an open mind means you're willing to change your mind! It doesn't mean you're willing to believe something crazy just because you like it. Well, it can do . . . they can be the same thing, but they often aren't. And finally, there are also – rather few, but very valuable to me – scientists who believe in the paranormal, or who do research on near-death experiences and are totally convinced that that proves life after death but are still open-minded. There are some like this who are still friends [of mine] and I can talk to them and enjoy their ideas and the differences we have . . . We can argue about it and enjoy it. That's nice.

Is that something that you value and believe in, that sort of argumentative life?

Yes. Okay. Maybe we've found something I do believe in, although I'm not sure 'belief' is quite the word, but it'll do. Yes.

Committed to?

Yes, I find myself doing it and smiling at the same time. 'What! You believe that?! Come on ... Now, what about this evidence?' Yes, I enjoy that.

A sort of joy of arguing.

It's an enjoyment, but in what sense is it a belief? It *is* a belief ... You're forcing me into finding out what I believe, as I thought you might! It is a belief that that kind of argument leads you somewhere, that you learn something from that kind of argument. You learn to firm up your own arguments, your own beliefs, your own ideas; you learn to take note of other people's and either go, 'Oh, I must think about that some more, as it might be true,' or, 'That's absolute rubbish. Now, how can I find out it's rubbish? Is it really rubbish?'
That's the way you learn. I keep going into, 'What is the point of life anyway? There's no point. So why is learning important?' And I think, well, you've got to make *something* important, because there's no ultimate importance. And you're smiling while you're doing it.

That's a brilliant description of how you know what's giving you happiness in life – you find yourself smiling while you're doing it.

Yes, yes. I get quite a lot of emails from people who are really distressed by my not believing in free will, and I've been writing to someone recently, who said, since he's watched lots of my videos and read stuff I've written about no free will, that it's made him terribly depressed. And one of the things he said is, 'You always look so happy talking about this.' So I tried to explain how it *does* make me happy to think there's no free will. And it is possible to live a happy, moral, kind life – or one attempting to be kind and moral – without having to base that in free will. So I hope I'm managing to explain it to him.

***

I want to come on to talk a little bit about drugs and their legalisation, because that's one of the many causes you're associated with. There are two aspects there that I think it might be useful to find out what you really believe. Firstly, the use of drugs generally, because I think you think that drugs can have life–enhancing effects in various ways. And secondly, the whole policy question of legalisation of drugs and what's going on in the world, and in our own country, with this losing war on drugs. So, do you think drugs can be, for many people, an ingredient in a good life?

Oh, absolutely, they can. But I would first of all say you can't just say 'drugs'. Nicotine has precious little use, but is very addictive, and it spoils a lot of lives. Alcohol is very mixed. Heroin's fantastically effective sometimes but horribly addictive; morphine is great for painkilling and when seriously needed, but not in people who use it only to escape from the miseries or difficulties of their lives.

The drugs that I'm really interested in are cannabis and the psychedelics. I find them especially inspiring for creative and original thoughts. And I'm so pleased that, at last, there is enough willingness in government and grant-giving bodies to allow research on psychedelics such as LSD, psilocybin and DMT. This should have been going on since these drugs first emerged into the West a century ago – or certainly, since the research that was going on when LSD was discovered in 1943. There was lots of research in the fifties, and then it all had to stop with the passing of the drug laws in the late 1960s. This research was already showing some fantastic things. For example, the use of LSD or psilocybin, or any of the major hallucinogens, for end-of-life care. Many people facing the end of their life, who know they're going to die with whatever disease; they can be terrified, upset by wondering what was the point of it all, afraid of the pain. They might be feeling guilty about things they haven't sorted out beforehand, or angry about things they remember. All the usual stuff that we have as humans, can be much worse when you think you're going to die. These drugs open up your mind, and this can be horrendous, terrifying – but if you have people sitting with you who know what to do, the horrible thoughts, realisations and visions can be very useful and need not even last very long. This can mean opening up to questions like 'Who am I? What have I done? What's important to me?', and the sense of self can change dramatically . . . can be transformed. Research on this was effectively banned for decades but now there are people trained to help the terminally ill in a safe environment. Typically they have two sessions of the drug – occasionally three – and the transformation in how those people face their own death can be profound.

Take also the use of certain psychedelics for depression, or for helping release from addiction. Again, it's the insights that happen during the trip that are important, and they very often continue during the following twenty-four to forty-eight hours. In depression, those changes to the self, to how you feel about things, how you feel about your past, can be quite dramatic. Addiction can be helped, too, with one, or two, or three trips. Then you need quite a long time after each one to integrate it. But you don't need to keep on taking the drug. This is important because it means that these substances are of no use to the drug companies. Drug companies are never going to make money out of something that you can get from a mushroom in your garden … well, probably not your garden, but somewhere. Or that you can just go and buy once they're legal. They're never going to be able to make money out of drugs that you don't take very often. I was at a wonderful conference, long ago. There's a website called Erowid. It's an anagram of 'WEIRDO', because the people who run it are self-professed weirdos. But at this conference, they were doing mega online surveys. And they asked users of LSD, 'If LSD were cheap and readily available, and you could buy it any time, how often would you take it?' Now, what do you think their answer was? I mean, the average answer; obviously, they varied.

Once a month?

Not bad. It was about once or twice a year on average. You'd probably find, if you started taking it once a month, that it was a bit much. I don't know. I tend to have it every two or three years. I've actually had long gaps, and then I might have it two or three times in a year, and then another long gap. But again, it's not something that most people want to do very often, because the changes take a long time to integrate with your life, and a trip can be quite an undertaking as well.

That's your position, then: that it's like learning a new thing, or taking a new idea, you take time then to integrate the experience into yourself?

Yes, that's true when you take psychedelics with that sort of attitude. Alternatively, you can just party with drugs and people. I've never been to a party drinking alcohol, smoking dope and taking LSD all at the same time. I wouldn't; I think it would be a waste of all three of them. So I don't know very much about what that's like. But yes, as far as these drugs are concerned, we can use them well in our lives. We can use them rather than abuse them. And we need to learn more, which is why I am so glad about that. At last, the research is going on.

Then, about legalisation. Well, the whole war on drugs is an utter disaster – always has been, right from the start. I don't blame them for not realising at the beginning, but I certainly blame them for not realising after five years, or ten years or twenty years, that if you go on, what you're basically doing by making drugs illegal is handing the power of very powerful substances over to criminals who have no interest whatsoever in what happens to the people who take them. They don't care if they contaminate them with poisons of various kinds; they don't care if they keep changing the dose, the strength of it, so that people take overdoses and die because of it. Of course they don't care. We would have more control if it was all legal. We're going to get there. As a country, we should be able to look at different methods used around the world. We should be having, in Parliament, serious debates about this! Which way should we go with it?

I have noticed that in Parliament, a lot of the prominent parliamentarians who are advocating drug-law reform have often been members of the humanist group. Maybe there's a tendency here.

I think there should be, don't you? I would think, in my idea of what a humanist is, you are compassionate about other people, you care about what happens to them and what their lives are like. Now, if you look with that attitude towards the war on drugs, you see ordinary people using drugs sensibly who shouldn't be in prison: you see the kids who get sucked into county lines and have their teenage years utterly ruined; you see violent criminals making money out of other people's suffering. These are the consequences. If you cared about people's lives, you'd make the drugs legal, controlled, and taxed. You'd work out ways to make it hard to abuse those drugs, you'd share ways of learning to use them well, and you'd help people who did get into trouble with them. And you wouldn't have the criminals making all this money and exploiting people. So I think it's quite understandable that the humanist view coheres so well with an attitude towards drugs that says, 'Let's make a way in which drugs can be positive in society, not the opposite.'

Richard Wiseman on understanding ourselves

April, 2020

> Richard Wiseman is a psychologist, author and magician known for his work on the psychology of luck, perception and illusion. He holds Britain's only Professorship in the Public Understanding of Psychology at the University of Hertfordshire.

I was invited to be a speaker at a sales conference, and somebody won an award for being best salesperson of the year. I chatted to them and I said, 'What's the secret of selling?', and they said, 'Find something that everybody wants to buy.' And I realised that nobody wants to buy scepticism. It's fun to believe in ghosts, or it's nice to think that a psychic can tell you all about your future, or it's comforting to go to a medium who gives you proof of the afterlife. And there I was, telling people that none of these things were true. And so, that's when I started to look at the psychology of luck and how you can lead a luckier life. It was straight psychology and science, but you're selling it in a much more positive way. And so, I spent a few years doing experiments into luck and change and happiness, and then started writing books about that.

I think we'll come back to that, because that is certainly something that you've written and spoken about a lot, and I think it might tell us something about your view on things more widely, but just to stay for a moment with the sceptical period in your life – what did you come to believe, then, about why people believed in the paranormal? You seem to be saying that it basically boiled down to, you think that people believe in it because it makes them feel good.

There are various ideas about why people believe these things. Some of the work takes a cognitive approach and basically argues that there's something wrong with their thinking. It assumes that believers are not thinking rationally, that they've got lower IQs, and so on. Over time, I drifted away from this approach, because many of the believers I knew seemed like perfectly nice people who were often very successful in other domains of their lives. I started to buy into what psychologists would call a motivational approach, which is that they *want* to believe. They want to believe in ghosts, or want to believe in psychic healing, or whatever it is – and then that motivation clouds their judgement and thinking. Actually, I think that's true of pretty much everyone. If we want to believe in something, then we don't look for disconfirming evidence. And if some evidence comes along that challenges a cherished belief, we give it a really hard time. So, it's not that we're not capable of rational thoughts. I think we all are. It's just we're not motivated to think in that way.

And did you – or do you – feel that's a shame? Or just how it is?

It's just how it is. We're all like that. I don't think anyone is rational about everything. I spent some of lockdown making pop-up books. I've done an online course on making pop-up books, and I've made lots of little pop-up cards. I've shown these to people, and they've been kind enough to tell me that they are

22

amazing. Now, there's no way I'm going to kind of cross-examine them and go, 'No. What do you *really* think?', because I want to believe that my little creations are great, and I want to believe people when they tell me they're amazing. It's just part of who we are. We like to believe certain things because they make us feel good, and then all sorts of mechanisms come into play to keep that feel-good factor going.

Let's come on to your work on luck. The biggest output of that was your book The Luck Factor. *What did you end up believing about luck by the end of your work on it?*

My argument was that, for the most part, people make their own luck. That was based on a decade of working with incredibly lucky and unlucky people. They were an amazing bunch to get into the lab because, as you might imagine, the lucky people were very optimistic about the world and very positive. The unlucky ones, not so much. The lucky people just seemed to encounter one amazing opportunity after another, while the unlucky people never got a break. And when we started to run experiments with them, we could see that a lot of that was about the way they were thinking and behaving. So, we ended up arguing that lucky people were often creating their own luck and, perhaps most importantly, that there were things you could do to increase the chances of being lucky. And that formed the basis for my first sort-of popular book, which was *The Luck Factor*.

And can people increase their chances of being lucky, or of feeling lucky?

The first thing is getting someone to *feel* lucky, because that then leads to a sort of self-fulfilling prophecy. Let's imagine that you're a fairly positive person, and you start to think about yourself as lucky. What impact does that have? Well, our emotions are contagious, so other people will feel good when they're around you, and there's a couple of very positive things that come from being socially well connected. For example, you will probably become more resilient. When bad things happen to you, your friends and family will support you. Also, more opportunities will tend to come your way, because you have more conversations with people. So, the feeling of being lucky causes people to genuinely become luckier.

I wonder how that stacks up with some of your earlier work, because I've heard you in talks – and, I think, read you as well – questioning the idea that if you think positive, better things will happen. And that what you actually need to do is to take action.

You've probably heard me say that I'm not a fan of just positive thinking. There's this movement that came out of America which is 'just be positive'. In fact, that doesn't have much impact on people. What you need to do is to know how to operationalise that thought. It's not just enough to tell someone to cheer up. That doesn't tend to work. Also, as you just sort of touched on there, I am a massive fan of taking action. Lucky people were very energised. They just did things because it felt good or it was an interesting thing to do. The unlucky people often wouldn't take action, and tended to over-analyse the situation. Then, by the time they decided to do something, their analysis was out of date. I love the phrase, 'Things happen when you're doing other things.' Just doing stuff, getting out there, linking up with others, starting projects and so on. In my experience, that tends to be the catalyst to some of the most interesting adventures that I've been on. So yes, I'm a big fan of *doing*.

Being sceptical, taking action, being positive, creating your own fortune. These are obviously values and convictions that hang together pretty well. Do you ever think about what your values are when it comes to relating to other people? Are there any? What would you say has guided your life in that area of our existence?

I suppose the old idea of treating others as you'd like to be treated is probably helpful. I think the comedian Simon Munnery has a very nice line (and I am paraphrasing here): 'Religious-wise, you can call yourself whatever you want, but if somebody throws a baby to you and you don't catch it, you're not a very nice person.' Judging on behaviour is important. We all love to say we're kind, nice people, but it really comes down to how we behave. I try and keep myself in check on that. First, I don't go around saying I'm an especially kind and nice person. But second, I try to do things which are helpful to people that I care about. And also, I think it's all right not to be a good person all the time. I'm a social psychologist, and so I don't think there really is a strong sense of person. I think we're different people in different situations. You go to a party, become more extrovert. You go to a library, and you become a bit more introvert. I think it's the same with kindness. People can be very kind in some situations and unkind in others. So, I'd jettison the idea of a single sense of kindness or niceness or whatever, and probably argue that we are different people in different situations.

And we are all like that?

We all love to think we're kind and good people. I suspect that there aren't many people in the world who would say, 'No, I'm a nasty bit of work.' I'm sure if you go into prisons and talk to people who've done some very nasty things, they'll still tell you that, deep down, they are actually very kind and good people. People are complicated. I'm complicated, and so are you. We can all be kind, and we can all be unkind. But I think that responsibility is very important. If you do a terrible thing, I think it's important to accept the responsibilities of your decisions and actions. Sometimes that sense of responsibility will have very negative consequences for how you think and feel. And I think you just have to accept that. I never really get forgiveness; I don't really understand it.

Oh, really? So what are the good consequences of not forgiving yourself?

There may not be any. I just don't like the idea of saying, 'I did this terrible thing, but I can forgive myself – so actually, it turns out, I am a good person.' Just go, 'No, I did this terrible thing, and maybe I can change and be better in the future, but I did that. That's the type of person I am under certain circumstances, and that's how it is.' I don't think it's always good to feel positive about yourself. I think that if you have done something bad, then feeling bad about yourself and just admitting that's part of your make-up, and part of all of everyone's make-up, is a more realistic and constructive approach.

I suppose sometimes, when people are talking about forgiving yourself, they're talking about actually trying to be at peace with yourself; you know, not hating yourself.

Oh, there's no reason to hate yourself.

REASON, SCIENCE AND TRUTH

But you're taking a sort of middle route. A sort of realistic approach to yourself as a moral being. You know: you've done this in this situation, you've done this in that situation. There's no point blaming or praising yourself?

You can ask yourself what you learned from it and what you are going to do in the future to not do it again, but my worry about forgiving yourself is you end up doing it again, because you end up forgiving yourself again. You take a group of people that have behaved badly, and you come up with an intervention where they think good of themselves – so they have their cake and eat it. They behave badly and feel fine about it.

You wrote a book called 59 Seconds: Think a Little, Change a Lot.

Yes, I did.

And that embodies what you've begun to talk about.

I've written lots of books, and that was the easiest one. From day one, that book knew what it was. I went to my publisher and I said, 'Look, I'm going to describe all of these techniques which you learn in less than a minute,' and I went home and I wrote it, I think in about two and a half months, and it's probably still the most popular book. Originally, it was called *60 Seconds* and then somebody said, 'If it's things you can learn in less than a minute, shouldn't it be called *59 Seconds*?' But then we could not come up with what's called a by-line, the second title. It's really weird how these things kind of come about. How the muses speak to you. But yes, *59 Seconds* is about small things you can do that make a big impact.

And it's had a big impact itself, as a book. I mean, I know a lot of people who have well-thumbed copies. So, I mean, there obviously is a taste out there for self-improvement and to read things by psychologists that will help you be better and develop personally.

Yeah. But it's important that it is all supported by evidence. For me, it's important that any project is innovative. When I did *The Luck Factor*, there was really nobody doing the science of self-help in quite that way. Instead, there were lots of practitioners saying, 'Oh, I think this works; maybe give that a go.' We were one of the first ones to run experiments. *59 Seconds* then focused on the idea of quick, evidence-based, interventions. Now, lots of writers are into that, and it's a very well-worn path. So, it's nice to do things that feel innovative. And it's lovely, because people email me saying that they have found it very helpful.

That's nice, isn't it? I can imagine that, because if I said to someone at the office that you were coming to speak at an event, I feel like I would mention that book and they would go, 'Oh, yeah! That's him.'

... 'That's the last person we want at our conference.'

(Laughter) What motivated you to write a book like that?

Well, I did *The Luck Factor*, and then I think I did *Quirkology*, which was all about sort of quirky psychology. I normally have my best ideas when I wake up, and one day I just woke up with the idea for *59* in my head. I knew that there were lots of psychology experiments that had important and quick take-home messages. I pitched it to my publisher, and we got it straight away. Again, it

28

was thinking about what people want. I can tell you about psychology experiments until the cows come home, but people may not be very interested. However, the moment I say that some of these studies yield techniques that can make you happier, more productive, have better relationships, and so on – then people are listening.

So do you want to help people become happier, more successful?

The most important thing is for people to realise that they are plastic, that they're malleable, that they can change. What saddens me about a lot of psychology is that it represents people as a brain, an unchanging brain. It suggests that you are a certain type of person, and that you don't change. That doesn't sit well with me. We all change and learn. That's what's phenomenal about our brains. We are astonishingly agile and adaptable. Then the question becomes, 'Well, *how* do I change?' And then you get into the psychology of change and growth. Both *The Luck Factor* and *59 Seconds* speak to that theme.

Rebecca Goldstein on knowledge and what matters

June, 2020

> Rebecca Goldstein is a philosopher and novelist known for her exploration of the intersection of philosophy and life through her critically acclaimed novels and non-fiction. She was awarded the National Humanities Medal by President Obama in 2014.

Your current life as a humanist philosopher, living in the world of ideas, is quite different from the world you were raised in, so I thought we might start there.

Yes, sometimes I will sort of come to in the midst of my life and think, *What? This is the life I ended up with?* There was no way that I could have anticipated this when I was growing up in a very religious Orthodox Jewish family with my life mapped out in front of me. That used to give me great despair, even as a child, thinking that this is how I was going to end up, the predictability of it. Then I was sent to an extremely stringent high school. It was the kind of place where the girls got engaged while they were still in high school, as I did, and were discouraged from going on to college. But I had already been bitten by the bug of knowledge and was already an unbeliever. I became an unbeliever at about the age of twelve or thirteen.

Was that what motivated you, the lust for knowledge?

Absolutely. This is a lust, a longing, a hunger. It's never satisfied. Never. It still drives me mad that there are whole areas of knowledge that I'm entirely ignorant of. It is the greatest joy for me to learn things and then to integrate them, to bring it all together into a maximally coherent world view, to plunge deeply, but then always to try to see which of my other beliefs have to go now, so there's maximal coherence. This has just always been a driving force for me.

So it's more than just curiosity? It's the integration of knowledge, the creation of a view?

I don't think I'm special here at all. I think that it is part of what it is to be human. I actually do believe that we are a species who are trying to get our bearings in this world, but we can live with inconsistency, and that is something, I think, that was a little bit different with me. Inconsistencies, I'm alert to them. They bother me. I can't live with them. I'll give you a story. I had a dear sister. We were four children, and I had an older sister who died relatively young, and she held all sorts of beliefs. She was very belief-friendly. Never met a belief she didn't find compatible. I would sometimes demonstrate to her the inconsistencies – and my sister, she was very smart - I would demonstrate to her the inconsistencies, and then she would say, 'Oh yeah, I see it,' and I would respond, 'Okay, so which one of these inconsistent beliefs are you going to give up?', and she would say, 'Oh, there you go with your philosophy!' It always baffled me. It's not that she couldn't see the logical situation. She saw it, but she could live with the inconsistency.

What bothers you about inconsistency?

Both things can't be true! When we're believing, what it means to believe is you believe that some proposition is true. Truth is just built right into this attitude, this propositional attitude which is belief. How can it not bother you that something you're believing can't possibly be true? How can you accept it? It's interesting. I have this grandchild. He's three years old, which is a fascinating age. Things are kind of in place, but they're still very fluid, all the conceptual schemes. I see that when he plays make-believe, he knows he's playing make-believe, but it's also kind of real to him. It's not that things are either real or not, true or not. There's this kind of middle ground where the law of non-contradiction just doesn't seem to hold. One of the things I am entertaining now is that maybe a lot of people never completely emerge from that stage where you kind of know it's a mythology, but you're still willing to entertain it as quasi-true.

Have you never done that? Some children of a certain age feel like that about Father Christmas. They know it's not true. They know it's a story. But, on the other hand, it's part of their experience, as if it's true somehow. They know it's not true, like 'if you go out your door, you'll be outside and see the garden' kind of true. Have you never had anything like that in your life?

I can't remember having it, no. My side profession is a novelist. I have an extremely vivid imagination, and there is a way, when I am creating a novel and creating characters, [that] I'm living their lives and they are decidedly not me. There's a sense of reality to it, but I'm very aware that this is not truth. But watching my little grandson, I'm thinking, *Oh, maybe this is what I've always been missing* – or just, I don't know . . .

33

Are there any beliefs from your upbringing that you've retained? That you are conscious of actually still having?

My sense of epistemic responsibility: that we have to take responsibility for our beliefs. As I was just saying, when we believe something, we believe it's true, so we really ought to be caring about that. Also, we act on our beliefs, so they are morally pregnant, our beliefs. Whenever we act, there's always both a belief, and a desire motivating us. There is such a sacredness; there's a responsibility to really keep examining your beliefs. From the very beginning, this was something that was motivating me, and it still is. More and more.

Was it a family principle to be thinking that way?

It was a very intellectual family. I take umbrage sometimes when my fellow freethinkers speak about religious people as if they're dumb, as if you just have to explain it to them, what they're not getting, and that's not the case. I know that's not the case, because I come from a family of Talmudic scholars who could think circles around me about many, many things. It's not intelligence, it's something else.

So you've carried over a certain intellectual rigour. You've just deployed it in a different direction?

I would think so. Here's another thing that I truly carried over from my family. Within Judaism, intellectual endeavour is seen as a moral activity. So that is what you do if you're a man in this tradition – you study, you sit, and learn. The word *yeshiva*, which is the word for these academies where you're studying the Talmud and such, derives from the Hebrew word for 'sit'. That's what you do, you sit. We're not a very fit people. It is seen as a moral activity, that you are coming to delve deeper and deeper, making all sorts of logical distinctions and thinking out the implications, and doing the kind of work that I do as an analytic philosopher. That is moral activity. I do believe something of that. I think to see clearly, and to come to know brings about changes in your behaviour, and if it doesn't, it's not gone deep enough. I certainly believe that about philosophy: that philosophy is supposed to expand your mind, to expand your whole being, and to ultimately, hopefully, make you a better person. I believe that, and that is something truly I got from my tradition.

I went to a very Orthodox school, an all-girls' school, and we were learning – I don't know if I ever told you the story, but anyway – we were learning Jewish history. I mostly played hooky. I hated school, but I was there one day, and we were learning Jewish history. We were learning about modernity (we were against it). It was all downhill from Babylon. Our teacher told us, 'This is a very bad boy, little girls. This is a cautionary tale, little girls. This very bad man, a Jewish man, named Spinoza, listen to the crazy stuff he believed! He felt that nature was God, and he thought that God didn't write the Five Books of Moses.' And suddenly certainly my ears pricked up and I was like, 'Who is this dude?' When I played hooky, I was going to libraries and just reading randomly, desperately trying to get myself an education. That's why I was playing hooky.

You've said there are two questions in life: what is and what matters. You've explained your view on what is – you're committed to the scientific method, to the scientific world view, a materialist in that sense. What is it that you believe matters?

There is something I do believe matters unconditionally. Each and every single human being. Unconditionally. That is the clearest thing that matters. Every human. Wherever there is human life, there is something that is deserving of extremely close attention, the kind of attention that we feel is coming to us right now. That is, to me, just the fundamental fact of morality. We can pay lip-service to it, but to actually live according to this truth is different. In Kant's categorical imperative, one of the things that he said, one of the ways that he formulated the categorical imperative, the thing that we absolutely must do, is to regard each human being never as a means to an end, to our own end, but as a kingdom of ends in his or her own right. That 'kingdom of ends' – it's almost using this religious language. I love that. It's sort of getting that sanctity into it – not the on high, not the transcendent, but into each other.

I think knowledge matters tremendously. Knowledge and ethics. These are the things that matter, that ought to lay out responsibilities for all of us. What matters to me is to add to it in some way, add to knowledge and add some value to particular people's lives. It is so hard to be human. It really is. I want to somehow do something to add some value.

How do you defend, when people ask you (as I'm sure they do, because they ask me and they ask all humanists), the proposition that every person matters in that equal way? Is it because, as you've said already, that the concern that we expect to flow in our direction, we ought also therefore to let flow outwards as well? Is that sufficient? Or are there other reasons that you give, opinions that you have, for defending that really quite, as you say, radical proposition?

Don't you think that's kind of the heart of humanism?

I do. But people ask how to defend it quite often.

One of the ways that one can defend something is that it's a thing that one must believe, in order to pursue one's own life coherently, and then it has further implications. That's a kind of defense. For example, we can't actually justify that the laws of nature are going to continue into the future. But we have to believe this, or we can't live coherently. Am I really going to say that just because gravity has always worked before and I can't justify that it will continue to work, that I should step off this cliff? We can't justify that the future will be like the past, but, obviously, to live coherently, we've got to be committed to it. Same thing with logic itself, right?

Worthiness of moral concern is something like that?

I have to believe that my life matters. I have to. Even if I'm in despair because I think I don't matter, I still therefore think my mattering matters; that's why I'm in despair.

And you're choosing to carry on.

Exactly. I'm choosing to carry on. I'm pursuing my life. That in itself is a commitment to my own mattering, my whole emotional scheme. All of it is bound up with my feeling of being committed to my life, pursuing it and therefore believing that I matter. That is as ingrained in our pursuing a coherent life as all of these things like believing in the laws of nature. It is already a moral commitment. I will be outraged if you don't recognise my mattering.

Okay, so how do I defend this? What do I say? That I'm somehow special? Sometimes people do that. 'I was born into the right race, the right gender, the right whatever. I'm so smart, or I'm so beautiful, or I'm tall, I'm short.' Some people have this way of saying, 'Yes, I'm special.' But if you're looking at it honestly, that's not why you believe it. You believe it because that's what it is to be human. Everybody believes it. Everybody has that same commitment to self. So if you're going to live coherently, you've got to realise you have no more grounds for this than anybody else. So just widen it to everybody. Those are the implications. We try very, very hard – the whole history of bias is trying very, very hard – to say, 'No, no, it's me. I'm a member of the kind that matters, others not so much.' That doesn't hold up.

So, you think that this moral concern for others follows from a genuine outworking of what are the facts?

I do believe that. The facts that, in some sense, we find in ourselves and look at ourselves, and what we have to believe about ourselves in order to pursue our lives, and then think about how that is justified. You realise it's got to be at least extended to all human beings – which is to say that they all matter, in the same way that you do. Which is not to say that only humans matter. This is a terrible mistake.

Yes. We've been saying humans, haven't we, but I know that you and I both mean suffering animals.

Exactly. Yes.

Actually, this is something we've never discussed, and I'd be interested in your point of view. I've always thought that in spite of the word humanism and what it can seem to denote to many people, actually the consequence of humanist beliefs is what helps us to expand our circle of moral concern beyond human beings and to other animals. I think it's actually quite a unique feature of what we say about morality, what it is and what it's for.

I think that's absolutely true.

Not a coincidence that Jeremy Bentham, Peter Singer, and other philosophers who have shown concern for other animals have been humanists!

I entirely agree. What you get from the Bible, from Genesis, is that we are made in the image of God, and therefore that is what makes us valuable. As a matter of fact, when people challenge me with, 'How can you say that all humans matter?', it's Genesis they bring up. But that puts a boundary between us and other sentient creatures, so that there's really no way to use that same kind of reasoning to expand beyond our species. If you rely on Genesis to justify that all humans matter you do end up with a speciesism.

Steven Pinker on science and human nature

June, 2021

Steven Pinker is a Canadian-American cognitive psychologist, linguist, and popular author known for his work
on language and the human mind. He has written 12
books, many of which advocate for reason and science.
He is a Harvard Professor.

I was a little too young for the 1960s activism, but it trickled
down from older brothers and sisters of friends. In those days,
the nature of human nature was very much in the air. Should
we be anarchists? Should we be Marxists? Should we be Ayn
Randians? Do we need money, or would people, left to their
own devices, just take what they need? Do we need police? Do
we need armies? All these ultimately boil down to questions of
what kind of species we are. In college, I explored a number of
the disciplines that approach human nature from different angles:
anthropology, sociology, philosophy and English literature. I
settled on psychology as hitting a kind of sweet spot between the
intellectual interest of the questions and tractability of setting
them. As a laboratory science, it meant that you could take at
least some types of those questions and gather data as to what
was true and what was false.

***

Do you think that as human beings we take a lot of our own capacities for granted?

Absolutely, and that's precisely because they work so well. From the inside, we open our eyes and there's an interpretable world. We hear other people talking, and we go from words to meaning effortlessly. We have no access to the machinery in the boiler room. What's actually responsible for our ability to grasp a carton without crushing it or dropping it, to recognise faces and objects, let alone driving and hiking, to putting our thoughts into words or understanding other people when they do the same – it goes on beneath the level of consciousness. It seems easy, because it is easy if you're a human being with a human mind. But when you go down into the boiler room, when you pry open the black box, I consider it to be an epiphany. One of the great scientific epiphanies. It's like when Leeuwenhoek, the first scientist who looked at a drop of pond water through a microscope, saw it teeming with microscopic things, or like visions of distant galaxies and then nebulae through telescopes. It's the same as us trying to ascertain what is going on in the human mind when we accomplish everyday feats. It's a question that you're forced to ask when you do artificial intelligence, which is duplicating it, or cognitive psychology, kind of reverse-engineering it. You become impressed by how much complexity there is to our ordinary mental processes.

Do you think that is something that's widely realised?

Not widely enough. You began the conversation by asking what drew me into cognitive psychology and, of course, I've gone well beyond studying people visualising three-dimensional shapes in the lab or writing down baby talk and looking for syntactic errors. That launched me into asking bigger questions about how the mind works. Historical trends in violence, human progress, which in turn brought me very closely into the humanist movement. I think that the consciousness-raising of asking what makes us tick – not just what it feels like if you are a human, because most of it is concealed from you; everything seems easy and natural when you yourself are a human doing it – but that kind of species-wide self-consciousness. What is human nature? What are the bugs in the system, as impressive as it is? What are the patterns that we naturally fall into? Perhaps we would do better by sitting back reflecting, looking back on ourselves. That, I think, is a source of enlightenment and empowerment. I like to quote Chekhov: 'Man will become better when you show him what he is like.'

Do you still think that psychology is the way to answer these big questions about human beings?

Not just psychology, because academic disciplines are really there for the convenience of deans and vice chancellors, because they can't put everyone into one building. They kind of divide it up, but the landscape of knowledge is continuous.

I've always drawn eclectically from my base in experimental cognitive psychology, but, depending on the thing that I'm studying, I'll draw in whatever information is relevant. In the case of language, most obviously, the field of linguistics is highly relevant, but also the field of artificial intelligence, natural language processing, the philosophy of language, the neurobiology of language, the genetics of language. In the case of vision, the history of the depiction of three-dimensional space in art was relevant. Why did it take so long to invent perspective, if we see in perspective? How do fiction and literature draw on our ability to visualise things in the mind's eye? Then, in the case of other domains of psychology that I blundered into later in my career, like violence, the neurobiology of violence is relevant. Because some of our circuits go way back in evolutionary history, and we share them with other mammals, but then there's kind of the software, the psychology of violence. What is the person thinking when he thinks it's a good idea to harm someone else? What's going through his mind? How can that be inhibited? What are the mechanisms of self-control? What is the psychology of empathy? Those are all from social psychology and effective psychology.

Then, of course, history is relevant. I began my book, *The Better Angels of Our Nature: Why Violence Has Declined*, with observations that, contrary to most people's understanding, violence when measured quantitatively has declined over many long stretches of history. That itself is a kind of psychological datum, even though it comes from political science and history and quantitative social science. Among other things, it tells you that we are not pinned at a constant level of violence. Whatever human nature is, it's not something that's going to make everyone commit the same amount of violence all the time. That historical fact – that violence has changed – raises psychological questions. Number one, why are we so apt to harm one another? Number two, why is it possible to inhibit whatever that tendency is? So I had in that book two chapters on psychology and neuroscience: one of them called 'Inner Demons', namely, the different motives for violence; the other called 'Better Angels', what are the ways in which people have inhibited those drives?

One very important idea for a humanist approach to life – and you touched on it there, in relation to that particular book – has been the idea that progress is not only possible, but it has been made and is being made. How did that come to be such an important article of belief with you?

The questions of human nature and how it manifests over different periods of history drew me deeply into humanist questions. One of them is, as you say, 'Is there hope for progress, or are we doomed to the same amount of violence and ugly competition?' And always, 'What is the scope for improvement?' Of course, we wouldn't need a humanist movement if things weren't changeable. We would just all be observers of the human condition, and sit back and deplore it and write plays about it and spout aphorisms about it.

What tells you that it's possible to make things better? Well, I suppose you could have a kind of an optimistic temperament, you could see the glass as half full, but that's not very reassuring. Much better is the evidence of what we've done in the past – and if we did [it] in the past, then why can't we do some more? It very much energises and motivates humanism as a progressive aspirational movement, as a worthy cause for all of us. It also made me realise that whether or not we call it humanism, we're embracing humanism.

A very common experience for people who encounter the idea of humanism is exactly that, isn't it?

We're delighted that we were speaking prose all our lives!

I think it's a good idea to put a name on it. It's a name for certain strands of historical development and thought since the

Enlightenment: that the ultimate moral purpose is to enhance human wellbeing, human flourishing, life, health, education, freedom, safety. That's almost what progress consists of. If I'm challenged to say what progress is, the answer that I give is really a humanist answer. It's not bringing the kingdom of heaven to Earth. It's not achieving the dictatorship of the proletariat. It's making humans healthy and happy and safe and well educated, leading the kind of lives they want to lead. A lot of the progress that we've seen in practice, whether or not it sports the humanist label, is a humanist development.

Our educational institutions, our hospitals, our research organisations, government, when it's humane in the best liberal democracies – whether or not they all say that they are advocating humanism, that's what they do when we treasure them, when they work. A hospital is there to make people better, and a school is there to teach kids stuff. That has been a historical shift. A lot of these institutions came out of religion and began with religious aims, which, interestingly, they tend to kind of water down over time without necessarily announcing it – a positive development. Likewise, governments which simply exerted the authority of some ruling dynasty have been, when things go well, redefined as institutions that we implement in order to maximise our wellbeing. So both progress as an aspiration is what we ought to work for, and progress, when we see it and recognise it and we say, 'Oh, that's a good thing', realising we're really appealing to humanist morality when we do so.

Religious people now, by and large, especially in Europe – and it's slightly different in North America, but in Europe they're speaking humanism all the time in ways that you sometimes think would be unrecognisable to a Christian of a few centuries ago. George Orwell said the difference between a religious person and a humanist is that the religious believer always has to be thinking about not this life but the next life, whereas the humanist thinks about this world and how it can be made better. Now, less than a hundred years later, that would be an almost unrecognisable distinction to be made between religious believers and humanists, because everyone's really moved over to the humanist side of things.

Indeed. And historical developments that haven't been called humanist really are, like the Second Vatican Council in the early 1960s, the changes within Mormonism where they retracted the idea that African Americans are descendants of Cain. That kind of thing happens in religion.

You think that there are certain historical events and tendencies that have been particularly beneficial for human progress. I think particularly of something like the human rights revolution, that you have written about, but what are some of the others in your view? What are some of the big things that have pushed us in the right direction on that level?

Well, certainly, science when deployed towards humanistic ends, the development of public health – that you've got to keep human waste away from the drinking water so you build sewers, vaccination, artificial fertiliser, antibiotics, blood groups, anaesthesia, the Green Revolution of Norman Borlaug, the agricultural revolution of the eighteenth century – all ways of coaxing more human wellbeing out of nature. Of course, science can also be applied to more and more destructive weapons, so the very act of understanding the world doesn't, by itself, lead to human betterment, but when tied to humanistic goals, either explicitly or implicitly, science is an enormous force for human betterment.

Rights, as you mentioned – the concept that individuals are morally equal by virtue of being conscious and having the ability to suffer and flourish. Despite the tendency in human nature to favour ourselves and our clans or tribes, that is indefensible once you start to rub shoulders with other clans and tribes. When you have to come to a working agreement, then you can't say what's good for *me* is good, because that's just not going to fly, so you're kind of forced into an expanding circle of rights and sympathy.

Democratic government: a concession to some of the darker sides of human nature. I'm not an anarchist because I think in a state of anarchy, as Hobbes explained, it's often misunderstood; it's not necessarily that we are all always out for blood and are immoral selfish predators. But all you need is the suspicion that some of your neighbours might be, and then you're going to start arming in self-defence. Then your neighbours are going to start worrying about what designs you might have on them, and they'll start arming in self-defence. You can have an escalation of weaponry and aggressive posture, a willingness to prove the credibility of your deterrent by lashing out against any insult or sign of weakness. If you have a disinterested third party, a government – as long as it is empowered by the people and it's constrained to serve the interests of the people – it can keep people from each other's throats because neither has to worry about the other if there is a referee. It's not just government, and I think Hobbes didn't quite get this right, but once you've solved the problem of deterring people from preying on each other, you've got the problem of government preying on the people, and so you need constraints on government. I think of liberal democracy as threading the needle between the violence of anarchy and the violence of tyranny. That is, the power of the government, just enough violence to deter people from exploiting each other without the government being able to exploit people itself. That's another engine of progress.

I think any kind of mechanism of cosmopolitanism, of ecumenicalism, of people seeing the world from other people's points of view, rubbing shoulders with them, makes it a little harder to dehumanise them or to demonise them. So a more connected world, all things being equal, will push towards progress. Then there are institutions that are dedicated to human wellbeing, like health organisations, scientific societies, a free press, think tanks, intergovernmental organisations, global institutions for cooperation. Institutions, I think, are crucial. Again, this relates to a running theme of human progress despite human nature, and it's the subject of my book *Rationality*.

We are a species that is, in so many ways, so rational. We stay alive despite a rather harsh universe that we're born into, we bring up our kids, we've populated the globe, we've seen all of this progress over the centuries, we've built a pretty respectable science. On the other hand, people can be daffy, fall for conspiracy theories and fake news, and to resolve that, I think the main answer is that we form institutions that make us collectively more rational than any of us is individually. We're all saddled with biases and prejudices and fallacies, but if we agree to the rules of a game where we can spot each other's fallacies and call them out and criticise each other, if you've got a diversity of opinion, if you've got free speech, if you've got the accountability, then people, no matter how egotistical, can spot the flaws and other people's egotistical thinking, and collectively we can arrive at more and more objective understandings of reality.

It sounds like you're rejecting both the idea that we're actually instinctive, irrational creatures that happened to have been able to develop technologies and so on, but also the idea that we are automatically rational. You're saying that we're capable of rationality, but it has to be worked for quite hard?

Precisely. I have a rather dark view of human nature. I don't think we're angels. I don't think we're basically good. (As Lily Tomlin said, I try to be cynical, but it's hard to keep up. All the more apt in the last few years.) On the other hand, we've done something right. We do mostly coexist a lot of the time, and we've reduced violent crime and we reduce war, and we've reduced racial prejudice and gender prejudice. So we're not all bad. The question is how do our better angels – as Abraham Lincoln put it in the speech that I co-opted for the title of my book – how do our better angels manage to overcome our dark side? It's very much with the help of norms and institutions that strengthen our self-control, our empathy, our application of rationality to the problem of reducing violence and prejudice. That is, we can see it as a problem to be solved. There are some people some of the time who will try to rob and rape and kill and demonise. How do we set things up so that they can't do it – or, where they do it, it's a lot less than they used to? Deploying our reason to this human-istic goal of cooperation, peace, health, happiness and so on, is the route by which we can better ourselves, and it's the answer to the question: how can such a flawed species, in principle and in practice, improve its condition?

You're asking both how it has happened historically, as a fact, and also how it can therefore be employed further in that sort of collective rationality?

Precisely. And it is hard work, as you mentioned. I think there's a kind of constant tendency to backslide, and we see that in threats to democracy, threats to human rights, threats to scientific understanding, just because it doesn't come naturally. We don't think scientifically, we think magically. We don't think naturally humanistically, we think tribally, and we do have to be reminded that it actually is better to resist those temptations to fall back into tribalism and magical thinking, authoritarianism, and realise liberal democracy takes work, the scientific outlook takes work – but it's well worth it.

Helen Czerski on all being in the same canoe

January, 2021

> Helen Czerski is a physicist and oceanographer at University College London with a particular interest in the physics of the everyday world and the oceans. She is also a broadcaster, mostly for the BBC, and the author of three books and a regular science column.

I was always interested in the real world, but the thing that, I guess, made me different from some physicists is that I was actually out in the real world quite a lot more. There are definitely people that go into physics because it lets them sit in an office and look at equations and they can hide. I was not that person. I was out and about. I thought about doing geology, because I wanted to understand the Earth, but there was never enough physics in it. I wanted to understand at a more fundamental level, but I eventually came back around. I did different types of physics, and ended up studying bubbles. I now work at sea and I go out into the outdoors and I study the physics of the outdoors, which is perfect. I like that.

My bit of philosophy that's interesting, I think, has only come along in relatively recent years, and it's because I learned to paddle outrigger canoes. My academic research topic is breaking waves and bubbles, on the ocean. I also do a lot of different sports. And I came across these people paddling Hawaiian canoes in

London on the Thames and I thought, *Well, they are mad, they're bonkers, and therefore I will be friends with them, because they are the right kind of interesting.* You know that anyone who paddles a Hawaiian canoe in the centre of London, that's an interesting person. And I was right. So I learned to paddle these canoes, and it was a sport and it was interesting, but it also comes along with a philosophy. I didn't really think about this at the time. I noticed that they talked a lot about friendship, that they talked a lot about a smooth canoe as a happy canoe, statements like that. It was only some years later when bits of this came out and I started to find the story of the canoe. It kind of made these two parts of my life join up around the back.

The Hawaiians and the Polynesians were fabulous navigators. They crossed oceans in these small boats, they navigated without modern instruments – this is five hundred to a thousand years ago. An incredible technical achievement without having modern technology. They live on small islands in the middle of a great big ocean. What is interesting about that is, if you're in a small canoe and you have to get somewhere, then it is not enough to be technically very good in the canoe. Yes, you have to put your blade in the water in the right way, and you have to be able to read the waves; you have to be able to do these technical things. But they realised that the human side – the team work – is just as important as the technical stuff. So I was finding out about this combination of approaches, that they're reading the waves, doing this thing that I do in my academic life, but they see it differently. They see the waves differently because it's observational. They don't write it down with equations, but they certainly spot patterns that scientists wouldn't. And then there's this pragmatism, which is that, yes, you have to be very good technically in the canoe, but if you are a mean git, your canoe is not going to go anywhere, because everyone else in the canoe is going to be grumpy and is going to hate you. All this other nonsense is going to happen and you're not going to go anywhere.

What's interesting about the canoe is it's such a good analogy, and that's how they use it. This isn't me putting stuff on to them. They are very explicit about this, and it comes from two things. They have this phrase, 'A canoe is an island, and an island is a canoe.' You can imagine that if you're on a tiny island in the middle of the Pacific, surrounded by potentially dangerous ocean that can help you get somewhere if you want to, and you're with a small number of people, and you've got whatever you've got on your island, that's very much like being in a canoe on a different scale. In both cases, you've got a small number of people, you're in the middle of a great big ocean. You've got to get on with things using both technical skills and human culture. To my mind, as a scientist, Earth is a canoe. It's the best analogy ever.

In Polynesian culture, the canoe is the way they talk about how to live on land. Once you see it, it's underneath everything. The way they talk about how to welcome people into the group, and how to treat people, and how to encourage people to behave well – and what to do when they don't – it's entirely driven by practical knowledge of the canoe, because it's the same problem. You're vulnerable. There's only a small number of you. It's not that the Hawaiians and the Polynesians haven't fought great wars in the past, but they tend not to because you haven't got loads of territory, you haven't got very much, you've got to understand very explicitly that being a nice person is just as important as any technical survival skill you might have.

I go to sea on research ships, and you see the same thing on oceanographic vessels. Oceanographers are nice people in general, because if you're not nice, you don't get asked back. It's one of the things that makes studying my science fun, because the people are brilliant. They're good team workers because they want to get things done. They're very good technically. So I talk a lot about canoes these days. It's not a religious thing. It's just such an obvious and good way of thinking about the world.

You're quite interested in general in the impact of the ocean on human civilisation and human philosophy.

Yes. We are citizens of an ocean planet. We call it a blue planet, but nobody ever looks at the blue, and it's far more than just where the fish live. One of the things about the ocean that we don't talk about is that this engine drives almost everything we do. The ocean is what makes Earth habitable. It stores energy, like a battery. If energy comes in from the sun, it's stored in the ocean, and a bit later on it's released somewhere else, and so it evens out the energy supply from the sun. That heat drives weather; it drives the patterns that we see on land and where we can have agriculture and where we can settle. This massive blue spherical engine sits right there. We've all looked at the surface of it, probably, and we never think about what's underneath. What's underneath is the engine that's driving Planet Earth.

I see us almost as little insects kind of carried about on the surface. There's a current going. Like sometimes you see a duck on the river and it's just carried off down the way; sometimes they stop swimming for a bit and it's very funny – they go whoosh, and you know, they're off. Humans are a bit like that, except humans assume that they're doing all the hard work. They took a current, but they didn't necessarily think to ask why the current is there. The current is there because there's an engine underneath it that means that, specifically in that place, the current is going this way. We take advantage of the currents of where the fish are, the things that the ocean brings to the surface, and yet we don't ask the question 'Why is it here and not over there?' Fish are not evenly distributed throughout the ocean. The ocean has its deserts and its rainforests, just like we do on land, except they're a bit more mobile. But there are 3D patterns written into the large-scale structure of the ocean, and we're just moving about on the surface of something much more intricate than we appreciate.

So the thing that I feel is missing from the general concept of us as citizens of an ocean planet is that we're just riding on top of the ocean; we're getting carried along by it and we don't see the engine underneath. There's something big missing in our philosophy.

What is missing? If we accept that what you've said is a fact, a truth about us on the planet, what are the implications?

The first thing is, obviously, how you see your own agency. Are you the all-powerful one that makes all these decisions? Or are you part of an Earth engine, which has been doing its own thing just fine for a few billion years, thank you very much? If you understand this, I think you have to understand you're part of the system, not separate from it and not sitting at the top of it. People are always saying science is always taking humans away from being the most important thing. We had Ptolemy and Copernicus, evolution, and Darwin, each one coming along and saying a version of, 'Oh, we humans aren't that special.' In a way, it's another one of those things. There's this massive, great big ocean. That's what determines how Earth works. We live in its shadow.

So first of all, I think it makes you see your role in the world differently. There are two big rules that our planet has. The first is that energy flows through. The ocean is its biggest reservoir as it flows around. That's where energy is stored on Earth on its way through. The second rule is that stuff goes round and round. The ocean is a massive recycling system, just like the land is. So the way that we design our society needs to fit in with this. We need a system where energy flows through, and stuff goes round and round. Of course, we know we're not very good at that yet, but if you have that bigger concept of how it works, actually, them's the rules and we're stuck with them. Energy flows through. Stuff goes round and round. So then that says to you, when we do something with some stuff, we have to bear in mind that it's been somewhere before and it's going somewhere else afterwards. Basically, we're all made out of poo. That's what I'm saying.

Humanists UK should put it on a T-shirt, maybe.

Yeah, because poo is incredible. It's the best thing, right? I'm using 'poo' in the general sense, meaning everything that has been something else before – waste from another process. But it's *not* waste, because it's raw material for the next process. That changes how you think about the way we live. You don't buy copper and some copper just appears like a rabbit out of a hat [. . .] you borrow copper, and you're gonna give it back. You borrow copper from the global sort of pantry, and it's going to go back and it's got to be turned into something else afterwards. So really, you're not ever taking virgin copper. You're always taking copper that perhaps was in chlorophyll before, or perhaps was in something else, and you're reusing it. I think this thing about the ocean is really helpful, because it shows our place and it shows how we can be better at being us. It shows how we don't need to dominate, we can fit in. The system already has very good rules. We don't have to invent the rules of how to live on planet

Earth; the rest of the planet knows exactly what they are, without anthropomorphising too much. We've already been shown what works, we just have to help ourselves fit in with what works. The advantage that we have is that we have human culture and history and science and all these interesting things, so we bring that to the table. But it doesn't mean we're going to change the rules of the planet. So I think this thing with the oceans is good for fitting in with all of that.

You describe how human beings are part of this system, the implication being that we should feel at home on the Earth, but also part of a bigger complex. Then you touch on something that makes us quite different – our ability to understand that system and to be scientists. Do those beliefs disrupt each other? Or do they integrate?

To come back to the Hawaiians, they're not anti-science, because they understand there are two different ways. One is how you see the world and determines how you behave. The other is the tool that helps you do things in the world. Of course, that also feeds into your understanding of the world, but the two are not a threat to each other.

I have the enormous privilege of being a trustee of Royal Museums Greenwich, which is the National Maritime Museum, the Royal Observatory, the Cutty Sark and the Queen's House, all these amazing sites where history and culture have woven together. The brilliant thing about those museums is that you can see that the things that changed our knowledge – our knowledge of longitude, for example – were the same things that changed the concept of art, and they were the same things that influenced social history. These concepts, they're not isolated. The brilliance of being a human is the culture, it's the variety. Separate subjects, fine, you have to study them like that a little bit just to stay sane, but they're different perspectives on the same thing.

But we do have a responsibility, I think, that comes with this enormous collective human achievement, and there's far more joy in seeing it as a responsibility than a rod for your back. Either you say, 'You have to behave because you've only got so many resources, so stay in your box and be good,' or you say, 'This is brilliant, what can we do with it?' What humans are best at is being inventive, and the thing that spurs invention is actually constraint. If you put an engineer in the middle of an open field with a massive workshop and say, 'You can do anything you like,' they won't do anything. If you say to them, 'We've got two weeks. We've got a specific problem. You've only got half of what you want; make that work,' that's where the real inventiveness gets going. So, actually, I see it as a spur, the limited resources and the limited energy flow. That is the thing that brings out the best in us. I find that an enormously positive thought.

Tim Minchin on being sceptical and giving up polemic

April, 2020

Tim Minchin is a composer-lyricist, actor, comedian, pianist-singer-songwriter, screenwriter, public speaker, poet, children's author and critical-thinking nerd. He has an AM (Order of Australia) and a few honorary doctorates.

The first thing I heard of yours was your poem 'Storm'. That lays out a pretty sceptical basis for a world view. Does it embody your own views?

I think so. At the time that I wrote 'Storm', I had been playing around the edges of trying to outline in my material that world view. Obviously, the place where it's easiest to play if you're trying to do slightly confronting comedy is religion. I wanted to do something that talked more about the inexactness of many world views, not just in the language of religion, but in the language of general spirituality – anti-science, anti-medicine, the kind of thing that I grew up with studying arts and studying music and being surrounded by various types of hippies, where people would wear as a badge of honour their rejection of boring old data, and an embracing of some grand, bigger-than-me thing. And they put all these lofty words to it. The more inexact the language was, the more spiritually elevated they would feel. I wanted to wade into that a bit. So 'Storm' starts with small, seemingly unimportant claims about homoeopathy and stuff. The protagonist, my guy who's an irascible, pompous twat – it's based on the sort of person I would be if I was less filtered, if I was less worried about keeping the dinner party going – it gets more and more under his skin. She, Storm, expands outwards from her small claims to bigger claims about knowledge, and he, too, expands outwards to bigger appeals. His appeal that he ends up on is, 'Isn't this enough justice? This world.' It had a bit of an impact, that poem, and all these years later, there's nothing in it that I would take back. I might just say, I don't have the energy to be so strident any more.

I keep fearing my material will date but, in fact, the things you and I were complaining about over beers in 2009 have, eleven years later, come home to roost. The criticism people like me would get back then, about something like 'Storm' – and I was sensitive to this criticism, because I wondered if they were right, with both my dismantling of soft religious ideas like prayer and my satire of soft spiritual ideas like homoeopathy – might be, 'Man, chill out, bro. People are allowed to just believe stuff. You don't have to throw data at their faces.' There's a criticism there to be listened to at times, and another discussion that maybe we'll have about what happens if you go hard at soft beliefs, and [there's] the backfire effect that makes people double down on their beliefs and get harder. But that's a different conversation.

I look back now and think that what we were noticing, what people have been noticing, is something that has got much more problematic post-social media, post-algorithmic editing and filter bubbles. This post-truth world, the world we live in, it's in part because of entry-level, gateway soft ideas that reject the basic tenets of critical thinking. I really do believe that. I think a reasonably harmless idea that you have arrived at through poor thinking and that you sustain through special pleading and through confirmation bias and because of the backfire effect, those things are your training ground for dangerous bad ideas. 'Maybe bleach will help you cure Covid,' or 'Donald Trump is an intelligent president,' [are] dangerous ideas that have been arrived at using the same techniques as the idea that the afterlife might exist.

Let's talk a little bit about the backfire effect. You mentioned Donald Trump. Isn't one of the possible explanations for his election the reaction of people who had been told that they were wrong, they were dumb, that they were stupid?

Yes, I definitely think so. I've been touring this show called *Back* for the last eighteen months, and the main rant I do in that show is a rant criticising us progressives, educated progressives ('lefties', I suppose, but I don't like to use the term 'left', because it's conflated with a bunch of other stuff) but progressive liberal intellectuals, or whatever, you know what I mean?

I know what you mean.

My main rant in my show has been that [just] screaming 'Where is your evidence?' at people who don't know what you know isn't helping. I'll shortcut to the end of my rant: we have to understand, whether we like it or not, that when the internet democratised the conversation, when it democratised the ability for people to communicate their ideas to one another, at the same time, it democratised diplomacy. The reason that we had diplomats before the conversation was democratised, the reason we spoke to people who were trained, wearing special clothes, trained to grit their teeth and speak politely and with respect to people whose ideas they loathe, the reason we had those people is because to get forward movement, you need to not be screaming at each other. So I am furious with the left and the progressives – and I include myself in the group of people who have, at times, been too vociferous in voicing their disagreement. We need to be the bigger tribe, because we are the ones who have the privilege. We are statistically more educated, and we have to do better, because I have no doubt that Trump exists because people are sick of smug assholes like me telling them how to think.

The difficulty, I suppose, is trying to frame a reaction that doesn't sound like the reaction of a smug asshole.

And I have been smug! I don't think I'm a smug person; I don't think that manifests itself in my life particularly. But, my stock in trade, my craft, was 'What if I take this idea and utterly dismantle it with words that the people who want to defend it can't even fucking keep up with?' It was preaching to the choir, and it's fine, because I know for a fact from the letters I've received that hundreds of kids have discovered humanism and atheism through my work. Young people who are trying to form their ideas, people like me give them an organisation like yours, and it gives them somewhere to go to solidify their suspicions, to put words and arguments around the things that they discover. I think ranty assholes, like me, are important, but I don't think I would like [to do] that in the second half of my career. I think in what I've been writing in the last ten years, I would like to try and be one of the people reaching across better.

So you believe in trying to be more diplomatic yourself in the future?

I do. I built a career on polemic, and now every fucker is a polemicist and I don't want to be. I want to jump out of there. Now, when I was doing it, the way I was doing pro-science, pro-sceptical, atheist polemic was unusual – or, at least, for someone with a funny piano and lots of rhymes to be doing what the New Atheists were doing in their books was unusual enough to give me a career. Now everyone is shouting, and I have largely stopped shouting. I'm trying, anyway.

Is that the spirit of the age? It's interesting that you mentioned the different situation ten years ago. It does seem like our times call for a more cooperative, collaborative, diplomatic approach. I don't know if everyone is capable of being a diplomatic envoy for their ideas.

I think nearly no one is. That's the challenge. You are! I mean you, Andrew, as well as the organisation – and yet how hard is it to make any inroads? If people can reject outright the ideas of Humanists UK, then they're definitely going to reject me or people who are more strident.

And there's a lot of bad faith as well. You can spend a lot of time engaging, but . . .

There's an assumption of intent all the time on both sides. I think that, firstly, the binary is bullshit. There are 'two sides' more than there has ever been before, but that's because the binary is generated by the myth of itself. Because we believe it's binary, it's becoming binary. I think we're as bad as each other – or, if not *exactly* as bad, close enough to as bad as each other. Because we assume nefarious intent in others. We assume that other people are deliberately bad. And, that is nearly always wrong. Mostly, people think they're doing something good, and, mostly, people are trying to progress an agenda that they think will make [others] happy. Most importantly, if your approach to the problem of trying to spread your world view is that you happily take out-of-context stuff that the other side says and dog-whistle on the basis of an out-of-context quote – which we all do on, both sides, all day, every day on social media – then you are part of the problem. And when I say 'you', I mean me, and nearly everyone I know. We must not respond to the dog whistle. I'm passionate about this, because two weeks ago I had thousands of messages of hate from fellow Australians for making the gentlest, quiet, laid-back comments about our Prime Minister's mediocrity. A bunch of news outlets put a headline on it saying I 'lashed out' and everyone just responded. I thought to myself, *These bloody right-wing fools, dogs go barking as soon as someone blows the dog whistle*, and then I sat down. I thought to myself, *Are we any better?* I looked through the internet with that filter in mind for the next week or two.

But you didn't just think that, did you? I kept an eye on some of those interactions, and I saw that, at least in one or two cases, maybe because of the contemplation you've just talked about, you took the time to respond in good faith to a number of people – and you actually got quite a good reaction, didn't you?

Yeah, so when you get a backlash, you can turn off and walk away, like I did with the Cardinal Pell song, because I knew that would be too hot to touch. But I find it very hard to turn off and walk away. I care very much that people know my intentions are good. I care very much what people think of me. I would like not to, but I do, and so when I know there are thousands of people saying 'You're just a leftie,' and mischaracterising me and my intent, I find it almost unbearable and impossible to walk away. So I spent a good few hours responding. And I think I want to die having my online footprint being free of abuse, so I am very careful these days – and have been for years – to treat politely even people who are making death threats, and I had a few really good successes in that. If you say to people, 'I read this, and I just want you to know, that's not who I am and that wasn't what I said,' [...] it can be tiresome, because people don't like being wrong, so they'll come back at you with something else, and they'll sidestep the argument, and do all that shit that we do. But it's sometimes worth it. At the very least, you put on the record your position.

So, is this what you do believe in? The opposite of this type of zero-sum, aggressive, polarised activity online – the thing that you do want to advance is this honest engagement or gentle engagement?

Absolutely gentle. I believe primarily in honesty, I think. I think we are very easily tempted to dishonesty, not as in lying, but as in sort of taking up a sword on behalf of our tribe rather than genuinely trying to illustrate our thoughts.

Most of what I'm trying to do as an artist now, apart from just make interesting art that is entertaining and makes people feel things – and, definitely, making people feel things is my main mission – is in my TV show *Upright*, which is just a story of self-forgiveness and family and perseverance and generosity: learning to give to someone else and stuff.

What values do you think it conveys?

Like everything I do, whether I like it or not, it is a very humanist text. I mean, the first episode, the very first sort of monologue, the first thing anyone says is Lucky talking about chance. The kid says, 'Everything happens for a reason,' and he does his big monologue about the cellist from Electric Light Orchestra being killed by a rolling hay bale, and just stats, and then the whole show unfolds. You don't learn until the very end what the protagonist's issue is, why he's got such a massive chip on his shoulder, and we realise that his entire life was upended by a tiny chance occurrence, which he's never – despite his sort of humanist world view – never really been able to get his head around. That is the humanist battle, that is the battle of living a materialist life: building narratives around the terrible things that happen. My friend over here, Julia Baird, has written a book called *Phosphorescence* which is about this very subject, about finding light in the darkness, and that is all I do, really. I'm trying to make work that shines a light on the question of how to live a meaningful life in a meaningless universe.

Some people who are brought up to be religious find they have to rebuild a scaffold upon which to brick in meaning. I've never had that. I don't really understand the question. When a religious person says, 'Well, why are you good?' or, 'What's the point of life?', I literally don't understand the question. I don't really get what someone means when they say, 'Well, where do you get good or bad from?' I just want to go, 'What do you mean? Are you saying you are morally bankrupt but for a book of two-thousand-year-old fables? What do you mean?'

I just don't get it. I have no idea what people mean when they say the word 'God'. I always want to start with, 'Well, let's break down some attributes. So we can at least talk about it.' I always want to say, 'Does God poo?' Let's start with 'Does God poo?' and work from there. I can't accept that 'God' always seems to be someone's word for nothing. I think I know what you mean by 'God'. And I think it's just the question mark for something. That's it. I really do have a linguistic, rhetorical block.

I guess all I'm saying is that I think I get meaning where everyone else does. It's just that the stories I tell are my own analogies and fables. I get from art what people might get from their religion – and everything else is the same, right?

I get joy from cuddles with my kids and my dog, and laughter with my friends, and a huge amount of joy from the natural world – and, conversely, a massive amount of despair at its abuse and decay and the overpopulation of our awful invasive species. But I also see myself as a machine, the inputs and outputs of which need to be carefully monitored. I am very aware that I can get a little down if I don't sleep the right amount and if I don't exercise every day and if I eat poorly. Or, if I attach great value to my relationship with my partner of twenty-seven years and acknowledge the challenge of monogamy and therefore take rewards from achieving monogamy. I am obsessed by my work as well. The fact that I'm allowed to write songs and scripts and act and play and wank along on podcasts and spend my life trying to unpack and articulate ideas is, to me, just the most incredible stroke of luck. I try and not take it for granted. I really like wine. I don't have as much sex as I used to, because I'm old.

Well, it might make a comeback.

That's right! Now my happiness is completely linked to my children. Now, when they're distressed, I'm distressed, and when they're happy, I'm happy – with very few exceptions.

Paul Sinha on family and the joy of facts

May, 2020

Paul Sinha is a comedian, broadcaster, and professional quizzer on The Chase otherwise known as 'The Sinnerman'. He is also a qualified doctor.

My parents are West Bengali immigrants. My dad was a doctor. My mum was a nurse. They met in medical school. They were part of, I wouldn't call it mass immigration, but a sizeable immigration to the United Kingdom in the fifties, sixties and seventies, of people whose primary motivation to work in Britain was to create an environment where their children could be educated to the best of the best. So, it was kind of like a future investment: that they'd make a good life being doctors and nurses, and as a result, their children would want for nothing. When I say want for nothing, I don't mean in a financial way, I mean in an educational and emotionally nourishing way, in that Britain was associated with good schools and good education. That seemed to be very much, when it comes to the generation of my dad's doctor friends, the big motivating factor. When I was a kid, I wasn't the kid that loved to play games, I was the kid that loved to read books, because my mum and dad felt that buying me books was the best way that I could make the best of my life. And so I was always, from a very early age, a quietly knowledgeable kid. I think that is the best way to describe it. That has always informed the way I think about stuff.

Is the value of education something that you've carried forward as important to you?

I consider myself incredibly fortunate that my parents always put my education first. It was the be-all and end-all; [it was] why they were working hard to earn money and bring home money, to see their children educated as best they could. So, yes, I think the pursuit of academic excellence and knowledge is a big part of my life.

And is that where the quizzing has come from? The love of knowledge?

I think that in many ways, a lot of us are prisoners of how we saw life between the ages of about eight and thirteen. I just loved a quiz. I just watched them all on telly, and I remember, at about the age of eight or nine, my mum and dad buying me a small book of general knowledge quiz facts, and it just kind of grew from there. I was the kid that my dad's friends would always know at Christmas, don't get him a toy, don't get him anything enjoyable, just get him a copy of that year's *Guinness Book of Records*. I was one of those kids – everybody knew. Everybody knew that what I liked was to read facts.

What do facts do for you?

Well, life is fairly different now because I'm a professional quizzer, and as a professional quizzer, you have to be pragmatic and realise some facts aren't remotely interesting, but they get you a point in a quiz – and there's absolutely nothing more to it than that. But there are other ways in which it's quite enriching.

The one thing that I always say is that before I went into quizzing, I had only a passing interest in art, and now I absolutely love it. In the last five or six years, I've been to all the world's major art galleries, with a greater understanding of the context of what I'm looking at from an artistic, cultural and historical perspective. I think in that sense, knowledge can only improve your life, because it increases the scope of stuff that you're actually interested in.

So, I've gone from when I started quizzing being somebody who would know facts just to get points, to [being] somebody who likes to know about the history of the world, the context in which we all find ourselves, but particularly how everything connects. In that sense, every day is a new day, an exciting day, because you know that you're going to find out something that enriches your soul.

Literally half an hour ago, I found out that Benazir Bhutto started a degree course at Harvard University at the age of sixteen because her dad, the former President of Pakistan, pulled strings with the economist J. K. Galbraith. That, for me, is more interesting than knowing what the second-highest mountain in the Urals is. That's a more interesting approach to quizzing, where what you learn is that nepotism has gone on for a lot longer than you thought. That's kind of what I mean when I say there are two types of facts. There are facts that get you a point, and there are facts that make you feel better that you know the facts.

Because they open up new vistas. When your parents were concentrating on education, was it for them a virtue to be interested in education?

Absolutely. There's a Hindu goddess called Saraswathi, and she's the goddess of learning. In my family background, she is as revered as any of the pantheon of Hindu gods and goddesses. And when I was a teenager – I think it was around every January, the festival to the Goddess Saraswathi – my parents, who are not religious especially, would make me just take a few moments to worship at the Shrine of Goddess Saraswathi, because for them, it was an important thing to do. It was more about . . . I'm looking for a word here that I can't quite bring to mind, when you're trusting in faith rather than religion . . . superstition! It was more superstition than a genuine belief in Hinduism. To me, anyway, 'Hindu' is an identity rather than a belief system. For my dad, Hinduism is his identity, but it's not his belief system. I don't think he believes there was actually an elephant god called Ganesh. I don't think he believes that people with ten arms are in control of our fates and our emotions, but I think he believes that he lives life as a Hindu and he will always be Hindu. For him, it's an identity.

Is there any way in which that identity is important to you personally?

Yes. I don't consider myself not a Hindu; I consider myself a Hindu, by identity rather than belief system, because I was brought up a Hindu and I was brought up with my parents' cultural values, which have enriched my life. I don't think I get to sit down now and say, 'Actually, that doesn't exist,' because it was a crucial part of my heritage and my growing up. I'd be doing my parents a disservice if I said that I wasn't a Hindu. What I am is a non-practising Hindu. Apart from one or two festivals every year, Hinduism doesn't affect my life in any way.

This is something we encounter in Britain, amongst humanists in Britain, more now than we did a hundred years ago – people with

REASON, SCIENCE AND TRUTH

Hindu backgrounds or Sikh backgrounds or Muslim backgrounds, where those identities are important to them ethnically, and who say what you've just said, that they've got a humanist world view, but at the same time, they've got a culture and ethnicity that they don't jettison because of that. That's quite different from humanists of Bertrand Russell or E. M. Forster's generation, the inspiration for this series, because they felt they must reject the Christian aspects of their parents or grandparents, because they were about belief, not about culture, and so they had to go. But that's not the case for you?

In 1999, we went for a family holiday to India. It was at the same time as West Bengal's biggest Hindu festival, which is a festival to the Goddess Durga. (We don't do Diwali. No one's ever quite explained to me why West Bengalis don't do Diwali, but we don't do Diwali. We do this big thing called the Durga Puja.) In Calcutta, the whole of the city [is] turned into a massive twenty-four-hour shrine to the Goddess Durga. On an aesthetic and artistic scale, it's an extraordinarily thrilling thing to see, to see these people going from shrine to shrine, having a whale of a time, enjoying themselves. We turned up to one of the shrines and my dad's sister's husband, whom I get on very well with, my dad's eldest sister's husband, turned to me and went, 'Of course, it's all nonsense.' And I just looked at him and, for the first time, I realised that not everybody taking part in these viscerally powerful religious festivals believed in the background to it; they were just doing it because it's what they do, and because it's fun. It's socially strengthening and uniting. A religious festival, well done and politely observed, is, in my opinion, a socially enriching, cultural thing.

Is that something you believe? That religion is like any other product of human culture, and, divorced from belief, at least, can have a social use?

Yes. I don't know how many humanists you hear say these words, but I am not anti-religion. What I am is anti anybody who thinks that their religious beliefs should apply to other people and how they live their lives. As far as I'm concerned, you're entitled to your own religious beliefs. You're absolutely entitled to turn to me and my husband and say, 'I wish you well, but I don't agree that you got married, because God said this and God said that.' As far as I'm concerned, they're entitled to that. What, in my opinion, they're not entitled to say is, 'The government should ban gay marriage.' That's where an arrogance has set in – when you believe that your own religious beliefs should be applied to everybody. For me, religion is your own personal choice. You're entitled to live your life by those personal choices, but the idea that other people should live their lives by *your* personal choices is, in my opinion, the most extraordinary example of hubris and arrogance you could possibly imagine.

A lot of your beliefs that seem very important to you are about this question of not compromising your personal identity, being aware of your identity, of its value and also how it's used. Is that fair to say?

If there is a belief that tends to unite the various strands and make up the humanist movement, it is a belief that, in all likelihood, we're only here once. And I don't want to waste my time on this planet and have regrets when it's my turn to shuffle off the mortal coil. This has been very much exacerbated by my diagnosis last year of Parkinson's disease. It didn't come as a shock. I knew that my body was behaving in what can only be described as unusual ways. It didn't come as a shock, but what it did was, it just switched on a button – and that button basically just said, 'Right, do what you like now. It's absolutely time to do what you like.' By 'do what you like', what I mean is, don't have any fear in expressing yourself; just be the person that you've always wanted to be, because you have no idea now when your time is going to run out.

Mortality was a spur to self-expression for you?

Absolutely. I don't really tend to hold back now when it comes to expressing opinions out of politeness. I just tend to go, 'This is my chance to say what I want to say.' I literally have no idea when my faculties are going to start to go, and I want to say as much as humanly possible before that happens, so I've been very much unleashed in the last twelve months, just doing what I want to do. I don't mean I'm going wild. There's an episode of *Beat the Chasers*, a spin-off show, where I perform a rap to one of the contestants. Literally all there was going through my mind before I did the rap was, 'This is the only chance you're ever going to have to perform a rap on a television programme. Just do it! If it doesn't work, they'll just take it out of the edit.' This would have been an inconceivable way of thinking to me two years ago.

So you found this empowering?

Yes. I've recently had Covid-19. The first two weeks of being in lockdown, I was in bed with a swirling fever and a cough and absolute physical exhaustion. As a result, I wasn't getting any of the side effects from my Parkinson's medication, which are slight anxiety, difficulty sleeping, [being] constantly alert, constantly awake and constantly creative. Now I feel all these side effects have come back, and I'm delighted. Not many people say they're delighted to have the side effects of their medication come back, but I've been living with the side effects of my medication for a while, and I like them. I like the person that it has made me become, just a little bit more impulsive and a little bit more alert and a little bit more creative. I actually enjoy this – and the Covid-19 knocked these symptoms out of me. Not many people would celebrate sleeplessness and anxiety, but I've just spent eleven months embracing them, and then they just sort of disappeared. I'm really glad they're back. Yes, it means that my husband has to deal with a lot more tantrums and emotional breakdowns. But that's his problem, not mine.

The idea that this diagnosis and these facts have been empowering for you . . . Do you think there was anything about you that set these things up for being empowering? Some people might fall apart with hopelessness at a diagnosis, or at least wouldn't have the same response as you. Were there any beliefs you had going into this that . . .

Do you know what? It's not so much a belief as having a family who've always coped with every bit of stress with grace, magnanimity and calmness. I think the most important thing, in terms of influence, is the fact that my dad has had three heart attacks and two coronary artery bypass operations, and my mum had a double mastectomy for breast cancer. They've provided me with a template of how to behave in life: [one] of being calm and pragmatic and just getting on with things. That isn't necessarily the template that I've lived my life by in the past, but one that I'm determined to live my life by now, because when I was diagnosed with Parkinson's, all I thought about was my mum, waking up from a double mastectomy, and my dad, waking up from his bypass operation, thinking, *I've got to be as brave as them*. I can't be an insult to their struggles; I need to do everything I can to cope with what I've been dealt.

Hannah Peel on music and meaning

December, 2020

Hannah Peel is an artist, composer and musician known for her explorative approach to electronic, classical and traditional music. Her work spans solo albums, soundtracks including *Game of Thrones: The Last Watch*, and collaborations with artists like Paul Weller.

I was born in Northern Ireland and then we moved to Yorkshire. One of the very first experiences I had was that during that period, the early nineties, there was this initiative where they would give children in primary school free lessons, mainly in brass, because they wanted to continue the brass band tradition and get kids playing and joining groups. So one of the first connections that I had to living in a different country was music. I'd gone from the kind of Irish upbringing where my cousins and everyone all played different instruments, seeing that from a young age, to moving to Yorkshire and being thrown in from the age of eight into that brass world. There's always been this kind of connection of place and what it means and that communication, so although I might speak with a different accent (I moved there with a very strong Irish accent and it very quickly moved on to fit in), I guess that musical language can work across everything. There's a mutual kind of respect between people, which I find fascinating. I guess until you're older, you don't really realise that, and [then] you can start to assess things properly.

What was the music doing for you in those situations, then? Was it connecting you with place or connecting you with people?

Both. From an instrument, you can kind of feel a history. Especially in Yorkshire and Barnsley as a mining town, the brass band just kind of releases every single chemical in your brain that tells you where it is, and I haven't found that with many styles of music, because there's so much amalgamation. Then, it was so apparent that this was the music of that town, and that was the world I was stepping into. So yeah, a total understanding of people and community. As I said, at eight years old, I didn't really think about that, but you do start to recognise, okay, this is a different place and it has a different sound.

It sounds like you think that music is a sort of language, or at least that it's communicating meaning.

Definitely! You can attach yourself to different lyrics and language, but sometimes, I think more so with instrumental music, you can listen to a piece of music and associate your own feelings with that in order to express something, sometimes things that are too hard to express in words. A piece of music can bring about an emotion or a memory or a feeling, or maybe even offer hope and an answer to something, just by listening to it. Isn't that insane? What I find fascinating is when you analyse that, that breaking down of the sound molecules and the duration of a piece, the pitch of a piece of music, the timbre, the rhythms, the volume, even – they all kind of feed into your brain in a subliminal way. I do find it quite magical at times. So sorry Andrew, I will get quite hippy on you.

It's interesting that you use the word 'hippy' there, because from what you've just said, it does sound like for you there's, not mystical, obviously, but a very organic feature to music, and obviously in the way that you make music and experience it. But then you also seem to be talking about almost engineering it. So it's an organic thing that exists and reaches us, but it's also something that you engineer, you bring method into it.

And I guess as you learn, you can kind of engineer what you want to say to someone to connect. It is just that kind of experience of formulating it. I guess what I found fascinating, and maybe what we'll come to at some point in this chat, is that there was a certain moment a few years ago that I really started to think about science and the brain and how we actually are processing sound and music. The fact that there are brain regions that are actually older than the use of language is amazing. You are absorbing sound from the moment you are conceived, so that has to have a play on how we communicate and how we talk and listen. The engineering, I guess, is me trying to artistically shape things for you to understand, as well as for me to understand. It's a process just as much for me as it is for the listener.

Let's talk about that now, then. What you're saying seems to be that you believe that there's a primal quality to music, that it reaches parts of us that other things can't reach.

Going back to the basics, the first part of your brain to be developed is the auditory cortex, which is the most central part of your brain – so that is there from the beginning, and that is the place where sounds are stored, and those sounds are then associated with smell and taste and place and memory. That is the primal aspect of it. It is the way that we would have communicated thousands of years ago through sound. I also think that our ears right now are blasted with too much information and too much noise. I think the appreciation of what music actually is has diminished. Especially as we live in a digital age where you can have it at your fingertips at any point. There is something special about when you find a piece of music and it really touches you or it moves you or it makes you want to cry, or it makes you think of another human or a relationship. I can't think of any other art form that touches all the senses in that way.

At the same time, I think it's an open source to be interpreted. As an artist, when you put music out there, you have to be expectant of different people liking or not liking it, and the memories that that can bring about. My grandfather was one of the first choir boys to ever make a recording on wax. He made it in Manchester Cathedral, I think it was in 1921 or 1923. He was only eleven years old at the time. I found this recording, it was on YouTube. I'd known it was in the family, but nobody seemed to have a copy. But, anyway, it was on YouTube. I ripped it off. It's my granddad; I should be able to.

I was writing a piece of music and, actually, going back to the brass band, it was commissioned by a brass band. It was for brass band and synthesisers, and it was to do with the connection between music and travelling into space. So what I'd done was, at the very end, there was this piece called 'The Planet of Passed Souls', where this character that had been taken on this journey went to this planet, and ... the airwaves in this alien landscape would drag out the memories and the sounds from your past.

And in the clouds of dust, it was the voice of my grandfather that came through. When we performed this live, it was the first performance in Manchester and I literally – as soon as I heard that voice, I couldn't stop crying. It was so hard to stand on stage and not just cry. There was this kind of overwhelming feeling of shivers down your spine, and when I looked about, it wasn't just me. Nobody knew it was my granddad, but there were people in the audience that were crying, and I just was blown away by how something like sound could release that kind of emotion with no context to it for other people, the way that they were attached to it or adapting to it as well.

So music for you, it's open to interpretation. It's how people receive it?

Yes.

At the same time, interviewed elsewhere, you've talked about how, when you're making music, you're using it also to explain what's going on in your mind. That does sound like there's a message at source as well. It's not all about interpretation. Is that a flexible dynamic between the music-maker and the listener? Or is it all one way?

I mean, there's definitely not a 'You can think of this as anything.' There is always, with music that I do, some kind of narrative attached to it, or some kind of thought process behind it that has led me to that point. I don't intentionally sit down and decide, 'I'm going to write a piece of music that has this effect, or deals with this question on our society,' but usually, after a while, things start to become apparent, and then I start to piece puzzles together. Like, why have I been looking at imagery of rocks for a while, and why am I obsessed with rocks? Oh, okay, I think I'm trying to look into the roots of our existence in a huge way. But then how do I make that part of a narrative or a story? Or make it like a human connection to myself and a listener? Like, one person, another person. What story would I tell to that person? There is an element of this being the framework, or the narrative, which I think is really important. I think we, as a society, love a narrative.

And that's not through lyrics in your case, is it?

Not any more. Strangely, I have just kind of deviated away from lyrics. I find them very hard, or I have done the last few years.

Why is that?

I just find it very hard to place a thought, one's thought, into a piece of music and have it so descriptive. I'm finding it increasingly difficult to write down a set of words and have them as the lyrics. Sadly, that also means that I'm battling with myself, because I love singing and I really miss that side of my music. At the same time, maybe it's just the period that I'm going through; I'm still discovering quite a few things. Maybe it will pass, and I'll go back to actually writing and talking in that form, and communicating in that form. It's just one of those things. Maybe it's like one of those insecurities that you get used to, and then you build it up in your brain.

At the moment, you think you convey more meaning through sounds other than words? See, that's fascinating to me, because that's so distant from my own experience. It's really interesting to consider that.

Oh really?

Yeah. Just because, like lots of people, I suppose, I think that words are my only way of communicating. That's my starting assumption, but it's such a different idea you're expressing . . .

If you remember a song, do you remember the lyrics or do you remember the melody?

I remember the lyrics. I used to write lyrics down when I was a child, actually. I'd stop songs so I could write them all down, so I could understand what was going on.

I can still listen to a song and a hundred times later, think that they're singing about sausages or something random. I will get the lyrics wrong every time. I think that is a common distinction – you are either a person that does remember all the lyrics, or you are actually only listening to the music. There is a double brain in action. I need to look into this more; I have seen some writings about it. I'm definitely more the other way.

You've written about, or been interviewed, at least, about the effect of music on your grandma and how it unlocked – or, I suppose, sustained – a relationship with her in a very difficult time. That struck me as a really interesting concept and idea. I wonder if you'd mind saying a little bit about that.

So, kind of working backwards, it relates to an album that I had out in 2016 called *Awake But Always Dreaming*. Previous to that, the few years leading up to that, my grandmother had been living with dementia for roughly about ten to eleven years. Over that time, she had gradually disappeared from us in terms of we didn't know how to connect with her. You kind of get to a stage where it gets so far back into her childhood memories that you just really felt like you'd lost that person. It was so devastating, and so many people have to go through this. But it always fascinated me, because she could always remember the words to certain poems that she'd learned as a child.

One Christmas, we all went to the nursing home and I'd said, 'Why don't we all just sing a Christmas carol and get the room kind of going?' – and we did. She kind of went from a position of head down, very distant, not communicating, not really aware of where she was or what time of year it was, to, as soon as she heard these carols and the singing, her eyes just opened and her head lifted and she started singing. It was just the most glorious moment, but also so sad, because it just unlocked a door and I couldn't understand it. I was like, as a musician, why do I not know why this is happening? This is why I kind of went off into more brain studies and got in touch with Alzheimer's Research UK. I started working with some teams that they had working in the Wellcome Collection in London, and some scientists in UCL as well. Actually, another girl that was from my year in Barnsley is one of the lead researchers. She invited me to her lab, where she takes samples from various different people and grows brain neurons in the lab, and then analyses them to try and find the cure for the disease. When she invited me there, I just couldn't believe it, because when you look down the microscope, it just looked like the moon or the universe. Following that, I found out about the auditory cortex and how the brain is formed, and where music and sound come into that, and how important it is. Various charities – there's one called Playlist For Life – they help you become a music detective . . . if someone is living with Alzheimer's or dementia, to try and find out the music that they like to make a playlist to kind of bring them back into the present so you can communicate with them. It was just amazing. It's all kind of stemmed from there, and that science side of the music has gone on from there.

So it was that experience, really, with your grandmother that developed this investigation for you and this journey towards the beliefs that you currently have about music – and it sounds like not only its effects on the brain, but also how it connects people?

Definitely. I just thought it was such a magical experience. I didn't know that kind of thing could exist, and I only wish that I'd known sooner, because I would have had many more years with her, being able to talk with her or communicate with her via song, because she was a singer. This was the saddest thing. She loved music. She was a singer. And we'd never explored that, because it was a bit of a taboo at the time, so I made it a kind of mission that no matter what the album did or what people thought of it, that I would talk about it, and if someone wrote to me and said, 'I've tried this with my grandmother or grandfather and it's changed me,' then I would be happy because I would have wanted that. And it did go like that. It was beautiful. It just wasn't all about making art for the ego. It was about doing something that actually felt like you were making a bit of a difference to somebody else.

Joan Bakewell on curiosity and being interested

September, 2020

Joan Bakewell is a journalist, television presenter and Labour Party peer known for her insightful interviews and cultural commentary. She has contributed to public discussions on arts, ethics and society for over six decades.

This is a little intimidating, because this is a podcast called What I Believe, *and you, of course, presented a series for the BBC for a long time, very similar, called* Belief. *How did you tend to open up the discussions?*

Well, I did come to find that a lot of people's beliefs today were based on their background. You can't get away from your background. You are shaped by the culture and your family life, particularly if it has been a happy one, because then you draw on it without any reservation. If it's been unhappy, you often rebel against it, which is to say, of course, it is just as influential as if you were happy with it.

Let's start there with you, then.

I grew up in Stockport in a very conventional lower-middle-class family, very eager to conform to the values of the time. We belonged to a church, in a nominal sense – the name was on the church register, as it were – but my parents weren't particularly keen to go to church. We went on special days, high days and holidays, and we went at Christmas, and we knew all the hymns and we knew most of the prayers at the Church of St Thomas, which was nearby, which was the church where I would subsequently get married. So, I grew up accepting and believing the Anglican Christian story. There was no reason to challenge it. It was perfectly acceptable. A lot of it was very charming to a child, with angels and nice disciples. Nobody seemed to do anything wrong, except the wicked people who you were meant to hate, whom God took revenge on so it all seemed quite satisfactory, and a rather nice tale.

Well, then, as I grew up, I did begin to question things, because curiosity makes you wonder why everybody believes this, and I enrolled for confirmation. We had to have classes to instruct us for the confirmation, exchanges of prayers and answers that will be presided over by a bishop. I remember as we finished one session – it had been a little bit confusing about spirituality – saying to the person instructing us, 'How do we know any of this is true?', and there was a quiet gasp among the other children, because I was stepping outside accepted behaviour and nobody asked that kind of thing. I think one of the answers was the weight of tradition. How could it not be true if two thousand years had not demonstrated that its survival power verified the actual truth of the message? I took that in with a certain reservation, and then, of course, they went on about the values that we'd learned through it, and the values which, of course, I still share, because those values are very universal. That was when I was, I suppose, fourteen or fifteen.

Then I went to university, at which point I collided with people of all sorts of different faiths and, indeed, a good deal of scepticism on everybody's part. That was very good for me, because I was studying economics, and then I studied history under Eric Hobsbawm, who was a distinguished Marxist and a very brilliant mind. He didn't bring his Marxism directly to bear on my tuition, but I always remember him saying, whenever I made some statement, 'And what is your evidence for that statement? What is this based on? What are you going to offer up in your essay, or your account, as a justification for making such a remark?' That hit home, very much. In fact, when I was moving among people of ideas and intelligence and intellectual status, one of the things they acknowledged was the importance of evidence. That started to impinge on my rather parochial set of beliefs, and I started asking around for evidence – and I never found satisfactory answers.

You say that all your beliefs were still quite parochial when you were at university, but you were the child who asked the question in that class and the other children gasped. Why do you think you were the child who asked the question?

Well, I was stepping out of line.

That was your way, was it?

I grew up at a time when you were taught to have respect for your elders and not to speak out of turn and not to upset anybody by the things you said. So, I was brought up to be amazingly conventional and conformist. I've had trouble rebelling against it ever since.

But you asked that question. Why do you think you asked that question?

I think the spirit of curiosity, which is very strong in me, even now. I find that I suddenly want to know about subjects that are completely alien to me. I'd quite like to know how an aeroplane engine works, or how a chemical reaction functions. I don't know any of these things, but I do find it worth asking, 'Why is that so? And how does that come about?' Of course, I apply that in my politics, as well as in terms of my ideas and my ideology.

You've had such a broad range of themes in your career in broadcasting. It seems you're always looking at something new and taking on a topic where you didn't necessarily know anything – and that's quite valuable, I suppose, in a broadcaster, because you're going on the same journey as your viewer or listener.

Yes, that's very true. It is useful in a broadcaster, because you ask a question from genuine interest rather than because some producer has drawn up a list of questions. I've never obeyed the list of questions, and I've always gone meandering off into interesting avenues of my own concern. People enjoy that. People respond to genuine interest. I've learned a lot of different things along the way. I've accumulated a lot of people's opinions into my own background, and began to look at people of ideas with enormous respect, because over those years when I did the series called *Belief*, I met really intelligent people who gave a very brilliant exposition of what it is they believed, whether they were Jews or Muslims or Hindus, [all] sorts of people, and atheists and people with strange beliefs. I interviewed a witch, and the programme was a little bit exercised as to whether we should include a witch in a programme that was run by the religious department.

But the point is, she came along to talk about being a witch, and we were all absolutely fascinated. She took it very seriously. She spoke about how she wasn't at all unique; it was quite a widespread shared set of beliefs. It operated in her life; it helped guide her and her beliefs, her relationships. And afterwards, we said, 'Well, shame on us for being so sneery as to think it wasn't worth talking about.' It was *really* worth talking about.

In the sixties and onwards, when your career in broadcasting was developing, you played quite an important role in building a more humanist approach to religion and ethics broadcasting. What was it that motivated that? I mean, as you've said, the basis of your own values in your personal development, at least some were Christian values. Where did the non-religious aspect come in?

Oh, I don't think I should be too proud or boastful about that. I took to it because they offered me the work. It offered me a job to work in programmes that were serious-minded programmes about what people believed. Would I like to do it? Yes, I liked to do it, simply as a journalist being offered a job. The more I did it, of course, the more I realised that it chimed with my interest in ideas in general, and my impulse to challenge everything anyway, so it suited me, and that was an accident. It wasn't a particularly high-profile area of broadcasting, the religious department, as it was called. It's not called the religious department any more. They did have a lot of people who were ordained: all men, of course. They had women who had studied theology but were not eligible to be ordained. They were interested in beliefs, but basically steeped in Christian theology and the theology of the Protestant Church. That was fine, because I knew enough, and I didn't feel I was betraying anything to do the programme, because I hadn't really asserted my independence from the Church.

Sometimes, in the middle years of my life, I called myself a non-practising, non-observing member of the Church of England. I always feel that I get along quite well with the bishops in the House of Lords – and, indeed, when I moved a debate not long ago about genetic engineering, there was a whole lot of development happening at that time. I proposed the debate, I got the space, and then I wanted to round up people who would come and speak. I went and knocked on the bishop's door – not something you would normally do – and said that I'd like the bishops to know that this debate was going forward under my name, and I would very much like if they would come and speak, and asked if they would find someone to come and join in that debate. I don't feel myself as a humanist cut off from the beliefs that people have in different religions, because I feel I have an understanding of what that is, because of their aspirations, their higher ideals, whatever they may be, their attempts to improve humanity's way of life, their championing of the poor and the neglected. I don't feel opposed to them, except I always have to make clear to them that I don't hold their beliefs in a whole set of supernatural happenings and events and possibilities. I don't share that, but it doesn't mean we don't have a lot in common.

Well, that sounds like a conviction in itself, a belief on your part. You think a large part of the religions and philosophies of the world is an overlapping area?

It's more to do with the pattern of behaviour that they set out. If you look at Islam, the duties of a Muslim, they're very honour-able. The whole business of giving alms, for example, which is an obligation of taking in the stranger. It's an obligation. Those are eternal values that are nothing to do with the actual nature of the person who founded the religion or the nature of their deity. I've got a lot against religions' accumulated wealth and their fantasy behaviour, but, instinctively, I feel sympathy for people who have given some thought to humanity's behaviour and misbehaviour.

You took on Labour values of the sort that you've described at university, and obviously now you're involved in politics. And when you were talking about the sort of Bevanite vision of society that you endorsed, it sounded as if that idea of progress was something that you were quite committed to, the idea that it's possible that it can happen.

One of the lecturers at Cambridge was Herbert Butterfield. His book prevailed very much in those days, and it dismantled the idea of the liberal progression that we are on some path of betterment, that will automatically come about through history. I grew to realise that there wasn't such a thing as progress, although it was part of a belief system that you went through as a child in forties and fifties England. Britain forever! We were at the forefront of all the progress that was to be made in human ideas and behaviour, and we took those ideas and forced them on a lot of other countries that didn't belong to us. I had to set that aside and say, no, human society is organised in a multitude of ways, many of which are self-contradictory. You have to find your way through, literally on an ad hoc basis. Do you think this is good? Or that is good? What about Belarus? What do you think of America? You have to solve each one to your own satisfaction.

Did you have a sense of loss, giving up the idea of progress? Did you still feel that during the sixties and the seventies, that progress was happening and was real?

No, I think I lost it much earlier. I think it was probably in my first year at university. First of all, I lost the sense that there was anyone out there looking after me. There was no Christ; I didn't feel that underneath are the everlasting arms, that I was cradled by someone who was looking after me. I suffered that as a great sense of loss. I'd come to the decision, and then I had to go into my life without this comfort, and I remember how frail I felt and how vulnerable without this sense of comfort supporting me. So that went, and then I studied history, and you learn that progress doesn't go as we want it to. We all have a sense of progress, and I do believe in aspiring to make the world a better place, and I still hold to that today, but it isn't surprising that empires come and go. We're now seeing the decline, to some extent, of the West, and we're seeing the rise of the East. We're not sure what's going on in Russia, but it's not particularly wholesome. That is how human society swings: one way and another, different groups, different power brokers. Different societies rise and fall and their people go with them, or they try to change it or direct it. That's why history never ceases to be fascinating.

It sounds like you took yourself out of the Christian story and sort of reinserted yourself into the big human story, with curiosity and looking for ideas and so on. Is that about right?

Yes, I think that's true. I didn't know it was called humanism at the time – and, indeed, when I speak to people who say to me, 'Humanism? What on earth is humanism?', and I set out what it is, they say, 'Oh, well, that's what I am!' So there are a lot of people walking this planet who are behaving, I'm glad to say, in accordance with humanist beliefs without actually giving it that name.

Can we talk about beauty?

Absolutely.

Poetry is one of the really rich elements of life which we can all reach, which reaches all of us, and perhaps we neglect it because we thought we had to learn it at school. I had to learn it by rote, which of course does more to turn you off than anything, but it still comes back to me, the poetry I did learn. I found that my son, too, had done that and we were saying, 'Oh, did you learn this one? Did you learn the "Ozymandias" poem?'

At the moment, with the vanity of all sorts of politicians, that poem is at the forefront of your mind all the time. Are you saying poems give you a framework to make meaning out of events?

They do. I'm also very fond of Cavafy, his 'Waiting for the Barbarians'. I've got anthologies of popular poetry, and they're very useful because there's a different poet on every page. You choose where you want to be at a particular time, and there's a great reward there.

I think it would be remiss not to say something about – well, you say it was a job, and it was work and someone offered and you did it, but I think there must be more to it than that. I think you must have convictions about public broadcasting, why you did the programmes that you did. Is there anything, looking back on that, that you would say united the work?

I've lived my life as a freelancer. I've not been on the payroll of any broadcasting authority. I worked for the BBC a lot, and I worked for Granada a lot, too, in the past. Looking back, I can see that the programmes I chose to do, what united them was the fact that I like ideas. I like to tangle with ideas. I like to be challenged by them. I like to share discussion of them with people. I see that now. I probably have turned down the more frivolous things that have been offered to me and forgotten about them. I remember one or two; it's just so silly, it's not worth remembering. I would turn those down because I did like something that gave me a bit of intellectual grit to get on with. *Heart of the Matter* was a classic case of that: that was literally going out and helping people make moral decisions for themselves. That was really important.

I did a programme with women who wanted to be priests before they could be priests. I did a programme with gay men who wanted to become priests who were not allowed to become priests. This was all in the nineties, when it was all changing, and the law, of course, has now changed, and I do feel that we have a little part in that. We [covered] things which needed the attention of the public conscience, and that was worth doing. We moved on from different topic to different topic. We went to Yugoslavia, as it was called, after the war there to discuss how you could decide which side was wrong and which side was right. What did that mean? The intervention of the United Nations, and so on. So, we posed moral dilemmas. I never came down on one side or the other. That was always the refrain of the programme: so on the one hand this, and on the other hand … 'That's the heart of the dilemma'. That was the refrain of the programme, and I never took sides. People would say to me, afterwards, 'Which side were you on?' and I would always think that I'd been a good broadcaster and that I hadn't revealed my own commitments. I hadn't revealed them, because that was to make people think.

Stephen Fry on uncertainty

January, 2024

Stephen Fry is an actor, comedian, writer and presenter
who has authored several bestselling books and starred
in numerous films and TV series. He is a vocal advocate
for mental health.

*Now, the name of this podcast is taken from the essay by E. M. Forster.
And I know that I don't have to tell you about that essay, because
some years ago now, when I presented you with an award for LGBT
humanists, you quoted that very essay in your acceptance speech, and
you mentioned some of the beliefs and values that were in it, as well as
some of your own. So I know that we're going to start off in the right
place. And I think we can leave it pretty open and just ask you, as you
look at your life, the way you've approached things over the years, your
world view, and what you think about the beliefs and values that have
informed and motivated you – what are they?*

Well, E. M. Forster was a huge influence, actually. I was blown
over by the novel *Howards End* when I was about sixteen, and I
read it several times. Then I found a copy of one of his collections
of essays, *Two Cheers for Democracy*, and that amazed me: the
mixture of wit, sternness, but also openness – it was so unusual.
And then I kind of understood that Forster was a satellite, rather
than a central figure, of what is now called the Bloomsbury

Movement, that includes, obviously, Virginia Woolf and Vanessa Bell, and Duncan Grant, and the artists and writers and poets. But also Bertrand Russell, the philosopher, who then became a big influence too. And he and Forster are rather similar, sort of querulously uncertain about things, and certain in their belief that uncertainty is the correct thing.

And why is uncertainty an important intellectual value to you? Is it almost a moral one as well – being careful, not being too firm on one thing or another, in case you're wrong, and being humble.

I'm very lazy when it comes to intellectual things, and therefore I almost don't bother with reasons, because I am pretty much fully an empiricist, rather than a rationalist. I don't need to explain why certainty is wrong by any logical or metaphysical twists and turns. I can just say, 'Look at what happens when people are certain.' It's empiricism, it's experience, what experience shows – people of certainty have nearly always, as far as I can see, got us into trouble. People who are more shadowed in doubt, and nuanced and uncertain, seem to be, if not more likely to provide solutions to world problems, at least less likely to contribute to the problems quite as much as the certain. I mean, really, all I'm saying is something I think most people instinctively understand, and that is that dogma and doctrine and ideology are pretty disastrous, and have been pretty disastrous for the human race.

We can look at the Enlightenment and the Age of Reason and say these got us a long way forward, but they were not doctrine. I suppose Immanuel Kant had one certainty, which was what he called 'the starry skies above me and the moral law within me'. And I kind of go along with that. This idea that we have within

104

us, somehow, in the same way as we have other instincts – like, it could be the sexual impulse or anything like that – we have also, as humans, this thing, this Jiminy Cricket on our shoulder that says, 'No, that's wrong.' And we can argue that it's our parents who teach us that. The religious will say it's from doctrine and text that we are taught what's right and what's wrong, but Kant understood, and I think most people understand, that it seems to be something inborn. Or, if it is learned, it's so profoundly and deeply embedded as to be almost the same thing. That's to say, it's not that one hears the voice of one's parents saying, 'That's wrong, that's wrong.' It's so much the whole chorus of humanity that instinctively understands that stealing is wrong, that lying is wrong, murder is wrong, meanness is wrong, cruelty is wrong, betrayal, deceit and all that. We just seem to know it. We certainly don't need to be told it by a hierophant or a priest! And I've always been aware of that. I believe I've always had a very high sense of morality and ethics – not that I've been a very moral and ethical person in my life, necessarily – but I've been aware of them, and they touch me and pain me when I fall short. Maybe I misjudge other people, but I do seem to know people who genuinely don't really seem to care that much about the moral or ethical mark they make on the world, or who may not, when they go to sleep at night, try to beat themselves up. And I do, and I've always had it, and it annoys me to some extent, because I'd love to be free of it.

How does that problem of other people's behaviour square with the idea that this sense of right and wrong is something that is in us, and is in all of us? If that's the case, and it is close to being an instinct, or at least in the grain of human nature . . .

Yes. That's a really good question. I love the question. Obviously, those of us who have been active in some ways within humanism, are most particularly annoyed by the claim of religion that without it, there would be no moral sense, because that just is empirically nonsensical, and rationally nonsensical too – and this was exploded, as I'm sure you know, by Greek philosophers, way, way, way back. But nonetheless, there is this idea that you need a god in order to guide your hand, and I think, looking around the world, we can see that it is something that is apparently inborn. One could look for the solutions, as we love to do, through evolutionary psychology and ethology, and all the ways that we try to understand how our behaviour genetically, and now epigenetically, is modified by what happens to us, and the circumstances of our growth and progress, as a species and as the various . . . the family, the group, the clan, the tribe, the race, however one wants to expand the identity of who we are. I suppose the question, really – and this is where we get to the Greeks – is happiness. We want to be happy, that's pretty obvious. It's best seen in how much we try and avoid unhappiness, perhaps. The lengths we go to, to avoid being miserable, if we can. And the question that exercised the Greeks was whether you could be happy, if you were not virtuous? If you are not kind and decent, and good, and thoughtful, and generous, and open and honest . . .

'Can you be happy if you're not good?'

And similarly, can you be good if you're not happy? That suddenly becomes a kind of political idea, that you can't be good if you're not happy. And Oscar Wilde and others kind of mocked Victorian morality by saying, 'If you're poor and you're suffering, the idea that you can waste time being good in a Victorian sense is pretty nonsensical.'

So is that your belief, then? You believe that human beings are set up to be good, if they've got the chance, or if the conditions are right, if they're happy, and it's things going wrong? It's poverty, or injustice, or kinks of various sorts that might warp us a little?

And the kind of territorial horrors we're seeing in the Middle East.

Loyalties, belonging.

Yes. It's so easy for me to sit here in my fat, comfortable, Western luxury, and talk about how moral the world is now, everybody's good, and yet we can see there's so much suffering, cruelty, abuse, terror, exploitation, etc. We know there are terribly wicked people out there who are sex-trafficking, who are selling arms right this minute. There is a lot of terrible behaviour going on, a lot of awfulness. Sometimes I think, rather than being a handwringing liberal – which is, I suppose, what I am ... I know that's an unpleasant thing to be for a lot. I should be more like Jonathan Swift, you know, a true *satirist*. Now, Swift was a religious man, as you know; he was Dean of St Patrick's Cathedral, Dublin, he was a man of the cloth, but he was a true satirist, in that he absolutely did not let humanity off the hook. He presented humanity as completely disgusting. He made satirical points that were remorseless, like his 'Modest Proposal', which was that we should eat Irish children, because it would solve the problem of the excess of children. And it was so beautifully and rationally put, that he never excused himself from the irony to say, 'Oh, boo, by the way, I'm being ironic.' He just stayed within it. And he said – and I think this is a thing that a lot of satirists can probably agree with – he said – and you'll have to forgive the gendering, but that's how it was in those days – he said, 'I loathe and detest the race called man. But I love Andrew and Peter and John.'

This is one of the things that's really interested me over the years: the nature of the difference between the individual and the mass. But let me just finish my point about satire. If I was a satirist, I would stop going on about morals here and morals there. And I would do similar things to Swift in terms of modest proposals. Here's my modest proposal, that would instantly make the world a much better place, a happier place, a less violent place, a less aggressive place, a place where more people are likely to have an equal share of everything, and in which there will be so much less violence and aggression. And it is guaranteed, by the way. I'm not necessarily a big one for this, but it's drug control. We have to outlaw the most dangerous drug in the world, which is called testosterone. Without testosterone . . . Have you ever seen a cat that's been spayed? From the yowling tomcat that fights in the alley, it becomes a little pudding, and you tickle it and it purrs, and it's lovely, like a eunuch in Shakespeare's *Antony and Cleopatra*: pleasant, pleasing, slightly tubby because the weight gets put on. And all these Andrew Tates, all these figures of toxic masculinity or however you want to describe it, would be fabulously reduced to cosy, warm, sweet, and they wouldn't have this territorial madness, this strange thing that testosterone adds to the human. It's absolutely failsafe. It would work perfectly.

Very modest.

Yes, a very modest proposal, but apparently, there are problems.

Anyway, the thing that interests me about the mass and the individual. It started when I was first in theatre and in the West

End. I remember the producer – a very experienced West End producer – and the play started as a moderate success, which is to say it was making money, but it wasn't an absolute sold-out smash every night. It was Monday, Tuesday, two shows on Wednesday, Thursday, Friday, two shows on Saturday, Sunday off, which was the old West End way. So, eight shows a week. I noticed that on Mondays, you would have about forty to fifty per cent, later in the run sixty per cent of the house full; on Tuesday, it will be sixty, sixty-five, seventy per cent. Wednesday matinee would be forty per cent. Wednesday evening would be ninety per cent. And then the rest of the later part of the week would be sold out. Now, why is it that the people who went on . . . Let's say you're looking at the month of April, and in the first week of April, on that Monday, fifty-two per cent, and then the next Monday, fifty-eight per cent. Why did not thirty or forty per cent of the people who went on the second Monday come on the first Monday? Why don't you have a Monday that is completely sold out, with queues around the block? But instead, it thins itself out. The individuals don't know that, that they're just behaving according to whatever they want and need – 'Oh, shall we go and see that play, darling?' And yet, it's always the same. Sherlock Holmes makes the point to Watson in *The Sign of Four*; he points out that although you can predict to a remarkable degree of accuracy what a mass of people will do, you cannot predict with any degree of accuracy, what an *individual* will do. And it is a most extraordinary thing.

So, is it the variability of individuals that fascinates you? And is that just an observation? Or is it something that gives you pleasure? That could give you pleasure, aesthetically, just thinking of all those different people and the wonderful sort of human diversity that there is, and everyone behaving differently? E. M. Forster, of course, valued it. In

Two Cheers for Democracy, *he thought that it was a good guarantee against conformity and control and totalitarianism. But of course, as a novelist, he also took pleasure in the individual, creating the individual, understanding the individual. Is that the same sort of thing as it is for you?*

Yes, I think that's right. Also, I'm sure most of us face this strange sense that the human race is almost like rabid dogs in a cage. And you get too close to the cage, and the fierce yapping, barking, the slathering, and the horror of this creature, is what you get an impression of humanity being. But when you go out into the streets, or you sit next to someone on a bus, or in the pub, or you chat to them, it's the opposite: everyone seems individually to be reasonable, kind of humorous, resigned about the mess of the world, not completely having swallowed a red pill or blue pill. There's a kind of openness ... Not all, of course – there are those who swallow all kinds of pills and conspiracy theories, and others who are loaded with prejudice against certain groups of people and all the rest of it. But, generally speaking, it's so hard not to think that if you wanted to look at it in a gardening sort of way, all the human seeds that you want to plant in the garden, there are only about two per cent that you'd say, 'Oh, that's a bit mouldy, throw that one away.' The rest are really good, and will grow into wonderful flowers.

But sometimes, the weeds are too strong. And of course, you have to be aware that you and I, Andrew, as we talk, someone might listen, who is not well disposed towards us – and we are the weeds, as far as they're concerned. We are the problem. And I'm fully aware that there are people further to the left of me and further to the right of me, who regard my kind of centrist and progressive, vaguely tolerant liberal beliefs; they're regarded as not just fatuous and weak, but genuinely dangerous.

You seem to be saying you're a woolly liberal, to use an old-fashioned phrase.

Yes – and maybe I shouldn't be, as I say. Maybe I should be really fighting for the prohibition of testosterone, and walking up and down Oxford Street with a big sign.

Well, you can be a hard liberal, I suppose. I mean, the alternative to being a woolly liberal is being a harder sort of liberal, and being more firm about the truth and necessity of liberal values. That's an inbuilt problem with liberalism, isn't it? You see both sides.

And it is what worries me about AI. It's taken us hundreds of years to realise that all human lives are of equal value, and that women are of equal value to men, and people of different races and outlooks and upbringings are of equal value, and there isn't a hierarchy of worth amongst humanity. And therefore, you must bake those values into AI, so that the Chat GPT-style and others, when they're scraping data from the internet, if they come across data that suggests women are inferior to men from somewhere, they must have an instinct, a prime directive to ignore that. Yes, we can all agree with that. But we forget that Russia and China have their own AI. They have a totally different ethical framework, one in which the citizen is subjugated by their duties to the state, and they should report neighbours who misbehave and mock the Supreme Leader. And suggesting that one AI can't sort of infiltrate another is like saying, 'If I put the yellow dye in the Pacific, I haven't put it in the Atlantic.' Well, there's only one ocean on Earth, actually. And there's only one internet, really. There are firewalls and national attempts to control bits, but, generally speaking, we have to be very aware of the fact that – and this is the bit that's so depressing for cowards like me – that these values that you've very perfectly expressed, maybe have to be fought for. And fighting for values is something that, instinctively, we tend to go against. The pure logic of Oscar Wilde's comment that the ability or the willingness to die for something doesn't make it any truer. It's no truer because you're prepared to die for it.

You implied earlier, when you talked about uncertainty, that intellectual uncertainty led, for you at least, to a certain type of tolerance. Would you say that was one of your moral values?

I think so. I suppose I would combine that with the things that have most compelled my attention and love all my life, and that is the arts, you might say: literature and poetry and music, and so on. They add another dimension, which is the ability to put yourself in the heart and mind and soul of another person. That's what imagination is. Imagination is not fantasy. It's not, 'Gosh, I pictured this planet in which the mountains are shaped like shoes, and there are seventeen suns.' That's not imagination, that's fantasy. And it can be very charming, but imagination is knowing what it is to be that person or the other person, to know what it is to be the rapist as well as the raped. And what it is to be the abuser and the abused, and to be the hopeful, to be the side-lined, and the ignored. The best artists are able to become other people, and therefore allow us to understand humanity and the feelings of others more than perhaps we otherwise might. And I think that, combined with uncertainty, is a very useful way of being in the world. You don't judge people, necessarily. I mean, obviously, you make judgements. If someone's a psychopath, and they're holding a knife, you don't say, 'I understand you.' But it is a mixture of . . . How would I put it? I suppose it's testing oneself. Not allowing oneself to get above other people. In the current mess of the world, taking a position is sometimes regarded as the ultimate good – you must declare what side you're on. In American politics, British politics, Brexit, the Middle East – all these terrible places where man is handing out misery to man, to misquote Larkin. It's wonderful to tribalise yourself on to one side of that and to make an enemy that is clear. But experience and knowledge of humanity, and the empirical ability to look back at history, I think shows us that that's no way to be moral. The most moral thing you can be is effective. And I think one of the crimes of our age is that people would rather be right than effective. And in that sense, it's a failure of being empirical about things, about wanting to solve things.

You're thinking politically as much as anything else there.

Yes, that's right. It's also very easy because of the clamour. And because I'm a sensitive soul, to worry about what's being said about one, and to fill in all the arguments against one in one's head. So you hear a chorus of people . . . So, let's see. It's easy for you to say, 'Stephen, look at your life! So you think it's better to be effective than right. So – what's your solution, then?' And you go, 'Yes, yes, yes. No, I know, oh God!' And you end up wringing your hands and feeling as Forster did at one point, since we're addressing that great man. When the Spanish Civil War broke out, a lot of British and American intellectuals and artists joined the international brigade to go and fight for the Republican cause in Spain against the fascists, and the young Auden and Isherwood, who both knew and were hugely inspired by Forster, decided they would go off to Spain. And they went to see Forster, and Forster was sitting in front of an electric fire with some toast and a cup of tea, in a very old tweed jacket, probably, and I dare say carpet slippers – because somehow, he always comes across as wearing carpet slippers. And when they said they were going, he said anxiously, 'Oh, do you think I should go too?' And they looked at him and smiled and said, 'Morgan' – he was always known as Morgan, his middle name – 'Morgan, your place is here at Cambridge with a pen in your hand.' He said, 'Oh, good.' Imagine him fighting alongside Orwell and Hemingway! But in that sense, I do think one of the wisest lines ever given in cinema was that of Inspector Callahan in the second *Dirty Harry* movie *Magnum Force*, where he says to Holbrook a number of times, 'A man's got to know his limitations.' And that is very important, you know.

And that's as profound an observation as any to end with.

Clint will always give us the answer.

LOVE, RESPECT
AND EMPATHY

Eddie Marsan on character and an immigrant mentality

February, 2021

> Eddie Marsan is an award-winning actor in both film and television. His work spans a range of genres, earning him critical acclaim for roles in films including *Happy-Go-Lucky*, *Sherlock Holmes* and *Ray Donovan*.

I was raised in Tower Hamlets, which is probably the most racially diverse and culturally diverse borough in the country. On a very superficial level, my family appeared to be white working class, although my great-grandfather came from Trinidad in the beginning of the twentieth century. He was a merchant seaman and he settled in the East End. On my mother's side, my maternal grandmother was born in Gibraltar, and her mother was Spanish. So I was always aware that our identity as white working class was quite superficial, even when I was young, from the stories we heard. Growing up in an area which is very, very diverse, where there's lots of immigration and lots of different cultures, I think the white working class, from my experience, roughly about thirty per cent of them adopted a racist tendency – supported the BNP or the National Front – and then there was a certain percentage who kind of were neutral. Then there were those who embraced multiculturalism and embraced their immigrant neighbours; they lived with them and they accepted them.

I think you see it in a lot of urban areas now in London; you see a lot of mixed-race children, which is very interesting. They say that the highest level of racial integration is between the white working class and other immigrants, but the white working class are also known to be the most racist, so, in a sense, it's a very honest, visceral response to change. Either you're repelled by it and fear it, or you embrace it and love it. There's no intellectual debate about it. You either want to fight somebody or you want to go out with them, one or the other.

I suppose that's because you're forced to be there. You've got no choice. You're there and you've got to make that choice, one or the other.

Yeah, it's not an academic choice. Poverty doesn't give you an opportunity to become detached and make an assessment. Poverty doesn't allow you to respond to things, it only allows you to react. When I was young, my parents had a very difficult marriage, and they went through a very difficult divorce for many years, and my home life was traumatic at times. There were times when it was good, but there were times when it was traumatic and I took refuge within a St Lucian family that lived on the same estate as me. There were four brothers and two sisters, and we all became friends. I used to call their mum Mum; she's still alive now. I still call her Mum. I had my mum, but I kind of took refuge in their family, and then I found myself taking refuge in an immigrant mentality. There's something about an immigrant mentality that was different from the white working-class mentality.

The immigrant mentality was much more long-term thinking. It was much more about an investment in education, a belief in yourself. I found myself more vulnerable and more in danger from the racist white working-class elements that I was trying to avoid, and I felt safer within the immigrant community. So very early on, about the age of nine or ten, I began to reject the orthodoxy that I was born into: not the religious orthodoxy, but the cultural orthodoxy. I remember my father used to go to the pub and come back and have impromptu parties. There'd be all these men in our kitchen when I was a kid and some of them would be racist. They would talk about supporting the NF and the BNP, or whatever it was. I knew that I felt safer with the people that they were disparaging. I knew that, actually, I felt more encouraged and more inspired and more loved by people who had embraced change within their lives. That was one of the earliest things of me looking around and realising that the culture that I was supposed to adopt, I rejected at a very early stage.

I suppose there's two things there, aren't there? There's the fact that at that point, you formed a belief that a person could choose their own way, and also that you would choose your own way.

I think it was a necessity, actually. It came from a feeling of anxiety and vulnerability. It was a desire and need to survive. I couldn't survive like that. I knew that what they were saying was wrong. I knew what they were saying was fake, and I couldn't live like that. I remember feeling anxiety, even as a child, and realising that I had to find my own way.

Did you challenge the old way out loud?

Yeah, but if I questioned them, because they were guests, I'd get sent to bed. You should be seen and not heard, all that stuff.

Then, when I was sixteen, I became a born-again Christian for about six or seven months.

I did not know that. Interesting!

Very interesting now, because if you think about it, most sixteen-year-olds need to rebel, and I did the opposite. I needed to find a very conservative or authoritarian, dogmatic belief system that gave me all the answers. I was so much looking for the answers because I was disorientated, even within myself, as a teenager. I never felt comfortable within myself. I never knew who I was. So I embraced this Pentecostal Christianity that I was introduced to, and at times it was very reassuring, like lots of them are. They gave me the answers and I adopted it. We used to go to different churches all over the country and pray; people would speak in tongues. I never spoke in tongues. I was waiting to speak, and it never happened. There was a guy within this church who I looked up to. I thought he seemed to be a really kind, spiritual guy. He told me that they were, we were, next week, going to Leicester Square to save homosexuals. I don't think I was even sixteen, and I said, 'Save them from what?' I didn't understand what he meant. Then he said, 'Why? You're not one are you, Eddie?'

It really shocked me, because I suddenly saw this guy who I thought was so spiritual and so kind, yet within his belief system, within his dogmatism, there was a bigotry. It suddenly frightened me. It really frightened me, because I thought, morality isn't only based on your belief system, it's the way that people are dogmatic about their belief system that informs as much about morality. You can have the most benevolent belief system, but if you demonise all other belief systems and think yours is the only way, that's immoral. It will create a dogmatism and a nastiness that cancels out all the good that you think you're doing.

It sounds like you almost saw the same thing there as you'd rejected in the racism.

It was, in a sense, because I began to realise I didn't know myself. I couldn't define myself, and for years I'd wanted to define myself. I see friends of mine now – the comedian Micky Flanagan is a friend of mine, and Ray Winstone is a friend of mine – these guys are quite successful within that white working-class culture. They're quite good at it. Danny Dyer is very good at it. He's very charismatic. I was useless. I tried to be like them, and I failed miserably. So I could never define myself. It wasn't until I became an actor. When I became an actor, I went to drama school, and when you go to drama school, they teach you to breathe, and we had breathing technique lessons for three months. In Bethnal Green, there was a Buddhist centre, and I went to the Buddhist centre and I learned breathing techniques and meditation. I remember discovering this Buddhist theory called *anātman*, and, suddenly – although I'm not a Buddhist and I don't believe in the metaphysical realm of Buddhism – there was something about the definition. I asked a Buddhist monk about it, and *anātman* means 'no self'; it means 'no fixed self', that human beings aren't fixed. We aren't eternal souls, we are just part of everything else, and we are subject to everything else. What that means is that we can change, that our environment affects us and we affect our environment. That suddenly freed me up at the same time as becoming an actor and realising that, in my job as an actor, even very early on at drama school, I was never going to be asked to be me. Some actors are asked to be them, because women want to sleep with them and men want to be them. Nobody wanted to sleep with me, and nobody wanted to be me. I knew I was never going to be a Paul Newman kind of actor.

There was a great line by Terence, this Roman playwright. He said, 'Nothing human is alien to me,' and I remember thinking, *That's it, isn't it?* I'd been so lacking in confidence because I couldn't define myself, and actually the fact that I can't define myself is my gift. Don't define yourself. Never define yourself. Have values, but people are pure potential, they're not fixed things. That's when I began to reject and I realised that all these religions, even though I can understand within certain communities that they form a function, and human beings need a sense of identity – a personal and a cultural and religious identity – actually, they don't correspond to reality as it really is. Reality is always much more complex and paradoxical than these binary religions.

Rather than that being an upsetting idea, it was an empowering one?

Very much so, very much.

Why was that?

I felt free. But also it was because I was beginning to learn a profession where I was being asked to take on other personalities, other characters. And therefore you began to ask the question, what is a character? What makes a character? So the idea that I wasn't restricted by my own character, because my own character was ultimately as impermanent as the one I was creating on stage or in front of a camera, was very liberating to me. Actually, it's helped me in many ways, all the way through my career. Then that informs a sense of social and economic and cultural morality about other people, because the truth of the matter is, if we are all just pure potential, we have to give people the facilities to fulfil their potential.

Is that a guiding principle for you socially? Giving people that opportunity?

Yes, and encouraging them. I always believed that when I saw a really famous actor, I always remember thinking, *If they can do it, I can do it.* Then, morally, I always had to say the reverse of that is true: *If I can do it, they can do it.* So that always informs me, in a sense. Also, because I was brought up in Tower Hamlets, like I said, and because I embraced the mixture of the cultures, I've always had a real aversion to any form of racism or prejudice. I've experienced it myself because of my class. I've seen friends of mine experience it both because of their class and race. When I was a kid, we used to experience some really frightening things, physical violence against my friends, which were terrifying. Because I believe we are all subject to our environment, I do believe in the idea of there being within every human being implicit bias. That's just an inescapable fact. Well, I think in this country, for the last thousand years, the only true human being who enjoyed full rights and privileges has been a white, heterosexual, Christian, able-bodied male. Everybody else has enjoyed, to a greater or lesser degree, different forms of privileges and rights below that. All of our institutions were created with that mindset, so we live within that mindset, and it will affect us in different forms in misogyny, homophobia, Islamophobia, anti-semitism, in racism, in all different forms. And it's subconscious.

In many of us, I believe it's subconscious. The way that we solve it is if we listen to those vulnerable minorities when they say, 'The things you're doing, even if you don't mean to do it, they're causing us this difficulty.' We need to listen to people. We are all born subjected to our environment, and if our environment is imperfect, then we will be imperfect – and the more perfect we make our environment, the better we will be.

It sounds to me like there's a lot of love in your world view. Mostly what you've said has been motivated by love. Love for all these different people that you grew up with, love now for all people.

Definitely. It's all love. I think love is seeing the potential in people. It's believing that all people are pure potential. I had to believe in my own potential to overcome whatever obstacles I faced, and that's what you should do for other people. I try to see people as potential rather than see them as fixed things. If there's no fixed self, then I think it's wrong to demonise people, to make them into fixed things, which is what tribalism does. It always creates an other; there's always an other to blame, you define yourself by what you are not, and I don't believe that.

I remember having a conversation with a Sikh friend of mine once, and he said a really interesting thing. He said that what people don't realise is we are all in an ever-changing world that's changing so rapidly, and we're all immigrants, all of us, in a sense, because we're all living in a world that we weren't born into. And cultural change, it's so quick now that we're all having to kind of adapt and behave like immigrants. What poverty did for my family, because you never had enough money to think beyond the next week or two weeks, [meant that] every decision was always made short-term. There was always a short-termism, even with regards to education. I mean, I left school at fifteen with no qualifications. It's not that my parents didn't care, they just couldn't – they never had the time. One of my sisters went to university, and she did that on her own, really. But when I was speaking to my Sikh friend and he was talking about immigrant values – that you think long-term, you plan long-term for your family, you think about the next generation, about education – that's one of the things that I think I've adopted. Because I now live in a world that's very different to the one I was raised in, [and] I hold on to that belief about my children and about the future. I try to adopt long-termism as much as possible, because it was something that wasn't afforded to me when I was young.

Janet Ellis on creativity and resilience

May, 2020

> Janet Ellis is a television presenter, actor and writer best known for hosting the iconic children's programme *Blue Peter* during the 1980s. She is now a successful novelist.

You've had a very varied working life: acting, presenting, most recently writing. What ties that together seems to be creativity. Would you say that creativity was something that was important in your approach to life?

Creativity, yes – and creativity as a way of exploring other lives. I think that's the other linking thread. Obviously, as an actress, that's what you're doing. You're finding out what it feels like to be someone else, to move like them, to have a different voice, definitely to have had different lived experiences. And in writing, I can explore that even more because I'm not limited by physicality. That was something, actually, that didn't occur to me initially. But in my first book, the protagonist is a nineteen-year-old girl. She's pretty determined, and has a very idiosyncratic approach to her moral compass, which is definitely skewed. It wasn't until I was published and somebody was talking to me about her and said, 'It's amazing. You've written this whole book about being a teenage girl', looking at me pointedly. I said, 'Well, I was once one!' I hadn't thought about anything other than what a great creative freedom to be able to just think like someone else without being constrained, first of all by how I felt, and most of all by how other people see you – because naturally, they define you by what they see ... It was a massive improvisation on the page, really.

And what was it that was particularly rewarding about it for you? Was it entering into another world and being another person?

Yes, especially the fact that it was a different mindset. Obviously, whatever you write, people think it's you, or a part of you or an element of you. And actually, it truly wasn't. She gets up to no good and she falls in love with someone (I have done that, so we have some things in common), but the way she deals with how she wants to be with her intended is not my path. What's rewarding, too, is that ability to tantalise myself with 'what ifs' – probably more so in the second book, which is again about a not-very-nice woman behaving badly, but also about somebody whose path in life does not go where everyone expected, and probably not where she expected either. It's fascinating to step into what you might think of as a parallel path.

***

The forces in my life I most believe in, though, are first of all love and kindness, and then humour, because I can't imagine a world without that.

What do you value in humour?

The fact that it reflects. It's a way of analysing things without having to commit. It releases rather than confines. My favourite people always make me laugh, and I think it is because even if they're making me laugh about something that might be deemed, in another context, deeply inappropriate (and after all, most of our conversations are not recorded), or if it's something that I've been analysing or worried about, or even snobby, when you laugh about it, it connects you. I find that enormously freeing. I can't imagine enjoying life with somebody who didn't feel like that, or cleaving on to writing that didn't have that effect.

And you believe, obviously, in self-reflection?

I think we're all – well, certainly I am – a work in progress, and I can't imagine ever thinking, *Right. Job done. Janet complete. Turn your attention to somebody else.* We're creating, all the time, ourselves. All the time! I think what first made me identify as a humanist was the importance of the present, the importance of connections *now*, how our actions *now* matter. Not that you would be punished or rewarded much too late for you to ever reap the benefits or even feel the fear. For a long time, I couldn't articulate it, and I think there's all sorts of reasons for that. I think that with a lot of my generation, it's a hangover, and something about a Christian upbringing. But for me, for a long time, there was a questioning about what I was feeling to be my – loosely, in other people's definition – 'spirituality', and me knowing it was definitely about people. It was definitely about people, their achievements, their thoughts, their values, and that overarching sensation that we are all each other has. When I

129

realised what it was, and when I could really put a name to it – 'humanist' – it was such a relief.

I think a lot of storytellers have that interest. And from a humanist view, our lives are stories, in a sense. Our own lives in our heads, I mean.

Yes, and I can see there is a plot – but on the other hand, sometimes I do think, *I wouldn't have written that bit. I wouldn't have given that bit to myself.*

When my husband was first diagnosed with cancer, one of our really close friends (and obviously a lot of my friends are actors or writers) rang me up, and he said, 'Oh my God, that's such bad casting. I wouldn't have given John that.' And I thought, *Yes, that's sort of it really.* It is a story, and we know how it ends in one sense, but we are still turning the pages all the time to find out what happens next.

Things happen to you, and have certainly happened to me in my life, that if I'd been told about them any number of years before, even months before, I would have thought, *I can't cope with that. That's too much. I can't cope with that.* Things that I would have thought would have been the catalyst for some sort of breakdown, for some sort of innovation, for definitely a feeling that 'I cannot be me in this situation.' But actually, you are, and that's the impressive thing. Well, look at the thing we're living through [the Covid lockdown in the UK]. We'd been told about this, but even when we watched it happening in China, in Italy, most of us said, 'But not here, not us.' And then it was, and we're dealing with it. So, yes, it is a story, but in a lot of ways it's almost not ours to tell, and the only thing we do know is the beginning and the end, and sometimes you can't even be quite sure about the beginning.

You say when we look back, we realise we've coped with more than we thought we could have coped with. Do you also find value in looking back?

I make it a value. I'll give you a very personal example. At one stage, I had a series of miscarriages. I wanted a fourth child. We wanted a fourth child. And it didn't happen, and I had a lot of miscarriages. When it went on I felt – and I was tested myself somehow by this reaction – not proud, that's wrong, but I was surprised by and grew with the fact that I could cope. I could cope. I mean, I wouldn't say I was proud of it, because it wasn't set up like that, but there definitely was sort of something in my marrow that I'd exposed [and] I thought, *Oh, that was there all along and I didn't know.*

If I'd been told that before – because I'd had children easily and I just thought another one would be nice, and even after the first couple of miscarriages, I thought, *Well, there's my miscarriages* – probably, given the choice, I might not have tested it like that. But I'm not someone who naturally revisits. I don't go back to places I've left unless I have to, and I don't go back over things, and I don't regret things. I try not to live like that, because for me personally, that's not the recipe for any sort of present fulfilment. But I do draw on the fact that I am able to be stronger than I thought I was.

We are all finding, all the time, a kind of core. We hope it's resilient. And if it isn't resilient – well, equally, I'm always saying to people that strength is an overrated virtue. There's nothing wrong with saying, 'I can't. I really can't cope with this,' and turning to whoever or whatever it takes to get through. Although I suppose that resilience and strength are not quite the same. Resilience is being able to get up again, and strength is probably standing there while the rushing brook hurls around you – and there, the point is, you don't *have* to get into it. You don't have to be there. You don't have to just survive. But I suppose for me – and this is just personal to me, only advice and not a tenet, 'This is how it should be' – there is something about that gathering of yourself every day, that regathering, too, which sets you up for the day to come.

It seems to me that a lot of your most precious beliefs are about human beings, our connectedness to each other, how we are created, what sort of thing we are, who we are. Everything you've said makes it clear that you think of the individual human being as a product, in a way, something that's continuously developing. I just wonder, do you ever become aware of the tragedy of that as well? Like, you think, Here's the human being, year after year generating this incredible personality, rich and layered and developed, just for it to come one day to an end. How do you deal with that? The individual human being is a story, a unique thing that is never completed, but then it does just suddenly end, and I suppose I find it a little tragic.

One of my chief pleasures in life is going through graveyards. I absolutely love graveyards. I walk, at the moment, every single morning, through quite a big graveyard, and I make a point of trying to read whatever grave is visible most to me – and obviously, a lot of it is sadly erased. When I was younger, certainly when I was a child, I used to think, *Were all of those people just okay with that being the end of it?* Setting aside any religious thing, just their actual lives ending with a stone that hardly records their name, and you have to really scratch around to see the dates. At that point, I was set on becoming an actress, and probably, in my mind, a very famous actress. It was a burning ambition to act. Nobody in my family has anything to do with that. So it just came from me, this real, absolute, strong connection I had to my future self somewhere on the stage. And I used to think, *I don't want a faded stone, I want more of a memorial.*

Now, I'm coming to a point where I think that is our contribution. That is our legacy: to be that entwined with other people with whom we have this common bond. Over the years, I have met people who ostensibly were ordinary, whatever that means, and yet no one is. Everybody's got some part of their personality – or, more often than not, some amazing or extraordinary or sad or remarkable fact that is theirs alone – and if you open that up, both of you can go, 'Good grief. I didn't know you did that, said that, thought that.' So we have this common link of all these individuals, who are all individual. Some of them, we elevate. We let them design our buildings or create our music or put things on our walls and I think what I got wrong as a child is the fact that not everyone wants to do that. That definitely did not connect with me then, because we were all jostling about trying to get not just on stage, but to the front, under the light. Actually, I think we don't all want that, or maybe we want it sometimes, but we don't want it all the time, and we are prepared – I'm thinking of my analogy of the moment – to be the trampoline for some other people. We're prepared to support the bounce.

So, yes, to go back to your point about the tragedy of the end, there are people I have loved and lost who would profoundly have enjoyed things that have happened since, or would equally have been incredibly useful, or would have been a real salve in things that have happened to me – but it was mostly the shared pleasure of their lives that I miss, and their view of the world. But I think we are that trampoline. Our ending supports the next bounce. I think I can only make sense of it like that.

Do you take anything practical from these beliefs, or this belief in particular? Does it have consequences?

It is not to say nothing matters, because everything really, really matters a lot, but it's more perspective that I suppose I've always wanted. Whatever frightens me or puzzles me profoundly, I want to get to the other side and have a look at it from there. I want to see it from all angles. I can't bear shapelessness. I've had to work really hard over this, because when the ending goes to a row of dots, that really doesn't suit. I'm quite good at thinking, *What's the worst that can happen?* I travel all that way a lot and have a look at it. It's pretty grim. But then I think, *Okay, now I know what it looks like. That's just one option.* The worst may well happen, but as I've said already, those bad things that happened, I did cope with, and I would put out exactly the same feelers and use, hopefully, the same coping mechanisms again. I suppose this is not a world view. It's quite tiny. It's a sort of step-by-step view. But knowing that even if the ground ahead isn't solid, something about it will be familiar. Something about it will be known.

Ian McEwan on being a novelist

March, 2021

Ian McEwan is an award-winning author of 20 works of fiction and many screenplays. Many of his books have been turned into well-known films including *Atonement, On Chesil Beach* and *Enduring Love.*

I've heard it said that every novelist is at least a little bit humanist, has to be interested in other people, to get inside their heads, to connect with them.

I'd go further. Novelists are primarily humanists. They have adopted a form that is fundamentally secular. It never really works having a *deus ex machina* in a novel's plot. The novel form grew out of the Enlightenment and established itself in the eighteenth century. Richardson, Fielding, Jane Austen do not have much recourse to religion, beyond conventional nods towards it. They examine moral values by what you might call a general human standard. If you want literature to worship God, then poetry is, I think, the perfect form. Otherwise, the monograph or the prayer and the hymn. The novel is too pluralistic for religion, too tolerant. It is indeed the ultimate humanist form.

That tolerance, does that come from a type of empathy?

Yes, novelists must get into other minds. They need that freedom. The form is virtually a celebration of individualism. It follows and focuses on a particular person or small group of people. Their fates must be open and that too militates against a religious sense of destiny, one that must be fulfilled before the eyes of a God. That open-ended quality is also what we find in life as well as novels.

You're speaking about your characters as if you need to give them what you would give real human beings: give them empathy, give them freedom. Is that how you feel about characters when you're creating?

It sometimes feels like that. For a character to come to life, to 'work', the writing process must involve surprise. One of the pleasures of writing a novel is recognising those moments when you've attained a degree of momentum and the force of events that you've imagined starts to deliver surprises. So yes, there is a parallel with life. I'm not sure it's true to say that novelists love all their characters, but they also know that they're extensions of themselves. Flaubert's famous 'Madame Bovary, *c'est moi*' rings true.

You see it as coming from your own creativity and your own imagination, even if it seems to be running away with itself?

Yes, it's down to the operation of the mind. You can set off walking down the street for three hundred yards and you cannot know what you're going to be thinking about at yard two hundred. The mind has a mind of its own. There is an aleatoric quality to thought which is one of its delights. Yes, on that walk you can address yourself to a problem, that's another matter. If the problem obsesses you, you can think about it in a sustained way. But in the daily nature of thought that's quite rare. Thought in an unstressed way has a meandering quality. We honour James Joyce and Marcel Proust and Virginia Woolf for teaching us how to capture that flow. This was one part of the modernist aesthetic revolution to which we are all indebted.

Are you ever doing that harder type of thinking in your novels? Some reviewers see some of your novels as being extended attempts to deal with some of the bigger themes. Are at least some of your novels a vehicle for taking on a particular ethical problem?

I think they illustrate a problem or pose the questions. Novels are less good at the answers. Most readers don't want moral messages presented on a plate. The problem is life itself is lived forwards, as Kierkegaard famously said, but understood backwards. Novels are written forwards at three, four or five hundred words a day but discussed backwards by readers and critics. That way, a novel's 'meaning' is artificially generated. But what, at that level, do novels show us? Iris Murdoch once said that novels boil down to saying 'nice things are nicer than nasty things'. We want novels to unfold convincingly the impression of lives lived and problems confronted.

As a reader, I want the complexity of life revealed, and the difficulties we may have in understanding each other, and how easily conflicts arise between rational people. Showing that process is not solving it. But somehow our experience of life is enlarged. In such discussions, I often refer to the novel by Saul Bellow, *The Dean's December*. The dean, an elderly American professor, is married to a Romanian. It's back in the coldest days of the Cold War. He wakes in the middle of the night. He's in his wife's home city, Bucharest. He hears dogs barking in the dark across the city and imagines that they're saying, 'Open the universe a little wider'. That's what good novels do. They open our universe a little wider.

This difficulty of being each other: you mentioned a moment ago that one of the things that the novel did was help us, to some extent, maybe not overcome but certainly understand the difficulty we have in understanding each other. Is this a particularly big difficulty, do you think, in the world today, or has it always been in the human condition, this difficulty in understanding each other?

Oh, it's there in the human condition. I don't think it's unique to our times. Since the invention of writing and before that, in the oral tradition, literature has probed human conflict, whether it's physical violence or simply the ways in which people misunderstand each other and fall out. Henry de Montherlant famously said, that 'Happiness writes white'. Novelists are never going to give you four hundred pages of happiness. Novels track individuals through time. It is not given to us to be happy at every turn. If you want happiness caught on the wing, again, turn to poetry, to lyric poetry. There we find the most sublime expressions of joy in landscape or by being in love. You'll get moments of that in a novel of course, but typically in life as in art, time delivers kisses, then blows.

We must never take for granted the miracle of language. It's an extraordinary thing. By breathing across a few threads of tissue in your throat, you can transfer a thought from your mind to someone else's. As with speech, so with writing. By dragging a bit of metal dipped in ink across a page, we can transfer the most complex ideas from one mind to another. We do fall out, we do misunderstand each other, we have conflicting interests, despite this material form of telepathy. We know a lot more now about the ways our emotional states affect our reason. We might be completely convinced that we're being wholly reasonable, but we're not simply calculating machines. We have feelings, we have vulnerabilities, we carry around the heavy luggage of memory.

You need only look at the turgid language of a legal agreement between companies or countries or individuals. The language is stultifying because it's building up defences against any possible misunderstanding. Within countries, between languages, across cultures, among individuals, misunderstanding stands ready to intrude. Literature is drawn to this friction. We need it to because we need to embrace our flawed nature and understand it.

One of the ways in which you're a little different from some novelists is you've got a very strong interest in science. I think you must be the only novelist whose personal website has a section not just about novels and about stories, but one entitled 'Science' where you've got various interviews in writing that you've done about science.

Science has, over the years, shaped my world view. I'd maintain it has shaped the world view of practically everyone you've ever met, including the most deeply devout.

Scientific thinking? The scientific mindset?

Well, most of us accept, for example, that the Earth goes around the sun. It took a while to get that established and some pain along the way. We know now about the vastness of the universe.

Again, it took scientific discovery. We know something about the world on a very large scale and the world on a very small scale and most of us know that the world of quantum mechanics is antithetical to our common-sense understanding. We know that germs exist and how they spread disease, that spontaneous generation does not spread disease and nor does wickedness create it in its victims. Such things had to be discovered and proved. They were established for us by scientists. Most people now, including the most religious, take for granted ideas that would have got them burned at the stake five hundred years ago.

You mentioned thinking scientifically, which is also thinking probabilistically. I'm fascinated by the nature of coincidence, of the random nature of events that can transform lives. It's the stuff of everyday life. How did our parents meet? Most of us are not derived from arranged marriages and if your mother had stayed in and washed her hair and not gone to the dance, she wouldn't have met your father. If your parents had made love two minutes later, you would not exist. In your place would be a sibling. It's almost too obvious to state how easily our lives could be other if we'd gone to another school or taken a different job, and so on. I know that's not quite what probability theory is about, but that sense of the contingency of life haunts and delights me when I'm writing. In *Machines Like Me* I decided to go back in time a little and play with certain political events, to see how easily they could have been different, often hinging on the tiniest things. For example, we could have lost the Falklands War if the Argentinians had primed their Exocet missiles properly. Our navy could have been destroyed. This would have had profound consequences for Mrs Thatcher's political future. It would have also meant, in Argentina, that the fascist junta would have survived. All kinds of other things social, but also personal, would have changed. Again, that's hardly really science but provides the reference point.

I can see how it's shaping your ideas about things. I was thinking of Enduring Love *when you first started talking about contingency.*

Yes. Pure chance in everything. It's so interesting really, social life, in that respect.

It makes it sound like it's almost a weird thing.

Well, once you step outside the view that your life is ordained by fate, by your destiny or your god, you step into an extraordinary jumble of possibility. It can be frightening to contemplate it, but it's also marvellous, quite wonderful. Nearly all of us who are married, for example and have had children have come at this entirely by chance – this partner, these particular children. Of course, how else could it be done? Everyday life is miraculous, and the novel's business is to remind us again and again how true this is. Or as the novelist John Updike famously put it, the novel's task is to 'give the mundane its beautiful due'.

Diane Munday on working for change

March, 2021

> Diane Munday is a humanist activist and campaigner who played a key role in the passing of the 1967 Abortion Act and the setting up of the British Pregnancy Advisory Service in 1968.

There was a period in my life, in my teens, when I just desperately wanted to believe. I thought I was an oddity – that there was something badly wrong with me. And I went visiting all the flavours of churches, and it wasn't until, quite by accident at, I suppose, eighteen or nineteen [in the late 1940s], I came across a book by Thomas Huxley in the library, and a great feeling of relief came over me. I wasn't an oddball; I wasn't alone. There were people who not only thought like me, but wrote books about it.

What was it that made you feel odd? Was it that everyone else appeared to be religious?

Yes, everyone seemed to believe these things or went to church. I had a couple of good friends who went to the same youth club I went to who were Catholics, and they took me to the Catholic church. My mother's family were Jewish, so I went to family weddings and things like that. It felt like everybody else was taking on something big, and there was just me who didn't believe any of this nonsense.

I remember reading that one of the moments when you first positively rejected religion was when you saw the strange behaviour of a Jewish 'uncle', who was a friend of your family but would eat ham – except on Saturdays! Is that right?

That's correct. I was quite young. And about the same time, I remember that my baby brother, who was nearly eight years younger than me, had been ill during the night vomiting, and my mother washed his bedding, put it out in the garden to dry, and it just so happened it was a Sunday. And our elderly next-door neighbour, who we were quite friendly with, came bashing on the door, and reduced my mother to tears because she was hanging out washing on the Lord's day. And I stood there, arms akimbo, and said, 'We're Jewish and Saturday is our holy day, so are you going to stop hanging *your* washing out on Saturdays?' That sort of thing stayed with me and made me very angry. But my uncle was in a different category. I'd grown up with the idea that Jews didn't eat pork. But when he clandestinely came round for his ham sandwich – but not on Saturdays – that just offended [. . .] something logical, rational, consistent inside of me. And I thought, *How stupid!*

So it was already in you, this questioning?

It was in me.

I want to talk about the times in which you first got involved with the organised humanist movement. I think it was the early sixties.

It was the late 1950s. When Humanists UK was called the Ethical Union!

How did you first get involved?

I think it was because I was undistracted. We had moved to North Yorkshire from London, where all my family and friends lived. I was pregnant for the first time, and we ended up in a small hamlet four miles from the nearest loaf of bread on the Yorkshire Moors, with one car and no public transport. I had joined the Ethical Union before we left London. They used to advertise quite widely and I wrote for some literature. Having abandoned religion at the age of seven or eight, and worried about it during my teens, and then discovered Huxley and other books, by my early twenties I had sort of pushed it to one side, because so much else was going on in my life, particularly being a mother for the first time. But I remember reading their literature, and only then discovering why my husband's middle name was Bradlaugh.

Oh, really? So did your husband come from a family that quite admired Bradlaugh?

Very much. His mother's father, in fact, had helped fund Bradlaugh, and my mother-in-law – and I do not know what's happened to them – had a pair of Annie Besant's earrings.

Oh! It's a shame we don't have them still.

Oh yes. She always said I should have them, but I've never seen them . . .

So, whilst in Yorkshire, I started reading a lot around human-ism/secularism and confirmed to myself that was where I really belonged. We then moved back down South at the time when the thalidomide tragedies were very prominent in the-news and I became pregnant for the third time. In fact, I was prescribed the drug to combat insomnia but kept the prescription on the mantelpiece but did not obtain the tablets. Realising that, if I was carrying a defective foetus, I would wish to end the pregnancy and how much linkage there was between the need for legal abortion and religious opposition to its availability, I joined and became involved with what was then the near moribund Abortion Law Reform Association.

Your work in the Abortion Law Reform Association and in the humanist movement on abortion is all a matter of the historical record. But I'm interested in finding out more about why you were motivated towards this work, and what experiences, values or principles really got you involved. It was a dark time, because abortion was a criminal matter. Was it outrage at that, was it a view of a better world – what was motivating you?

It was the same lack of logic and consistency that I objected to in people's religious practices. By outlawing abortion, you quite clearly didn't stop it. You sent it underground, where it became even more dangerous. And it was the fact that because I had a chequebook to wave in Harley Street, I could buy a safe abortion, but other women – they were suffering. And it was the same outrage I had at the stupidity of my uncle and the ham sandwich. I think it was the sheer irrationality of outlawing abortion.

When unintentionally pregnant for the fourth time, I personally felt a surprisingly intense internal drive not to have another child. I was happily married with children, but the minute I was pregnant, I knew that nothing and nobody would make me have a fourth child within four years. I just could not cope. And if I felt like that in my relatively stable, comfortable position, what about others who were not? I actually knew somebody who disappeared from school (and I was at grammar school; she was very bright). Suddenly, in sixth form, she disappeared. Many years later, we were on a camping holiday in Wales and went into a café, and there she was, serving. She had become pregnant in sixth form. She had been shipped off to her grandmother in Wales. So instead of going to university, she was serving in a tea shop.

So it's not just the irrationality, it's the injustice as well.

It was and is! I had bought my abortion in Harley Street; I was alive. A young woman I had known earlier, like me, she was married with three young children – and then she died because she could only afford a back-street abortion. The sheer hypocrisy of it, too, and of society. It was a mixture of all sorts of things. It was anger and a sense of injustice that drove me.

In those years, of course, there were all sorts of progressive reforms taking place. It wasn't just the partial decriminalisation of abortion;

it was also the abolition of laws against homosexuality, on divorce. And you were campaigning on all of them?

Yes, but often behind the scenes. Assisted dying was – and is – a very big concern of mine, too, and the older I get, the bigger it gets. But not for many years did I campaign openly on that. I did a lot, but I didn't want to tar other campaigns with the abortion brush. I didn't want them to say, 'That woman, she kills babies. Now she wants to kill everyone!'

So there was a sort of notoriety. But in the last couple of years, as we've been celebrating the anniversaries of partial decriminalisation, do you think there's still a negative connotation?

Certainly among some people there is, and I am still campaigning, because campaigning really consists of changing people's minds, I think. Now, I am a reasonable elderly lady, and I get further in that persona. Although with younger politicians especially, there is less stigma anyway, and they've grown up in a completely different moral environment. They are younger. There are more women. And they don't carry the post-Victorian baggage that my parents' generation had.

One of the concepts that unites a lot of the causes that you've been active on is the concept of choice. And I thought it would be interesting to know if that is a personal value for you? And if so, why? What is it about choice and freedom of choice that is so valuable?

Do you know, I've never thought that through. As you've rightly said, they do come together through something I believe in – in freedom for individuals as long as they harm no one else. But I actually always thought the thing that linked them is, very broadly speaking, there are fields that we tend to label as being about morality. My husband's death and my mother's death reinforced my theoretical belief in the right to choose to die. But what outraged me was that they were stopped by some other people's belief in this great, good, powerful, loving father in the sky. Because without that, there could be no reason for inflicting these agonies, which are inflicted on people, because of the fear about this entity and what he wishes you to do. But believing in choice and freedom is just part of me. Common sense.

Did that come at all from your family and your upbringing?

No.

That was completely absent from your family upbringing?

My mother had a very childlike naivety. She didn't go to synagogue, but I wore the Jewish Star of David; I had a gold one pinned on my vest. I used to say prayers when I went to bed ... Thinking about it, I think one thing in my upbringing perhaps enabled me to stand up against things and carry on my own way. We lived in East London when I was young, at the time of the fascists, at the time of the war. I had a German name and a Jewish mother, and I can't tell you the number of times I was tipped off my bike in the street, grazing my knees, and called a 'dirty German Jew'. So I got used to people calling me names. During the war, when things were pretty grim – I was there throughout in East London during the Blitz – this didn't stop. Also – and my mother didn't realise how much stick I got about this – she was born in South Africa. Her parents were English, and she had a lot of family there. She had a cousin who had twins, two years older than I was. And all the outgrown dresses and hair ribbons and other clothes were sent to us. And I stood out, because I had pretty dresses and big hair ribbons. She thought she was doing me a favour. But that did me no favours whatsoever.

So because of this, you got early lessons in being thick-skinned, and that made you more willing to be brazen in later life?

It made me brazen, yes. I became accustomed to being attacked, knowing that the attacks were unjustified, and just getting on with it. Someone did ask me how I felt when I had death threats, when I had red paint poured over my car – 'dead babies' blood' – when I was called names, when there were awful letters put through the letterbox. And I said, 'It just made me determined to ignore them and carry on.' My upbringing had given me strength. That fortified me when I saw what I believed to be injustice.

The mid-twentieth century has been called the humanist revolution in that it was all about freedom of choice being affirmed as long as it didn't harm others. You say you were ridding yourself of the strictures of Victorianism. Has that been quite a profound change that you've seen during your life?

I've perceived it because I was part of it. I don't think everybody will have perceived it. And now, of course, critics say it's the lack of religion which accounts for the lack of morality and all the terrible things that happen in society. I live in a small village. And there are still many people who I move among that don't see these changes as a good thing. But there has been a revolution, and I'm proud to say I was part of it, especially in the 1960s when I was most active in Parliament. It was a bloodless revolution. Abolition of capital punishment, homosexual law, divorce reform, legalisation of abortion and contraception on the NHS. It was a total revolution. And current Members of Parliament, many of the new intake, have grown up knowing nothing else. They haven't lived it.

And where do you think the big issues are, now? I mean, obviously, there's assisted dying and choice at the end of life. If you were twenty-five again, and you were embarking on getting involved in these issues, getting involved in the humanist movement today, what would be the agenda you'd see in front of you?

Assisted dying, yes. As we are getting cleverer at keeping people's bodies alive, I think it becomes more important. And so I think – and feel strongly - that is a continuing problem.

The rights of transgender people, that's important. And I think I would still be concerned about the role of women and racism. I was brought up a racist. My mother was born and brought up in South Africa. She had her 'boy' who carried her and took her around. His sole job was looking after her. And he went home for a holiday once a year, and one of his brothers came. When we lived in London, she asked the dancing teacher not to stand a 'half-caste' girl who was my friend next to me so I wouldn't have to hold her hand.

Really, and what did the dancing teacher do?

Didn't stand me next to her – that was absolutely acceptable. *I* found it completely unacceptable.

A. C. Grayling on the good life and the good society

A. C. Grayling is a philosopher and Principal of the New College of the Humanities, London. He has written and edited over thirty books on philosophy and other subjects, many bestsellers among them.

When you look at your life and what motivates you, what are the beliefs and values that are guiding you that you can identify?

They stem from this drive that I feel to try to make sense of things, to try to understand things. I'm curious about everything. About science and history and the world, politics, society, people, psychology – all of that just seems so fascinating to me. And it all connects up, anyway. The one true thing it says in the Old Testament is that the ankle bone is connected to the knee bone. This is true of pretty much anything.

So, right from a very early age – really, from the time I was a child – the huge relish that I'd always had for wanting to find out and wanting to know has been a big driver. And it feeds into this question of value, because the value of knowledge – of making sense, of finding out – and the values of enquiry – of matching what one thinks and believes to the evidence that one has for it, examining arguments, listening to what other people have to say, scrutinising them, bringing a kind of healthy scepticism to bear – all these things are part of the epistemic values, but they're also part of the values of life.

I remember reading something many years ago, perhaps when I was still at school: an essay of Plutarch, 'The Dinner of the Seven Wise Men' (it was always just men in those days). The essay begins with two of the sages on their way to this dinner party, and one says to the other, 'We know what the host's duty is. He's got to provide the food, the entertainment, the wine. But what is a guest's duty?'

The other one says, 'A guest's duty is to be a good conversationalist,' and that means he must be well informed, knowledgeable, and must have thought about his views. He must be able to articulate them, but he must also be a very good listener. He must really listen and really hear what other people say, so that he can draw them out, engage with them, debate them, challenge them, if necessary. So many of the world's problems arise from not really hearing what other people say, but only thinking you do. (This is certainly the source of pretty well all domestic difficulties in life.) And so, to be a good conversationalist is also to be attentive and curious. If you match the two things together, pushing the responsibility to be well informed together with the responsibility to be open and enquiring, you see what it is to be not just a good conversationalist at a dinner party, but a good citizen of the world.

When you try to do this, you very quickly discover the great diversity there is among human beings and the great variety of human nature. Even with people whom you immediately take a dislike to because you think their political views are so different from yours, or things that they've done are things that you find unacceptable, if you scratch away, you will almost always find something of interest. There are very few people who don't have some passion in life or some sort of intelligent interest in whatever it is. It doesn't matter what it is; if you get people on their home turf in that way, you can find that there is a lot of richness and depth in humanity.

So it all connects up, in a sense – the desire to know, to make sense, to stand on a mountaintop so you can see the view across time and space and human enquiry, and what it teaches you about this great variety in the world. All these things link up together and, as a result, constitute one set of values.

Some people talk about the meaning of life as if it's some standard out there and they're assessing their success in life in accordance with how far they've attained it. Everything you've just said makes me think that you care more about something else. A good life, maybe, a life well lived?

It's interesting you say that, because there is a significant distinction between the idea of a life that feels good to live and is worth living on the one hand, and, on the other hand, the question of seeking meaning in life. Because in some cases, the search for meaning could be painful, could be difficult, and life may not feel particularly good to live, but you're doing something that you think is going to be very productive. Of course, a life which is successful in the quest for meaning will turn out to have been a life worth living, even if it wasn't also a life that felt good to live. One does have to tease all these things apart.

Most people in the world are content – and justifiably so – with having a life that's worth living, even if they don't think that they are in search of some great meaning or creating some great meaning in life. For me, the idea of discovering something that is of true and lasting value – that is what constitutes the sort of quest for meaning in my view. This business of making sense of finding out is indeed what makes existence, my existence, meaningful for me. I'm thinking of what Schopenhauer said, that if you're going to want to keep on living, then existence should be better than nonexistence. In my view, trying to understand things and find things out and put together a view of what this world is, and what we are in it, is a very meaningful quest. It's what generates meaning in the lives of scientists and historians and philosophers and writers, and everybody who has tried to articulate some vision, some view of things: trying to find what contribution they can make to the overall picture.

As I say, I think most people may not be driven to do that kind of thing, but nevertheless they may feel that planting a garden and looking after a family, having a relative success in their careers and so on has made life worthwhile, providing that it hasn't been one in which the balance of sorrow, of grief, of loss, of disappointment outweighs the good things, and that's absolutely fine. People don't have to be urgently striving for the heights in order to have a life that's worthwhile. Although, personally, it always seems to me that the fact that there *is* something more, that there is something that one really could reach for, and that's worth reaching for, even if you don't get hold of it, that in itself makes your life something that does have that additional element: the element of meaning.

Is that something you think you've been in the grip of in your own life, needing to reach the next thing?

Yes, the reaching. I don't know about the success, the grasping part, but the reaching part? Certainly.

Why has that been important for you?

In part, it might be a temperamental thing. But when you look at the examples set by people who have made an effort and have achieved something, it's a remarkable fact that we remember the poets much more than we do the generals. It's a very heartening fact about human history. To want to be able to do something that is a putting in place of another piece of the jigsaw puzzle, to contribute something, to be part of the conversation, because all enquiry over time has constituted a great conversation that humankind has with itself about what matters and about what this world is: trying to understand the ultimate nature of reality, how we know it, how we can justify our claims to know it; understanding something about the major impulses that have driven human history, and which drive human individuals; understanding the place in our lives of things like our intimacies, our friendships, our participation in community. All these things are things that need to be found out about and discussed and understood, so to contribute something to that seems really worthwhile. If one could do that, if one felt that one had really put that piece of the jigsaw puzzle into the mix, then that would really be something.

It sounds like you also believe in hard work! Are you a hard worker? Do you believe in the value of hard work? It sounds like it; you're talking about things as an enterprise, as a task, as what's got to be done, with appreciation of the work involved.

I sometimes tell people that I've never done a day's work in my life, because it's not work, it's fun. It's what I love. So, as I tell people, I use that wonderful phrase from the Chinese poet who said, 'I leap from my bed and hasten, swift as a thirsty cat, to my work because I love it so.' For me, it never felt like labour, it never felt like effort. It's just been something always so fascinating, so gripping. Of course, there have been times, preparing documents, committee meetings, and so on . . .

You love a good committee meeting! I've chaired you in committees. You enjoy a good committee. I know.

Only when you're chairing it. That's the differentiator there. But my work of writing books, teaching, that kind of thing, doesn't feel like work at all. It feels like something both necessary and good. Now imagine that combination!

Where do you think this came from, this root value that you have of curiosity, finding things out, wanting to know and so on?

I can certainly think of one event which was a potentiator of it – although I cannot remember a time, and now I'm really thinking back to the age of seven or eight or so, where I didn't have this instinctive curiosity and desire to know everything. If I read something, then I wanted to know more and more. When I was fourteen, I think, we were set our first texts for English exams. They were Shakespeare texts. I was so bowled over by *As You Like It* and *Henry IV Part I*, that in the school holiday following, I read everything, I read the entire works of Shakespeare. I just had to. I was so gripped by it that I really wanted to get the whole context and to read more and understand more.

I'll tell you a little anecdote which is the source of this passion that I've always had for ancient Greece, Greek mythology and

Greek philosophy. I was at a boarding school, which I went to when I was about seven or eight. There had been some theft in the school, so the headmaster had made an announcement to the effect that no boy should go into any other boy's locker in the locker room, on pain of expulsion; this was a very serious matter. I happened to be down at the sports fields of the school when a big boy told me to go up to the school house and get something out of his locker for him. I said, 'I can't do that. I'm sorry, it's against the law here.' And he said, 'If you don't do it, there's going to be a more strict law that's going to come crashing down on you.' So regarding discretion as the better part of valour and so on, I went up to the school and was rummaging about in his locker when my brother (I have a brother who's five years older than me, and he was a great man in the school – he was a prefect, the head of boarders, captain of cricket), he marched into the boot room just as I was doing it, and he shouted at me.

Of course, in those stupid old days, we used to call one another by our surnames. 'Grayling!' he shouted at me. I'd been caught red-handed. He had under his arm a parcel. It was a present from my grandmother. It was a children's book of Greek myths, and he said to me, 'Right, I'm not going to report you for doing this, but, as your punishment, you have to learn by heart the first two pages of this book by tomorrow morning.' By the next morning, I could have recited to him the entire book word for word. I was just so gripped by it. It really triggered everything.

The thing is that every spring leads to a river, and the rivers lead to an ocean. For me, there's this sort of compulsion, in a way, to sail down all those rivers and to find out more and more, and to take huge relish and delight in it; it really is something which is self-feeding.

But the potentiator was an event that happened, a precursor of difficult things that happened in my family. When I was about nineteen or twenty, I lost my sister and mother at pretty much the same time. This was an appalling thing for my father, who was devastated by it. It was a real blow to our family. Because of the nature of the event – and it was such a difficult time for the family – I felt afterwards that I had to respond by trying to do something positive. If something is taken away, try to put back something even more than was taken away, if you can. Some sort of effort of doing something that might be really worth doing, intrinsically worth doing, which could constitute some kind of contribution in some way. From that moment onwards, I became, to the horror of my publishers later, a complete workaholic, over-productive.

You've written more and more recently about politics, about your own political ideas, your own ideas about constitutions and statecraft as well as about the immediate issues of the day. Is political conduct or political activity an important area of interest for you?

You're dead right. Just recently, I've produced a little flurry of books about democracy and the idea of the good state, the good society, and the kind of problems that the world is facing because of deficits in democracy. For example, look at the fact that we've not thought at all clearly, as a species, about the impact of this enormously rapid progress in technology, whether in war or communication, social media and the rest. We haven't really thought about how to manage them and how to respond to them properly.

And you see that failure as resulting from a democratic deficit?

Yes, because above all, we haven't had a discussion about it. Decisions have been made, corporations have proceeded with development of technologies, the impact of which has not been thought through. The way that AI, for example, is being rolled out will have very many positive advantages – very positive things will happen, but there will be some negatives as well. We haven't thought about those negatives. That's the problem there. I've always had an interest in being engaged politically, mainly in questions of human rights and civil liberties. So from the 1980s and 1990s, I did a lot of human rights work, especially in relation to China at the Human Rights Council in Geneva. I got very much involved in campaigns over biometric identity cards in the 2000s, at the time that the ID card campaign was going on.

But it was basically Brexit and Trump which made me think that campaigns about particular issues are one thing but we had to make the case, put the argument, that the framework itself is distorted. There's a lot of dysfunction, especially in our own constitution – and, indeed, in the US constitutions. I'm thinking about Westminster model societies, of which there are over fifty in the world (and one of which, by the way, is the US also). There is something rotten in the very floorboards of this way of doing politics and doing governance. I've been very keen to try to elicit what it is that's the problem there, and what should be done about it. Firstly, I did a book about what went wrong and produced Brexit and Trump. Then that made me think, *I've got to dig a bit more deeply into the question of how it should be and why it should be that way.* So there's this idea about what a good state would be like.

This has a connection, by the way, with the humanist view that I have, which is that the good society – the good, well-governed and self-conscious society, as the setting in which good individual lives can be lived – is very important. It's a connection made long ago by Aristotle, who said that ethics and politics are seamlessly one thing, because you can't have a good individual life unless you do so in a good social setting. Then it generalises even further to the point that I was making about technology, about climate change, about world poverty, about economic injustice as well as social injustice in our work. They're all connected, because we, the people, don't have enough of a voice. Government has become political. Government is about politics. In societies like ours and the United States, with very dysfunctional electoral systems, what we get is one-party government, party-political government, instead of government for all the people that acts in the interests of all the people of this country, and recognises that all the people of the world should be working together on things like climate change and so on.

All this sounds incredibly idealistic, but there is a hard practical point here, which is that if the G7 governments were governments that were really, each of them, not thinking of the economic competitiveness of their own situation, not wanting to be left behind in an arms race on weapons or AI or technological development, not wanting to be too active about dealing with climate problems because that puts them at a competitive economic disadvantage – that if the major economies of the world were to do what thoughtful people in them (and if everybody were well enough informed, then we would all be thoughtful about this) wanted to do about our world and putting things right, then it could happen. What's possible could be made actual. Of course, it's highly improbable that it will happen – so unlikely – but that's no reason for not arguing for it.

Nigel Warburton on clarity and freedom of thought

July, 2021

Nigel Warburton is a philosopher, author, and co-host of the *Philosophy Bites* podcast. He is known for his popular introductory philosophy books.

You're known not just as a philosopher but as a populariser of philosophy with successful books, newspaper columns, but also hugely successful podcasts. What was it that made you want to be a populariser?

I don't think I ever sat down and thought, 'I want to popularise philosophy.' I actually see myself as a writer – and now a podcaster – with a special interest in philosophy. Everything I've done, I want it to be accessible. I don't see the point of writing or speaking in a way that excludes other people unless there's some very good reason for going technical. So I guess the simple answer to your question is that clarity is a great virtue as far as I'm concerned, and that's what I aim at.

Why is it a virtue for you?

Because it's a matter of respect for other people that you speak and write in a way that they can understand without forcing them to do unnecessary work, without using obscure language, without alienating them. You could even see it as connected with humanism. There are some people who enjoy using very long, obscure words because it shows how clever they are, or using very long, convoluted sentences because it reveals that they've studied Latin and Greek and can handle those sorts of subordinate clauses and so on. I'm much more influenced by George Orwell's approach to writing, and the idea that you should say things clearly, simply, without unnecessarily complicating matters. In philosophy, where I've written most, it's very tempting to use the jargon; it's very tempting to nod to the names of authors without actually specifying quite what about them it is that you're referring to. There is an academic tradition of keeping philosophy away from a wider readership, although there are some excellent examples of philosophers much of whose work is readily accessible, including David Hume, our own Bertrand Russell, Daniel Dennett, Martha Nussbaum, and Peter Singer particularly – he's a superb writer, who doesn't usually get the credit for being a superb writer because it's almost invisible what he's doing, he does it so well.

It's about showing a certain respect to other people and treating people as your equal. The assumption is there isn't that much difference between human beings, and most people share quite a lot of common experience, so we should be able to communicate with one another about the deepest questions we can ask ourselves.

You wrote a book about essay writing, and you said there that writing well also helped you think well.

I believe that. Writing is a kind of thinking. Very few people have a fully formed idea which they then transfer to the laptop or to the page. It's the process of trying to create something that allows you to think, and revising and editing it that allows you to think clearly. It is one way of thinking. When people speak, they don't necessarily formulate what they're going to say. I'm not formulating and rehearsing what I'm saying now and then speaking. I'm just speaking. So I think writing, particularly for professional writers, is very much a way of discovering and refining what you think. It's not putting your ideas down on paper. It can be, if you've been for a long walk and worked a few things out, it can be like that, but for most people, it's the process of writing that is the thinking.

And for you, is that how your thoughts develop? On the page?

In as much as I have any. I often jot down ideas and then write, and the writing is better than the jotted-down ideas. Or I talk to people. Conversation is another very good way of clarifying thought. That connects very much with some of my thoughts about free speech as well. Dialogue is particularly good for human beings in lots of ways: socially, developmentally, but also in terms of thinking, when you come up against ideas which may not seem true at first, or which need a bit of clarification, or when somebody forces you to think through what you've just said and rephrase it so it's more accessible, easier to understand, or perhaps more watertight as an argument. Those sorts of interactions are the kinds of things you might try and have on the page with yourself, as it were, as you're writing, but there is a particular kind of thinking through speaking with other people that is an excellent way of developing ideas as well.

You mention free speech, and you've written a book about that. You've got a lot of thoughts about that value.

I've got other people's thoughts about that, mostly. I would say I'm broadly a liberal in the sense that I believe that free speech, by which I mean extensive freedom of thought and expression, is a very valuable aspect of society. It's important politically and it's important emotionally for most people, in the sense of their being able to express their viewpoint on the world. There are, however, limits, which should be set by law and by etiquette – it's not just 'anything goes'.

The default position should be in favour of extensive freedom of thought, even for the ideas of those people we think are absurd and even potentially dangerous. There's a point where you have to draw the line, but it's not where they're *potentially* dangerous in some vague sense, it's where they've actively become dangerous, and it's very hard to draw that line. As anybody who's thought at all about free speech will recognise, where you draw the line in each particular case is almost like case law in the sense that you have to take into account the details of the particular circumstances, the particular subtleties of what's going on, and the precise context. That's not an easy thing to lay down the law about, but I think the world is better when people can disagree with one another rather than being pre-emptively silenced.

Why do you think that is better? Is it because of the good things it gives rise to, or is it because of something personally satisfying in being able to speak freely?

I think both are important aspects for me. I'm not completely convinced by John Stuart Mill's optimism about truth emerging from the collision of error and truth, because it often doesn't. He recognised that it often doesn't, but he was pretty optimistic that kind of ongoing seminar would lead to less dogmatic thinking, at least. I'm tempted by that. It's true that when you don't have your views challenged, it's easy to fall back into what he called dead dogma.

But I've also got a strong emotional revulsion to being silenced, and I think a lot of people have that feeling: that as an adult, it's part of a mark of respect that we're allowed to have a viewpoint on the world and on the questions that matter, and that we should be able to communicate that with other people in a civil way. So there's an emotional aspect, and there's also the function of speech as catalysts to thought, an aspect that Mill drew attention to as well in *On Liberty*: people with whom you disagree are the best people to have a discussion with, in some ways, because they're the ones who help you work out what you actually do think and what matters. Whether you come to agree with them more or less, they still stimulate you. I think having a world of diverse opinions, like having a world of diverse viewpoints, including religious viewpoints, is better than having a monoculture in which everybody grows corn or maize. We want to have, as it were, a biological diversity of ideas, and the best way to do that is, I believe, to have extensive freedom of expression.

Also, I've interviewed a number of people who had been victims of oppression for speaking out in various countries, including Belarus and Myanmar, people who've been tortured for their views. In one case, my interviewee, Zarganar, a comedian, had been in solitary confinement for over two years. I was struck by how much they were in favour of extensive freedom of expression. Having been through all that, we're still prepared to stand up and say that this is a really important value. Even more amazingly, they would exercise that value again, in courageous ways, because they think that it's important that their views should be heard. They were treated abominably for speaking out. Those people who too readily silence other people are on the wrong side, I feel. The kind of puritanical, pre-emptive action that we sometimes see, when people with whom you disagree get no-platformed or forcibly removed from places where they're about to speak, that seems to me worse than letting even quite obnoxious views be aired and argued with. I'm all for the argument, not for the muscling of the speaker off the podium.

Part of your motivation for valuing free speech is that you almost feel you owe it as a duty to those people who are silenced around the world?

I've got tremendous respect for people who risk their lives when they express their beliefs. Most of us are lucky enough not to have been imprisoned and tortured for our views. I'm not saying there's a slippery slope that we're inevitably going to go down when we start censoring people, but it feels to me that some of the people in the UK who are so ready to censor, and are so sensitive to views which they dislike, are heading that way. It really does.

I do believe that hate speech is a kind of harm, and that there are certain kinds of psychologically damaging speech which should be legislated against. But at the same time we should be very wary of those whose immediate reaction to views they dislike is to try and silence them

What do you believe are justifiable limitations on free expression?

Well, I was thinking of the kind of hate speech where some-body uses words to damage somebody psychologically, where the motivation and the very likely effect is real belittlement of the person addressed that way. That's very different from having a discussion about something which somebody else objects to. When it's name-calling and using pejorative words about people over and over again with intent to upset, that's when we can speak of words causing harm. It's obviously context-dependent, so it's not easy to lay down a simple rule about this.

Is there an example you could give, then?

Imagine a horrible teacher who constantly belittles somebody for making mathematical mistakes over and over again, and says, 'You're stupid. You're an idiot. You can't do maths. You should go home now. You're a failure. You're never going to be a mathematician. You're not even going to get through this test. I don't know what you're doing in my class!' Those sorts of repeated statements, it's a kind of abuse and, because it's verbal, it's not merely causing offence, it's actually potentially damaging somebody. I've picked an easy example because you have a vulnerable child, but you can imagine somebody doing that to an adult.

And that person was specifically a teacher; they weren't just someone who happened to be saying to someone, 'You're really rubbish at maths.'

Somebody in a position of power can use words to harm another person who's in a more subordinate position to them, for sure. Famously, John Stuart Mill drew the line between causing offence which is tolerable but not necessarily desirable, and real harm. We all cause offence to people. Humanists cause offence to religious people a lot of the time, just by existing. Mill drew the line between that and inciting violence using words. Obviously, he didn't want incitement to violence to be a legal form of free expression, he made that clear. That was the limit for him: the incitement to violence. But I'm saying we have a more psychologically sophisticated understanding of the harm that words can do, and I think a kind of malicious, repetitive hate speech can be at least as damaging as hitting somebody with a stick, if not worse. There are lots of things that people do and say that offend me, but I hope I would be tolerant enough not to stop them doing those things and saying those things if they're not physically harming other people and if they're not psychologically damaging them in a malicious way.

Malice is the test?

I think so. It's an ingredient at least. That's my starting point.

So people's intentions do matter – not just the effects of their actions, but their intentions?

Of course intentions matter. If I flip a light switch and instead of the light coming on, I electrocute somebody next door, even though I didn't know you'd wired that up, that's a very different act from just turning a light switch on. But it's not because of my intentions that I would have electrocuted that person. You would judge me differently if I'd deliberately wired up the person next door to be electrocuted. We always take intentions into account. That's why the law is so interested in *mens rea* and the intentions that people have: the difference between murder and homicide, the difference between different kinds of physical violence that are accidental and deliberately done. Those are all taken into account in judging the severity of a crime and its punishment, or whether it even is a crime. That seems a very human thing to do. We live in a world of understanding each other not just through outcomes but through whether these were an accidental, unexpected or desired consequence of our action.

Are there other freedoms that you find yourself attached to? Freedom of expression, we've discussed. Are there other freedoms to which you find yourself particularly committed?

My more utopian commitment, which obviously isn't possible, would be for freedom of movement of people around the world. I think if it were possible somehow to open borders, I would love that. I find restrictions on immigration – which seem pretty arbitrary sometimes, particularly in Britain at the moment – very disturbing, particularly as I have a cosmopolitan outlook. I think we're just inhabitants of the world, we have cultural differences, we have localities in which we grew up, but people have very good reasons for moving away from some of those. There's no easy solution, but in an ideal world, there should be greater freedom of movement than there is now. I worry about the kind of national borders idea where people lock down and present all kinds of rationalisations about why such-and-such people can't possibly come in and pollute our isle. This is the kind of worrying rhetoric that we're seeing at the moment.

A local version of this is that I love going for walks and I love cycling, and I find the lack of freedom of movement – because some people own large tracts of land and keep other people out – very disturbing. There's something wonderful about public footpaths and bridleways and the like, which allow a certain kind of respectful freedom of movement across the countryside. Just around Oxford, I've several times encountered people who've put barbed-wire fences across what seemed to be footpaths, bridleways; they put up signs saying 'Private, keep out', 'Do not go through this lane', 'Do not cut through this driveway'. Again I have a strong feeling that we should be free of most of these restrictions; that owning huge amounts of land without good reasons for keeping other people off that land is not a good way to live – for either the landowner or the ordinary person who is kept out. Putting up those barbed-wire fences that stop people crossing a field when all they want to do is enjoy the countryside – and when they're not damaging crops and they're not threatening wildlife and they're not doing anything particularly disrespectful – seems wrong. The presumption that we should always favour the private landowner above the rambler is not a good one. I feel that there's something particularly important about having freedom of movement wherever possible. The default, as with freedom of expression, should be that we should be free, free to think and express our views, and, wherever possible, free to roam. Free, unless there's a very good reason, such as it's a firing range; it's a delicate crop; there are very rare orchids in that field that you want to walk across. Freedom should be the default.

Nichola Raihani on cooperation

May, 2022

Nichola Raihani is a professor of Evolution and Behaviour at the University of Auckland and University College London. Her work explores cooperation and altruism in humans and other animals. She is author of *The Social Instinct: How Cooperation Shaped the World.*

I started working on cooperation during my PhD, when I worked on a species of bird that lives in the Kalahari desert called the pied babbler. They are an extraordinarily cooperative species; they live in tightknit family groups, and everyone works together to a common goal, which is raising the offspring of the dominant pair. I think situations like this, in nature, often strike us as puzzling, because when we think about things from a Darwinian perspective, that tends to emphasise self-interest and every individual looking out for themselves. And what we see in species like the babblers that I worked on, or the meerkats of the Kalahari, that you might be familiar with, and lots and lots of other social species, is that individuals actually seem to put aside their own self-interest in pursuit of a common goal. Reconciling the existence of that helpful behaviour with this overarching theory of how we understand the world – which is Darwin's theory of evolution by natural selection – is something of a puzzle. So how do we, on the one hand, accept this theory of Darwinian evolution, which emphasises competition, and reconcile that with all these examples of *cooperation* that we see in the world around us, in our own species and in other species on the planet? And I think that answering that question and finding the ways that evolution has solved that puzzle is the thing that keeps me going research-wise, and is the thing that I think is so interesting about working on cooperation.

For a lot of people, the idea of 'the *selfish* gene' has come to support this world view that we live in a competitive world, that it's a jungle out there, everything is zero-sum. If you lose, I gain. If I gain, you lose. And to give us this idea of ourselves as nakedly competitive beings. In my book [*The Social Instinct*], I pick up where *The Selfish Gene* left off in a way, and start from the prem-ise that actually, cooperation is everywhere around us. When we look in the mirror, we see ourselves – and we are wonderful conglomerates of cells and genes that are all cooperating to make us individuals. If we look outside our window, we see evidence of cooperation all around. The streets we live on, the houses we live in, the trains that take us to work: these are all examples of how we've managed to cooperate to create the societies that we live in. In my view, cooperation is so pervasive that we actually take it completely for granted a lot of the time.

So this important concept for you, how would you define it? What are we meant to understand when you're talking about cooperation?

'Cooperation' is one of those terms that's become a bit hijacked by corporate-speak. If you type 'cooperation' into the Google Images search bar, you come up with a bunch of images of people doing, frankly, weird things with their hands: variants on handshakes and holding hands, and other weird things. And, in many ways, cooperation has become synonymous with this idea of teamwork and cheerfulness, and lots of other bland corporate metaphors. But in reality, cooperation has a much deeper meaning. And it is a much larger concept. In an evolutionary sense, when we talk about cooperation, we're talking about interactions where individuals work together, and where it often involves one party, or maybe both parties in the interaction, paying the cost or investing to help the partner, such that benefits are generated for all individuals involved. And so, we can talk about cooperation among the genes inside our bodies that put aside their own self-interest in the service of creating a unified organism; we can talk about cooperation among the cells of our bodies, some of which agree, as it were, to have a life of servitude and to be non-reproductive – and that's the majority of the cells in your body, actually, only a handful of which will be able to make it into the next generation as sex cells. And we can also talk about cooperation, of course, among individuals. And there are lots and lots of lovely examples, both in our own species, and in other species on the planet as well.

This idea of cooperation involving at least one entity paying a cost to benefit another is an important concept in your thinking about cooperation?

It's interesting, because whenever we see individuals paying costs, if we want to understand how those kinds of behaviours could be favoured by selection, we also have to understand how those costs can be repaid via downstream benefits. To make that a bit less abstract, one example that I think resonates with people is an example that concerns ants, a particular species of ant called *Forelius pusillus*. They live in really hot, dry regions in Brazil. These ants live in a big colony, like all ants do, and their nest is underground, but during the day, they come to the surface and they search for food. And when the evening comes, they go back to their nest. When they go back in the nest, the majority of the ants will go down the tunnel – they go into the safety of the nest overnight – but a couple of them wait at the surface, and they wait for everyone else to go into the tunnel before they then start dragging and carrying grains of sand and other debris to completely conceal the nest entrance from the outside. In doing that, they seal their own fate, because they can't survive overnight above ground. And, in fact, this kind of costly act of self-sacrifice isn't the final cost that these workers at the surface pay, because once they've ensured that the nest entrance is concealed from the outside, they then march off into the night and go off to die somewhere that won't attract predators to the location of the nest.

In this poignant example, what we see is a very obvious cost that's being paid by some individuals in that colony – the ultimate cost of sacrificing themselves to protect their relatives that are in the nest underground. And from an evolutionary point of view, we want to ask, 'Well, why would an individual ever do this? Why would they ever pay a cost to benefit some other individuals?' And in the case of the ants, the way that we can explain this is very obvious, because they are related to the individuals that they help. And so they benefit via what we call 'kin-selected benefits' by performing this act of self-sacrifice. But in many cases, individuals will pay these kinds of costs – maybe not the ultimate cost, but they'll pay all kinds of costs, like sharing food, sharing resources, things like this – to help other individuals, and they may not be related to those individuals. And understanding how those kinds of behaviours have come to exist on this planet, and why they're so common, is a central question in the research that I do, and that lots of other evolutionary thinkers are concerned with.

And your work is of relevance not just to these other animals that we've been discussing, but to human beings as well.

Totally. Cooperation is so much part of our societies. Every morning, you get on the train, and you can stand there with your face in someone's armpit; you're on your way to work. And it's a miracle in some respects, not only that the train and the platform exist, but that you can get on that train with a bunch of strangers that you don't know, in such confined circumstances, and reasonably expect to make it to your destination unharmed. There's a famous remark by the anthropologist Sarah Blaffer Hrdy, who made a comment about being on a transatlantic flight and saying something like, 'Well, what if I was sat here with a bunch of chimpanzees, and not humans? This would not be a pretty sight when the plane finally got to its destination. There would be all kinds of appendages and limbs strewn about.' We kind of laugh about it. But that's actually the reality. Chimpanzees are hugely intolerant of strangers; they really will attack individuals they don't know that are from neighbouring groups, and they will kill them or maim them. Humans are extremely cooperative in ways that we don't even really think about a lot of the time.

These are the opinions you've come to have about the nature of human beings: that we're cooperative, and that's amazing, and that it's a good thing?

I think I would caveat that statement. I believe humans are inordinately cooperative. But my view is a bit more nuanced than that. I also see that cooperation isn't always a good thing. Just to take some obvious examples: war is a hugely cooperative endeavour, and yet that causes lots of suffering and misery for people that are affected. And on smaller scales, we see things like nepotism and corruption and bribery, which are all also examples of very local-scale, cooperative interactions that generate wider costs at a societal level. And so, while it's true to say we are hugely cooperative, sometimes that is sort of taken as a shorthand for thinking, *This is great, and cooperation is this thing we should be aspiring to, and it's really virtuous and beneficial.* The reality is that cooperation can be harmful in some cases, and it can have victims, and appreciating that that is the case can help to reconcile this view we have of ourselves: that we are cooperative, but cooperation can sometimes be harmful. I think that's sometimes where people struggle with this idea of humans as cooperative, because they think of all these scenarios that seem bad, like war and harming each other and things like that. I think it's not intuitive to think that a lot of those bad things also stem from cooperation.

So cooperation is just a fact, and the results of cooperation might be morally negative or morally positive, or morally neutral?

Exactly.

The common ethical principle of treating other people how you would wish to be treated, is that a sort of result of our cooperative instincts, our social instincts?

Yes, there are certain moral values or moral rules that we see in pretty much every society on the planet, and I think are pretty universal in human society. So this idea of reciprocity, which in some places is called the golden rule, things like 'Tit for tat', or 'You scratch my back and I'll scratch yours', 'One good turn deserves another' – all these idioms we have that enshrine this principle of doing to others as you would have done to yourself is a very general principle that we see in every human society in which we've looked for it. We see that people generally endorse that principle, even if they don't always abide by it.

I think I'm also very much a product of having been brought up in a Western democracy and the kind of moral values and rules that are part of our cultural milieu that we all find ourselves in. So, our very particular notion of fairness, and the extent to which we perceive our moral obligations to everybody – we ought to treat people impartially, we shouldn't favour our kin or our friends with things like employment decisions, and things like that. All those kinds of moral values are very much like part of the cultural inheritance that the people were born in, in societies like the UK.

When we're talking about cooperation, quite often we will be running into trade-offs. It's not just a case of, 'Should we help or should we not help?' Often, we're facing decisions like '*Whom* should I help?' and 'Is it my duty to help these individuals over here, or is it my duty to help those individuals over there?' And sometimes those things are necessarily traded off against one another. I think that the source of lots of the disagreement that we have in society nowadays, where we can come into conflict over values and what we think is morally appropriate, concerns how we resolve those kinds of trade-offs.

So, to make that a bit more concrete, if I'd been born in a much more collectivist society . . . if you ask people questions along the lines of, 'Would it be right to lie in court to exonerate a friend who had committed a dangerous driving offence? Would it be right to lie to basically get them off the hook?' or 'Would it be right to hire your cousin for a job rather than a qualified candidate instead?' I have my own personal view of what I think is the right thing to do in both those scenarios. But if I'd been born in a different place, and been raised with a different set of moral values, and moral imperatives, I might answer quite differently. One thing that I believe, if you like, and also that I argue in the book, is that it's really important that even though we have our own view of what's moral in those kinds of scenarios – and that might be different to what another person thinks – it's really important to try to resist interpreting those differences with a moral overtone. So, to think, 'Well, we're right and you're wrong, and you're immoral because you think hiring your cousin is the right thing to do, or that lying in court is the right thing to do.'

So it's not just awareness of the relative nature of moral values that's important to you. Is it actually some degree of acceptance of the relative nature of moral values that's important to you?

I think it's massively important to accept that people differ on what they think moral values are, and what moral norms should be endorsed. Because if we can't accept that people will differ on where they think their moral obligations lie, then there's no hope for us of ever having productive dialogue . . . We'll just always be fighting about things. And I think, more than just accepting it, the thing that I find interesting, is to try to understand why those differences arise and where they come from. And one thing that seems to be really, really important is understanding why some people would prioritise morality as being kept within a relatively small circle: some people who would say that their moral duty is more towards their friends and family than it is towards others, compared to people who would enjoy some more universalistic kinds of norms.

Those differences seem to stem in large part from material security, which is basically the ability that people have to meet their basic needs on their own, without being reliant on others. So it's things like, can you get the food you need? If you fall ill, will you be looked after? Or will you have access to healthcare? Have you got shelter? Are you safe from anyone who might potentially want to attack you? So these kinds of things all feed into material security, essentially. And when people have lower material security, they tend to have to rely more on one another; they tend to have to rely more on their close social network to get by. So, you see, in places where people are less able to meet their own needs independently, food-sharing is much more common. So if I have food, I'll share it with you. And if you have food, you'll share it with me. You're much more likely to see patterns of what we call 'need-based exchange', where if I need something and you've got it, you ought to give it to me. And if I've got something and you need it, I need to give it to you without any expectation of repayment. So you see these really strong social bonds, where people are asking really quite a lot of one another. And it makes sense, when you think about it, that the more you're pushed towards that low-material-security end of the spectrum, the less likely you are to endorse impartial norms of cooperation, and the more likely you are to say, 'Well, actually, I need to look after the people that look after me, because I rely on these people,' and you don't have the luxury of extending investments and impartial cooperation to strangers and random people you've never met. I think understanding where those differences in morality come from will help us to understand and to accept why we have these differences.

Frank Turner on creativity and connection

March, 2022

> Frank Turner is a bestselling folk-punk singer-songwriter and musician known for his energetic performances and poignant lyrics. He has released nine solo albums and sold over a million albums worldwide.

It seems to be an inherent part of my character: a need to be creative in some way or other. Throughout my life, I've been fortunate to have discovered useful, and one might even say practical, ways of incorporating that into the way that I live my life – in fact, making it the focus of my life. I seem to have some sort of deep-seated need for self-expression and for making sense of the world through creativity, so that just seems to be how it is, really. It's so ingrained that it's difficult to question in any way.

It's always been the case in your life, you've felt that?

I think so. It's difficult for me to remember into the very mists of time, but certainly since I discovered rock and roll music in the broadest sense of the term when I was about ten years old. I fell in love, but also the very first thing I did was think, *How do I do this too? How do I get involved?*

There's always been something participatory about anything

that I love. Obviously, as you get older, you realise there are some things that you will never participate in, like Arctic fishing or space exploration, or whatever it might be. But I heard bands, and I wanted a guitar straight away.

You say that being creative or creating helps you make sense of things.

Very much. There's a degree to which a lot of the art that I make is catharsis, and is almost a sort of public form of therapy, if you like. Because I've got older, I've realised I could probably do with some actual real private therapy as well, but it certainly hasn't hurt. But there's definitely a sense that it's now become a kind of instinctive reaction. If anything happens in my life of any kind of significance, I find myself, maybe not automatically writing a song about it, but at the very least toying with phrases and expressions, and that kind of thing. It seems to be that that's my method of detangling the world, in a way, or at least figuring out what I think about it.

So you're thinking out loud in a way, with what you're creating?

Definitely. The process is – well, I always find it quite interesting. I'm in the middle of this right now. After releasing a record, the process of discussing it with journalists seems to be a collaborative one in the sense that I'm in the middle of finding out what it is I have to say as much as anybody else, and what it is I think about things.

'How do I know what I think about it until I've said it?'

Right. I'm not sure that's necessarily the best approach in all spheres of human activity. I would hope that negotiators, for example, might think that through more carefully in advance – but for myself, yeah. I've always been a fan of – and, therefore, a creator of – hopefully, unforced art. It's not quite automatic writing, but definitely I try and have as few barriers between emotion, thought and expression as possible.

When you were talking about creativity a moment ago, you branched out from this a little and started talking about the participatory nature of this and the way it connected you with others. Community and connections are also important values for you?

Very much so. To me, music becomes an interesting activity when it becomes, at the very least, dialogue rather than monologue. That's not true of all musicians. I'm old enough now not to want to sit here and wag my finger at people who have a different opinion about this – or anything else, really – but generally speaking, for me, the moment in the show when the creation of sound becomes collective (and that's a very pretentious way of saying a sing-along), that becomes more interesting to me than demanding silence from my audience while I perform. There's a sort of commonality to it. In a similar way – but I think a distinct one from the creative impulse that we're talking about – I do feel very strongly that all humans have this kind of communalist need, in a way. Historically, people have often taken it from religion, and that's fine. I don't have an issue with that, personally. Some people take it from sport, some people take it from computer games. I happen to take it from music, and there are no more powerful experiences in my life that I've had other than those moments when a real show becomes a collective performance. I say that both as a performer and as an audience member. There is this quite tribal sense of unity that can come together, and it becomes very kind of weird and exciting. I think that that's something I'm chasing very much.

Slightly less highfalutin if you like, for me, when I was a kid, one of the main ways I got into playing music was my older sister and her friends and some of my friends. I was into heavy metal, but they were into more song-based stuff, whether it would be Counting Crows or Weezer or the Levellers or whatever. I learned how to play those songs on acoustic guitar, because they were easier to play than Megadeth songs. I would play the guitar, but the thing about the whole situation – this was on summer holidays and on nights of trying and failing to get into the pub in Winchester, and wherever else – I would play the guitar so that we could all sing together. It wasn't me performing to a group of people. It was me facilitating a group activity. I think that something of that experience and that activity has remained constant in the DNA of the way that I think about music and think about performance. At its best, one of my shows is an opportunity for me to facilitate a group activity.

And why, for yourself, do you think you're chasing those moments of communion? Or those moments of unity with others? Is it a peak experience?

I think it's a really important experience. I think it's food for the soul. You could get quite existentialist here, if you like, but there's a connection between the isolated human experiences and, to a large degree, I think a lot of art is about empathy. Most art is about empathy. It's about that sense of connection between atomised individuals. I think it's important to say that this isn't an experience that I wish to have twenty-four hours a day, seven days a week. I think that you'd go nuts. I think it's really important to have moments of solitude and isolation as well. The Greeks said 'μηδὲν ἄγαν' – 'nothing too much' – like, trying to strike a balance of having a little of both. I think it's a healthy thing to do in life. Certainly – again, I'm going to the Greeks – euphoria is a real thing, and I think a valuable thing and a powerful thing. Again, one has to be a little careful with it, in the sense that I think that the twentieth century had quite a few dubious political movements that were predicated on euphoria and collective euphoria.

And loss of the self.

Right. So this is it: I think you need to strike a balance, that's important. Nevertheless, it definitely gives me a sense of orientation and meaning and value to have those moments in my life when I experience losing myself in a collective.

And it's much better to do that in sports matches and concerts than it is at political rallies and political movements.

Exactly. If we could somehow have turned many people in Germany and Russia in the twentieth century into kind of nerdy metal fans, that probably would have been better for the world.

You gave a talk for the National Prison Radio when we did a series when the [Covid-19] lockdowns were on. Humanists gave radio talks, and you gave one. You talked about kindness and you talked about it not just depending on reciprocity – treating others well because you want to be treated well. You said that you wanted, as a result of your assessments of your own actions, to be able to hold your head up high.

Absolutely. What I mean by that is (I suspect everybody does this, to a certain degree) I'm very self-critical. There's a comedy routine I saw once about somebody waking up in the middle of the night and despairing thinking about a careless word that you said eleven years ago when you were drunk. I do that all the time. Particularly if you've been through addiction issues, which I have, one of the things that gets taught – this is an aside, but let me get it – and one of the things that I think doesn't get talked about enough when it comes to addiction issues, is shame, in the sense that I feel oceans of shame for the ways that I've behaved at certain chemically altered moments in my life, because a lot of those chemicals make you careless, they make you callous – or, at least, the ones I was involved in do. So, I spend a lot of time hoping that I can just self-justify, and hoping that I can look in the mirror and not be completely disappointed. That's quite a strong motivating factor for me. I'm kind of reaching more of a sense of peace with it, in that I understand that it's an ongoing process and that everybody goes through this, and that there is no such thing as purity or perfection. I think that's very, very important, not to let the best be the enemy of good. The fact that I don't necessarily always hit my marks doesn't mean I shouldn't try.

But your motivation is that you want to be able to give a good account of your actions to yourself.

Yes. I think that this is possibly one of the things I talked about in the prison podcast, but Clive James talks about that, being on his deathbed, and saying,

'I should have been more kind. It is my fate
To find this out, but find it out too late.'

I do think, in a lot of ways, that the thing we leave behind (to the extent that there's any point in caring about that at all, which I'm dubious about) is a record of our actions – and the quality of our actions, perhaps more than the content of them. When I think about friends whom I've lost touch with, or who have passed away, or even just who are distant, it's not always the specifics of what they do, it's the way they do it that strikes me and informs my sense of their character. It is reciprocal, in some ways, in the sense that part of what we're talking about here is reputation. I feel like I'm not a terrible first evaluator of that.

It sounds like consideration of yourself is making you more generous to others as well, in judging their acts.

I hope so. One of the things that I've found very useful in recent years when assessing my own mental health and my own kind of self-regard is that I've long tried to be generous with other people and their motivations and their foibles – pluses, minuses, whatever it might – but a lot of people, myself included, don't extend that generosity to themselves. I think there's an interesting exercise to be carried out there, which is to try and evaluate your own scorecard as if it was somebody that you knew and cared for.

Christina Patterson on loss and suffering

November, 2020

Christina Patterson is a journalist, writer and broadcaster known for her commentary on society, health and culture. Her books, including *The Art of Not Falling Apart* and *Outside, the Sky is Blue*, explore resilience and the human experience.

I have been interested all my life in how we cope when life goes wrong. Largely because quite a lot of things went wrong for me. Of course, life goes wrong at certain points for everyone, but one of the big questions is how old you are when that happens. I think some people can be quite cushioned for quite a long time. I remember in my mid-twenties, when I had a pain condition that was quite immobilising, which turned out to be an autoimmune disease. Meeting people, it was clear that nothing at all had gone wrong in their lives, and I remember thinking, *How is this possible?* but of course it is.

By the time you reach middle age, then something will have gone wrong for you; you might have lost a parent, you will almost certainly have lost a grandparent, you will have lost somebody you love, you will probably have had some kind of illness at some point; but if you are in a Western culture, and you're middle class, and you're employed, and you're healthy, you can go quite a long time without having had too much go wrong in your life. In my family, my sister had what turned out to be schizophrenia, though we didn't know that for quite a while. She had a breakdown when she was fourteen and I was nine, and that had a big impact on us all, really. From that point, I don't think I ever thought, *Life is just going to be fine.* It wasn't fine. I mean, my parents were magnificent. My sister was, in many ways, a wonderful person. She died when she was forty-one. I think I became slightly obsessed by suffering, actually. She got ill, and then, in my early twenties, I developed really, really bad acne. I mean, really severe acne, so that I felt hideous, and then I developed this pain condition and various things went wrong. So I suppose I've just always been fascinated or obsessed with how we cope with pain.

Are you saying that early experience of pain and suffering changes the way you experience it later on in your life? That it builds resilience? Or are you not saying that?

I don't think it automatically builds resilience. For example, if you look at some of the research on the resilience of children who come from what would be called chaotic backgrounds, with not much in the way of parenting or not much money at home or badly fed or whatever, they actually tend not to do very well in future life. So it's certainly not a given that early suffering builds resilience. It's a complicated mix; there is no formula to it, but I certainly think that suffering when you're relatively young can build empathy and compassion, and practice at getting through tough times will build resilience for the future, I think – generally speaking,

Your book, The Art of Not Falling Apart, *is about how we cope when life goes wrong – and, of course, one of the themes of that question is*

that we meet it with resilience. What else do we meet it with? What do you think are our other tools for dealing with life's bad events?

I think probably the most important, or one of the most important, is relationships. I think if you feel alone in the world, when your world collapses and you feel alone, then it is almost unbearable – and sometimes literally unbearable. But if you have built relationships with people, whether they be family or friends, and if there is love in your life, and you have the ability to be heard, and to cry on somebody's shoulder, or to laugh, I think that makes a huge difference. I think friends are incredibly important, and also humour. A lot of the people I interviewed for the book were friends and people I'm very, very fond of who have been through tough times. They're not my friends because they are courageous and resilient, they're my friends because they're very good fun and they make me laugh, and I think that's incredibly important. I think if you lose your sense of humour, then that is tough, and I think one of the things we've seen in these past difficult months [of the Covid lockdown] is, it's really important to carry on laughing. Life is very difficult for many, many people at the moment, but you still have to find things to laugh about. Otherwise, you're sunk.

So it sounds like you think that relationships with others, they're valuable in themselves, but they also take us outside of ourselves.

Absolutely right. And again, the resilience research shows that if you have a good network of relationships, you're much more likely to be able to cope when things go wrong – but yes, absolutely. I think that's right.

Feeling better is obviously something for which there isn't a recipe. I got the impression from your book that you don't think it is just something you can switch on, but it is something that emerges eventually, and that the choices we make can help it emerge. Is that about right?

That's exactly right. Unfortunately, you can't just switch it on. There is talk about 'Fake it till you make it,' and I think there is some truth in that. I think, when I was younger, I was very, very 'heart on my sleeve'. Actually, I'm still pretty 'heart on my sleeve'. I remember when I lost my job, people said, 'Oh, you've got to go around and do all this networking,' and I remember going to a networking event and telling everybody that I'd just been fired and was feeling absolutely awful, which isn't what you're meant to do! We also have to be who we are, don't we? I think that's quite important. I think if you try to put on a huge act, at some point, eventually something will crack. You can't completely brainwash yourself into feeling something you don't feel. If you feel miserable, you feel miserable. This is where it gets complicated, because I do also think that one of the things we do learn as we gain a bit more wisdom and accumulate a bit more experience and have survived a few more knocks is that there is a sense in which happiness is a choice. I think, mentally, you can choose to focus on the stuff that makes you miserable, and if you are in terrible, terrible pain, whether that's physical or emotional pain, it is hard to get your mind out of that groove – but there are always things that can help, maybe, break a circuit, in a way. For example, fresh air and exercise – a very simple thing that we can all do. I've always thought that I hate exercise. In my head, I still think I hate exercise, but actually when I go for a run, I secretly quite enjoy it, and I feel much better afterwards. I know that when I don't go for a run, I feel much worse. So I think there are always small things, whether it's picking up the phone to a friend, or watching a funny movie, or reading a poem you love, that can make you feel different. So, I do think there's an element of choice.

What do you think it is that holds us back, then? If the choice is there to be made, if you believe that the sunshine is out there if we want it, but we have to choose to seek it. Why do you think that people choose not to?

That's a very difficult question to answer.

Yes.

I do think a lot of it actually comes down to habit. I think we build all kinds of habits that we're not really aware of, in our thinking, and just in our everyday lives. For example, one habit I was not aware of was that I have been single for most of my adult life. There's absolutely nothing wrong with being single. I had, in lots of ways, a lovely time being single, but some of the time I felt a bit resentful about that, and I would be envious of friends who were in relationships or friends with families. I realised that being single is also a habit. I think most of us can be in a relationship if we really want to be, and I don't mean that in a magical thinking 'you create your own reality' kind of way. I just mean that it's not climbing Everest. I always thought that having a relationship was like climbing Everest, and it isn't. It's about being with someone and getting on well with them, and being nice to them and them being nice to you.

But, if you think it's like climbing Everest, which I did, then it's quite difficult to choose to do that, because I definitely couldn't climb Everest and I'm not going to try. I think we can get into habits of thinking very easily. I'm someone who can easily be – and has been – very obsessed by work. I've been in cycles of working most of the time. I think obsessively about politics. I think obsessively about all kinds of things . . . At the moment, we're in the middle of the American election [of 2020]. I literally can't think of anything else. But generally speaking, we have a choice about what we put our mental energy into. So yeah, I think we can snap out of certain things. And we don't even think we have habits about what we eat and what we do, when we brush our teeth and when we go to bed and who we speak to. I think almost everything in our lives is a habit, actually.

I think we can always surprise ourselves by what we survive – and plenty of things feel like a catastrophe, and are pretty catastrophic. I've lost every single member of my family. My brother died last summer, and I'd already lost my sister and both my parents, and that was absolutely devastating. I mourn him every night, and I'm, in fact, interring his ashes next week, having delayed because of the pandemic. So, I can't claim that that wasn't a catastrophe. It was a catastrophe, but I'm alive and I'm here and I still love life. I suppose it comes down, ultimately, to how much you love life. I think, for me, having lost every member of my family, I value life all the more. I've also had cancer twice, which has made me value life a great deal. So I literally think that being alive in itself is an incredible, precious gift, and I want to live for as long as I can.

And is that what those losses gave you, that perspective? Or was it something else?

It's so hard to answer that. I don't know. To sum it up, I think loss gives you all kinds of things and, as I said earlier, I think a sense of empathy and compassion is part of what it brings you, because you can't help but feel for other people who also experience loss – which, ultimately, is all of us. I think it should give you a greater love of life. It certainly has in my case.

I remember when I had cancer the last time, which was ten years ago, and I had a big operation and it took me a long time to recover. It was a terrifying time. Obviously, I didn't want to die. I didn't know if the operation was going to work and what the results would be, and I was on my own. It was very, very, very tough. But, you know, weirdly, when I look back on the time, I have a sense of – the word nostalgia would not be right, but a sense of an incredible intensity to the experience, and intensity to the love and care of my friends who helped me through that time that I can't quite recapture . . . I think there is certainly something to be said for being reminded of how short and precious life is.

You wrote once in a column that the study of English literature was one of the things that made you realise the Bible wasn't the word of God. I don't want to talk about the Bible or religion. That's not what we're talking about on this podcast. But I thought we might talk a little about the value of literature. Humanists are well off for scientists and philosophers and all the rest of it, but sometimes our novelists and our writers and our artists get neglected.

I think that art is the most sublime expression of the human spirit. I'm sure a scientist or mathematician would say something similar, but I am not a scientist or mathematician, so I can't comment on the incredible sense of joy or elegance in a mathematical equation or even the theory of relativity, but I do know about poetry and literature and, to a lesser extent, the visual arts and music. For example, when I listen to Bach or when I read

Shakespeare, or a great contemporary novelist, like the American novelist Elizabeth Strout, who I think is absolutely wonderful, I think you sense that this is human beings at their best. I think that human beings are capable of such greatness, and that's why it's so heartbreaking to see our politics reduced to these popularising slogans that oversimplify, because everything in life is complex. What I think art does, at its best, beautifully or even sublimely, is capture the complexity of life, capture the doubt, the uncertainty, what we humans can't quite articulate but are constantly aspiring to articulate. I think of Keats and his negative capability, which is a phrase he used in a letter to a friend, which is being capable of accepting a state of uncertainty and doubt. I think that's what we need more of, in a way. Of course, populism is all about certainty, and simple (and therefore wrong) solutions to complex issues.

It's interesting that you've emphasised that idea of negative capability. How do you fit that together with what you said earlier about thinking about our own lives? It seemed then that you were seeking clarity and resolution.

I think life is all about that tension, about how to navigate the fact that we live in an uncertain universe where we don't know the answer to the most fundamental question, which is why we're here – and where did we come from? Well, the 'Where do we come from?' thing we can make some pretty good guesses about, but the 'Why are we here?', in a kind of metaphysical sense, we can only make some stabs at, and we will not get an answer in our lifetime. Since those of us who – I am a humanist, but I don't go around using labels particularly – but those of us who are broadly in the humanist camp agree that it's very unlikely there's anything after that, that means that we never get the answer at any point.

I think there are very few clear answers about anything in life, even policy in political terms; you're only trying to come up with better solutions rather than worse ones. I think that the clarity I was talking about earlier was about making choices for yourself, and trying, within all the uncertainties around, to clarify what's important for you – and that's where the values come in. We can't know what will happen in our lives, we can't know what choices will be available to us, but I think there's a kind of clarity you can have in terms of your values.

Sarah Bakewell on the biography of humans

January, 2024

> Sarah Bakewell is an award-winning author. Her books
> include *At the Existentialist Café* and *How to Live*.
> President Barack Obama listed Sarah's *Humanly
> Possible* as one of his favourite books of 2023.

*You wrote what was marketed as a biography of Montaigne. But it's
not just a biography, is it? Because the title gives away that it's about
a bit more than that:* How to Live. *Looking back at that – the process
of researching or writing, your motivations in wanting to take on the
life of Montaigne, or how you were affected – what beliefs and values
did you take from that as being important in your own life?*

I think my starting point was to just enjoy reading Montaigne's
essays, which I came across by accident, not as part of any formal
study programme or anything, just looking for something good
to read. My response was probably a reflection of what I believe,
too, because reading what he said about his life and his thoughts
on life, his experiences, reflections on his reading, and everything
else, and the general spirit of tolerance and curiosity – it all
immensely attracted me, and there was a feeling of recognising
something, either that I felt I was, or that I wanted to be. So my
initial sense was of a meeting of minds with somebody from the
sixteenth century – I mean, that's a hell of a time gap. There's a

tendency ... I think a lot of people do this, you read him, you think, *Oh, that's just like me!* And then as you immerse yourself a little bit more in reading him, you realise that there's also a lot in his writing that is strange to us now, very difficult for us to relate to. You tend to just gloss over those bits ...

What sorts of bits were they?

He was a nobleman living in France. He had servants, he had the big wine-growing estate to run. He, like a lot of people in the sixteenth century, was very much concerned with how to behave, how to be what we might call gentlemanly – matters of honour and a way of behaving immersed in the culture and the social structures of the time. You get that as well in Shakespeare, with somebody like King Lear thinking, *Who am I if I don't have the right forms of behaviour from those around me? Am I really a king?* We've now become much more inclined to think that everybody is at the same level. We don't think of that as a very serious thing to worry about: the comportment of those around you as a reflection on you. All of that is there in Montaigne. It's a very different world.

The fascination for me was to find the points of recognition with another human being who seems to share so much with me and with many other readers, but *also* the strangeness. That has always fascinated me about reading authors from different times. It's not just about cherry-picking the bits that match our modern sensibility, it's about also recognising and trying to make some sense of the strangeness. And from that, I also became fascinated by how people have read him differently in different times. And that became a big part of my book as well. The chapters move through what the Romantics made of him in the eighteenth century, and what the Victorians made of him in the nineteenth century, and what the twentieth century made of him – finding in him all this kind of anxiety that you get coming in the twentieth century.

What are some of your own points of connection with him? Mutual tolerance and curiosity. But what else?

I loved his level of fascination with what it is to be a human being: with the complexity of human responses and experiences; the fact that you can think something one day, but feel completely differently another day. He says, one day, he thinks the world is a wonderful place, but the next day, he has a corn on his toe, and he's bad-tempered and thinks everything's rubbish. And this is how variable we are. There's not a sense of a simple soul that's either good or bad. There's a sense of this fluctuating, changing, inconsistent thing through time. As you get older, you change as you interact with other people – they change you. As you read books, that changes you as well. You're in constant flux. It was very interesting to find that coming from that era, that sense of how variable and unpredictable we are. But also, I suppose it must speak to something in me.

What do you think it was that appealed? Because he was avant-garde and out of his time, or do you think you're connecting with something timeless, because he himself was obviously drawing on other, even ancient, thinkers?

He was drawing on earlier thinkers and changing them and then passing them on to his readers. But it's not that often that you come across somebody who just writes about what it is to be human. He says, 'I write about myself, because that's who I know. Each person bears the whole form of the human condition' in some way. It was unusual in his time. I'm not even sure that it's that usual in our time. I think there's an awful lot of revelation of yourself and all your emotions – we're perhaps far more familiar with that now than his generation was, but that doesn't necessarily amount to really reflecting deeply on what it is to be human.

That was a good reminder for me of what I'd come to love about philosophy. When I was younger, the kind of philosophy that I used to be attracted to was all about big ideas, theories that were abstract but exciting. There would be a system of ideas that you could immerse yourself in, with grand ambitions for what philosophy could do, but without reference to any particular person, just some cosmic thing. With Montaigne ... okay, he's talking about the whole human condition, but he's doing it by talking about one very particular person. So it was while writing the Montaigne book that I started to realise I was more interested in the particularities of people's lives, and what we share, but also what makes us individual and peculiar and eccentric. And how we live through our ideas in the course of living, rather than just sitting in an ivory tower and thinking about Being.

And your next book was about a group of philosophers who also had a very worldly attitude: At the Existentialist Café. *You didn't just look at the non-religious humanist existentialists. You looked at one or two who might be categorised slightly differently from that – but, again, a common strand between the two books is your interest in people who are interested in this world, this life and, in this case, in philosophy.*

There's definitely a connection between the two books via the question of how to live a human life, or what it is to be human, and how we are to live on this Earth, and a sort of disregard really for anything theological. There are some religiously devout existentialists in the book, but I was more drawn to the ones who were atheistic, because Jean-Paul Sartre, who's the most famous existentialist of all – and looms large in the book – once said that he lost his faith as a teenager when he was standing at a bus stop. So he devoted himself afterwards to figuring out how we deal with the fact that it's really up to us what kind of beings we're going to be, because there's no blueprint laid down by God. There's no order given to us on how to be a good human being. It's up to us to choose our path through life and to find meaning, and to find connection with others and ways of understanding ourselves. Again, I suppose this spoke to me. I didn't lose my faith at a bus stop, though. I never had any faith in the first place. I didn't have any to lose.

You were raised in a non-religious atmosphere?

I was. Both of my parents are completely without religious belief although both of them were raised within religious institutions. My father was raised in the Baptist Church; my mother went to a convent. Neither one of them stuck with it. And because of that, I didn't grow up with it.

My attraction to the existentialists centred on the way that they tried so hard to understand what it feels like to be alive. The first book by any of theirs that I read was Sartre's *Nausea*, which is a novel, but it features scenes in which the protagonist goes to a park and looks at the trees and feels how full of Being they are. It's just overwhelming how real they are, how they're sort of sitting there, full of reality. And, as a consciousness, how do you experience that? There's an awful lot of novelistic scenes even in Sartre's philosophical books, like watching a waiter delivering the

Parisian drinks and seeing how he behaves, how he presents himself. Little interactions between people. It's very observational.

Let's come on to your third book, Humanly Possible, *which is about humanists, both in the modern organised sense, and in the sense of people from before humanist organisations in the modern sense, who had humanist ideas and humanist approaches to life. How did you find yourself drawn towards thinking about and writing about humanists, as such?*

The starting point for the book was thinking about the things I'd been interested in before, people I'd written about before, and what they had in common. And it struck me that what they had in common was their humanism, of different kinds. So I wanted to understand, what is this thing that draws them together? . . . Well, it wasn't the first time I'd realised that I'm a humanist, too. The thought had occurred to me, somewhere along the line, that my feelings about life, my values, my sense of what's important, did very closely match what humanist manifestos and organisations stand for. So I feel, on the one hand, this is quite a personal book, because I do want to understand more about what that means to me. But also, I wanted to get a sense of all these different meanings that the word humanism has had. One reaction would be to say, 'Well, that's just a kind of an accident, the meanings don't have anything to do with each other.' Some humanists are people who study or practise the humanities: literature, history, reading, writing, the arts. Others are humanists found in modern organised humanism, with the morality and the sense of values, and the critical view of religious texts. These different humanists might not seem to have much to do with each other. But on some level, they have everything to do with each other, and that is down to that word 'human'. In both cases, the focus is on what our cultural, and moral, and interpersonal lives on this Earth are like. Language and the arts – that concerns ways of responding to each other. Morality is how we decide how to behave with each other. And the whole concept of humanities denotes the study of human things, as opposed to the study of divine things – and theology – or the study of just physical nature, as we call it. So I thought, *Wow, this is great. I can get all that into it!*

I remember thinking when we first met after you had started writing it, That's going to be interesting, to try and put it all together. Are there really such clear links between, as it were, the humanists in the Renaissance sense of the word, and the humanists in our sense of the word? I've always thought that there were, but that's because I'm humanities-inclined myself. I think that you analysed really adroitly the humanist tradition that unites these different types of humanists, and the analytical way in which they can be combined. Was that something you were conscious of doing?

Yes, it struck me early on what the challenge was. It's quite difficult to bring together very different meanings of a word, but I wanted to do it in a spirit of exploration. E. M. Forster, who is quite a personal hero of mine, and I think of yours as well . . .

Yes, absolutely.

. . . he came up with the great two words, 'Only connect', in his novel *Howards End*. I took that as my motto: are there connections between these ideas and traditions? Of course there are. There are also big differences. But I tried to make the differences part of the story too. It's not an attempt to kind of shove everything into a box together, but an exploration of how they differ, as well as how they are similar. I do remember thinking at a certain point – which is actually quite good advice for all sorts of writing challenges – if something is proving very awkward, and you think, *This is going to be the obstacle*, make a virtue out of that thing. Make it the focus of the whole book in a way. Why is this thing sitting like a lump in my path? Why is it going to be a challenge? It's probably because it's one of the most interesting things. So why not make it the heart of the book? So I tried to do that. I tried to say, 'Look, this is a hugely varied tradition. But that's a strength, that's not a problem. The immense richness and variety of this tradition is one of the things that is so exciting about it.'

Towards the end of the book, you blend in quite artfully, I thought, the moment at which science becomes an important part of humanism itself. Before a certain point, it's fair to say that anyone we might recognise as a humanist, even in the modern sense of the word, was far more likely to be concerned with human matters than they were to be concerned with material science. It's the nineteenth century that you highlight as being the great coming together of these things, and I think that's right: there comes a point when science is blended into the humanist way of looking at things, and instantly has an incredible impact on it.

I'm a great believer in science. I've suffered from not having a scientific education. I made the mistake at school of going for things like extra languages ... Well, it's not a mistake, but I'd try and replace all my sciences with things like extra literature modules and extra languages, and try and dump the science as far as I could. I really regret that now, because it was only later that

I realised just how endlessly fascinating and important science is. Actually, in a way, it is at the heart of my own world view. I'm a great believer in scientific method. Nothing is ever perfect, but that's pretty much the best method I think there's ever been for investigating reality. It's very robust and it's very good at outwitting our own tendencies to make mistakes, or to have prejudices and partial views.

Also, I'd love to know, as much as we can about what the universe is like, what makes it tick, why the cosmos is that way. I wish I understood more about it. With that nineteenth-century turn towards science, what interested me particularly were those figures who were important scientific thinkers, but *also* involved with humanist concerns, topics like ethics and morality, and methods of study and education. So a figure like Thomas Henry Huxley, who wrote an enormous amount about education and other humanist concerns – and he was an agnostic, and wrote about his agnosticism. Darwin himself was very interested in humanist ideas about ethics and morality. He didn't tackle it for a long time, because I think he was a bit nervous about responses, and his attention was elsewhere anyway. But the question of 'If we evolved, how did we evolve the system of morality?' came up in his book *The Descent of Man*. Those figures interested me a lot, because they were good humanists *and* they were good scientific thinkers at the same time, and they engaged with all the questions that science throws up about humanity.

We've talked about these three books as being books about ideas, but they're also, in a real sense, biographies. What draws you to that?

It's that interest in human particularity and human existence. People change through life, as I myself have enormously: that

Montaignean variability. They also *don't* change in some ways, as I also haven't. There are things that are carried through all the events that have happened to you, some sort of tendency, or a kernel of personality, that remains pretty much the same. I try to write about that in relation to the ideas, because when you're writing about writers – as, on the whole, these people were – you have a great chance to explore the lives of people who also reflect on their own lives and on the things that they experience.

***

Iris Murdoch, who was both a novelist and a philosopher, so she knew both sides, used the term 'inhabited'. It doesn't necessarily mean that you have a philosophical idea and then live it out in some consistent way – like, if you're a believer in utilitarian philosophy, you might try and live your life completely according to those ideas. There have been those who've made a pretty good attempt at that, but on the whole, we're never that consistent. An 'inhabited philosophy' is not a kind of acting out of ideas in a way. It's just one that is interwoven with your particular responses to the particular things that happen to you, the other people that you encounter, the world of politics and [the period of] history that you live in. Those things affect your ideas, and the ideas in turn affect how you respond and develop – then the ideas themselves can change through life. Most of the people that I've written about haven't had just one consistent idea in their life; they've had different ideas as they go on. I suppose it just comes down to what I find interesting, and that's people and life. So it's that which pulls me towards biography. I love reading biographies: they're enormously rich case studies in being a human being.

FREEDOM, EQUALITY AND JUSTICE

Alice Roberts on culture and equality

May, 2020

Alice Roberts is an anthropologist, author, and broadcaster, known for presenting various science and history TV programmes. She's written over 15 bestselling books on archaeology and other subjects, including with Andrew Copson, *The Little Book of Humanism*.

A lot of people, when they think about change in the past, when they're trying to analyse history or think about today, they think of events as being led by ideas: 'This idea came at this time and caused this effect.' But you see changes in our history and our nature as having been led by material conditions, as much as anything else?

If you look at the history of humanity, going back into deep time, we see that there are innovations. Let's take farming as a good example of that: the Neolithic, which is where you get the beginnings of agriculture. I don't view that as a group of people coming up with a bright idea and saying, 'We're going to take charge of our resources. We're going to control where our food comes from, and this is how we're going to do it. Rather than gathering wild plants and hunting wild animals, we are going to plant fields of wheat and rye and barley and oats, and we are going to go out there and catch wild cattle or oxen, and domesticate them, and wild goats and wild sheep, and we're going to start farming. Then we can take some of the risk out, because we've been in a position where, as hunter-gatherers, if the herds don't come through that year, or there's a massive drought, we cannot protect ourselves against that risk.' I don't think that's what happened at all. I don't think there's that degree of foresight. But that's one end of the spectrum, where you say it's all down to human ingenuity, people coming up with bright ideas, those bright ideas catching on.

Then, at the other end of the spectrum, it's all about environment. It's all about people responding to environmental change. So, the stimulus for the change doesn't come from inside people and from the bright ideas inside their heads. The stimulus for the change comes from existing in an environment. We see that farming comes in after some pretty extreme environmental disruption, climate disruption. It comes in after the last Ice Age, when the world is warming up. We have a period of a few thousand years where the world is warming up. We have more carbon dioxide in the atmosphere, and various plants are doing very well. We see hunter-gatherers starting to depend more on cereals. So, way before they become farmers, we see an increase, particularly in the Middle East, of the use of wild cereals, and even the development of things like grinding stones for grinding grains down to flour, which we can presume is used to make bread. So, we've got breadmaking before farming. We've also got some very early evidence of beer before farming as well. People have always thought that the bright idea of farming came first, then you have the great idea of bread, then you have the bright idea of beer. It seems to be the other way around. It also is very much people responding to a change in their environments. As the world warms up after the peak of the last Ice Age, you've got a few thousand years of quite nice weather and lots of nice resources. Amongst those resources are these cereals, which are suddenly easy to gather, and there's big stands of wild cereal. We

214

then have a downturn in the climate. It's horrendous. About one thousand years of winter returns, a mini Ice Age. At that point, people must have been under massive pressure. We're looking at the kind of conditions that would have caused widespread droughts, that would have caused a population collapse. People are forced to depend on what previously were probably a minor part of their diets, and maybe fallback foods. (Cereals are great fallback foods. When other things aren't around, these grasses will still be there. They're difficult to eat, but they're still there.) There's quite a good argument for the origins of farming happening against that background of a deterioration in climate, where basically you become completely dependent on these fallback foods and you start to bring home more of these cereals.

We'll never know, because we can't time-travel back. But if we think about what's reasonable in terms of the innovation and how people came up with those ideas, it could have been some bright spark saying, 'Well, actually, I could plant some of these seeds and I think they might grow,' but I think that what's much more likely is that people were bringing wild cereals home, threshing them to get the grains to do whatever they were going to do, make them into flour or whatever, and some of those grains would have fallen to the edges of the threshing floor. The genius is not coming up with the idea, but noticing that something has happened. What you notice is that around the edge of your threshing floor, over a few weeks and months, you've got little plants growing up. And you think, *Oh, hang on a minute. I don't have to walk all those miles to go and gather these wild cereals. I could just do it here.*

Do you prefer this explanation?

I think it stands against the kind of lazy narrative that has become quite embedded in the stories we tell about our ancestors. We love a heroic story, right? Let's face it. They're our ancestors, so we want them to be heroes.

Some of them might have been. They're people. Creating a narrative that says, 'Oh yes, and then they came up with farming' – it's triumphant. I rather like this idea that things happen by mistake. I think it's like cooking. I don't do much cooking – I'm not a very good cook – but I will occasionally follow recipes or go a bit off-piste. Sometimes the off-piste things turn out horrendously, and every now and then they turn out really well. Then you go, 'Oh, that works well,' and you didn't really plan it, but if somebody comes round for dinner, you might say, 'Well, yes, I decided to do it. I knew this would work. I knew it would turn out that way,' whereas actually it was chance and serendipity. I think we underplay the role of chance and serendipity in human history. We do it with evolution as well, of course. We can go back further in time and look at evolutionary processes. We massively underplay the role of chance. Again, we rather like the idea of species struggling heroically against the odds.

So what's wrong with this? What's the harm that you've identified that comes out of this heroic-pioneer-ancestor narrative that you're rejecting?

I think it instils a kind of arrogance. I think it stands against a position of healthy humility. I suppose, as far as my own broader political beliefs are concerned, it does feed into those as well. If we look at the species that are here today, we call them successful species because they're here. That's the measure of success as far as evolution is concerned – you're alive. But look at the dinosaurs. The dinosaurs were an incredibly successful, diverse bunch of animals that had expanded into pretty much every ecological niche you can imagine. Then a huge rock falls. You can't really mitigate against that kind of thing. So it doesn't matter how successful they were on a day-to-day basis, on a year-to-year basis; a rock falls out of the sky, that's it. So, mammals get their chance at that point. The idea that you could say that the dinosaurs were somehow ineffectual and the mammals somehow superior? It doesn't make sense . . .

We are a very successful species today. We're extremely numerous, and we've colonised the entire globe (and now we're slightly worried about the fact that we are perhaps becoming victims of our own success). Chance and serendipity played a massive role, and we underplay that role, both looking at human history and prehistory, and looking at evolutionary history as well, but the same principle applies in society today.

We tend to tell the stories of people who have succeeded, and you see this over and over again. So you see people who have become very successful business people, for instance, or very successful sports people in any kind of area or any discipline, and you look for the reasons for success. You think they have something – that there was something in them which means that they succeeded where others failed, and if we can grab on to that, then each of us can achieve that success. The flaws in that are, of course, that not everybody can be exceptional, and whatever you do, you're not necessarily going to be that exceptional person. The other flaw in it is that you've completely disregarded the role of chance and serendipity. A lot of that is where you're born and the family you're born into and your life chances. There's a huge amount of chance which underpins how successful you are as an individual in modern societies.

For me, this makes quite a fundamental point about equality. It's about saying that if you look at certain people and say that they have done well, that they deserve more, and they deserve more because they have worked hard for it, it's just not true. Yes, they *have* more, but there's so much chance involved in that. And actually, those opportunities should be spread much more evenly through society. A lot of it comes down to land, actually – it's bizarre. If you strip it all away, if you strip everything away and ask who should own the land, then I think probably fundamentally nobody owns the land. But looking at it historically, you have these constant clashes between groups of people who have used land because it's there and because it's available, and then other groups of people who have tried to enclose it and create territory because it's their source of income and their source of wealth. I think that goes back to the Neolithic at least, that clash and difference of perspectives about land use between farmers and hunter-gatherers.

You said something at the beginning about culture and nature, and the idea that culture is what we do as organisms. You've talked about cultural differences and stepping outside and seeing different cultural perspectives. How much is down to culture and how much is down to nature in the sort of things that we've talked about: our approach to death, or morality, or the way we organise our societies? Or is that the wrong question?

It is the wrong question, because nature and culture are completely inseparable.

I don't know whether it's something about Western thought and Western philosophy, that we're so weighed down by dualism – weighed down by mind–body dualism, as if the mind is not just

FREEDOM, EQUALITY AND JUSTICE

what the brain does. I think that it's interesting, as a humanist, having conversations like that with people who are religious, or some people who are not religious, who still feel very strongly that the mind somehow exists, outside of or beyond the physical brain, which, for me, is a completely supernatural belief with no basis in scientific understanding at all. So, there's that dualism on the one hand, and then there's this dualism about biology and culture. That's probably more understandable to me, in that human culture is so extreme that it appears to be something quite different from any other animal cultures.

But I would say, as an anthropologist and as a biologist, other animals do have cultures. We define culture as a sort of behaviour which can be shared within a group, which sometimes might be about survival, finding food, that kind of thing, but there may be other aspects of culture which don't actually appear to be anything to do with survival. They might just be about group identity. There's a fascinating example amongst a group of chimpanzees where one of the female chimpanzees stuck a piece of grass in her ear. For a while, she'd go around with this piece of grass stuck in her ear, and the people observing her are thinking, *What on earth is going on here?* After a while, the other chimpanzees in her group all started to stick bits of grass in their ears. What is that? That is chimpanzee fashion. It's not for anything other than they're just thinking they'll put a piece of grass on their head, or, *That looks good on others, so I might do that.* It makes you see human culture in a different way when you see things like that in other animals.

In terms of culture, I would say technology is part of culture as well. Then you say, 'Okay, humans make tools and use tools, and other animals don't.' That starts to fall down immediately when you look at chimpanzees using stones as hammers and anvils to crack nuts. As far as we know, no chimpanzee has ever made a stone tool – as in, ever flaked a stone tool – but that's the difference, not the use of tools itself. And all sorts of birds use tools: the very clever crows, for example. It's all about modifying your environment, sometimes to help you survive – medicine is part of it, all of our agricultural technology is part of it. There are things like art and music, which are more difficult to classify in immediate survival terms, although I think they help us as a group. They help us express ourselves in ways which transcend the verbal. You start to see human culture as being something which is not an absolute difference between us and other animals, but it's a difference of degree. Because there isn't such a gulf between us and chimpanzees, our closest living relatives. It looks like something completely different, but I don't think it is.

And what about our morality, our values?

Again, I think we can see the origin of human morality, human values, back in the past, but also by looking at our closest living relatives in the animal kingdom. Michael Tomasello, who is an evolutionary psychologist and developmental psychologist, has done a lot of work looking at the development of morality and values in human children and comparing that with values and morality in chimpanzees.

Do chimpanzees have ideas of fairness, for instance? He's looked at that with some really ingenious experiments and found that there's a point at which children overtake chimpanzees and they have more sophisticated concepts of fairness, but absolutely chimps *do* have concepts of fairness. We even see that with some monkeys as well, a little bit further away from us on the primate tree of life. There was a famous experiment where monkeys are given different foods as a reward. I think one of them gets some grapes and the other one gets cucumber. The one that gets a cucumber is utterly outraged and throws the cucumber – *This is not fair!* So they have this concept of fairness, of equality, you could say. You can see how our morality has evolved from that, and I think that, fundamentally, what it comes down to is having evolved as a species which is incredibly sociable. We've evolved as a species where we have to work together in groups, we have to be able to cooperate. That's how we've been able to be successful.

In order to achieve that cooperation, you first of all have to be able to think about what other people are thinking, so you have to have some theory of mind, you have to have empathy. Then you have to have an appreciation of fairness and equality. I think some of the moral values that humans have are less worthy and those we must try to reduce. If you identify different kinds of moral values, they include things like in-group loyalty. That, for me, is something that I've tried to get away from, and I would try to promote things like fairness and equality over in-group loyalty. But you can certainly see the roots of all those values looking back into our evolutionary past.

Michael Tomasello came up with this amazing quote; I absolutely love it. It's about the way that you can't really separate human nature and human culture. Yes, we are biological organisms, but culture is part of our behaviour, and our behaviour comes from our biology too. So, he said, and this is absolutely brilliant: 'A baby is born expecting culture, just as a fish is born expecting water.' You can't separate the two. You can't say, 'Right, how much of this comes from culture and how much of it comes from something that's biological and innate?' So the whole nature/nurture argument breaks down as well.

S. I. Martin on history and variety

May, 2022

> S. I. Martin is a writer and historian focusing on Black British history and literature. He has authored historical fiction and non-fiction including *Incomparable World* and *Britain's Slave Trade* for Channel 4's *Windrush* series.

I thought we'd start with something that no one else has talked about on our podcast before as a great passion, but I know it is a great passion for you: archives. Not many people can say that the great passion of their life is archives. But I think you would. Why is that?

It's because I like things that can be verified. I like to have provable stuff in my life. My interest in history is connected to the histories of people of African Caribbean origin. But in order to substantiate my positions and to have a comfort zone, I like the presence of documents, tabulated information, some factual basis, some way to frame arguments. And something to talk about multiply and reference multiply. It creates a comfort zone for me.

So the fact that it's reliable and referenceable?

Not necessarily reliable. But it's that you can have points that you can make relationships with, it's something to actually talk about, and create a framework for dealing with life. And, moreover, to a significant degree, it belongs to the public. Significant bodies of archive material in these islands, we pay for them, we support them, and they are about us, they're about our lives. And of course, if you're incredibly nosy, like I am, they're just wonderful insights into other people's existences and other times.

You're relating the common ownership of archives, in a sense, to our common ownership of history and who we are. Is that right?

That's exactly what it is. And it prompts us to engage in a really immediate and personal way, just on the most prosaic levels of the histories of the properties that we live in, of our streets, of our neighbourhoods, of our schools. All of this information is there about us, it's there about our forebears, those of us who have forebears in these islands. Nowadays, it's at the click of a mouse or a visit to a particular archive.

Accessibility, then – that's an important thing to you as well?

Yes, making sure that as many people as possible know that this material is there, and that we pay for it and it's about us.

So it sounds like you like archives for their material usefulness, but you also like them for what they represent socially.

Yes, it's the ability to link us to each other and to centre ourselves, and to be linked one to another in a meaningful way, and to have serious conversations about these relationships as well.

And is that the same sort of thing that you think about history? I mean, do you think about history as being, at least in part, a way in which we can connect ourselves?

Ideally, yes. But more honestly, I think it provides wonderful frameworks for great arguments. The more controversial, the better. Again, it's about how we describe ourselves. Who do we think we are? And why do we think or believe we are these things? And I think, of course, that's an infinite set of discussions. But the more grist to the mill, and the more controversial, the better. I really do enjoy talking to people, especially [those] who I'd say were my polar opposites, in terms of all my positions. This is why I think history is important. You really are challenged constantly, and you can challenge others.

Are you in history to find out what's true, or are you in it to find out different stories, different perspectives, to look at things through different frames, and maybe argue, maybe in a never-ending sense, about what might or might not be true?

The idea of having a finite conversation, which leads to a fixed body of opinions and thoughts, doesn't make sense to me; it's not my personal taste, and intellectually I just don't see the point in it. Unless you're a power-mad lunatic who wants dominion over bodies of opinion, then it doesn't serve any other function. For me, it's important to keep the discussions alive, and to keep things moving – not necessarily forward, but moving. To keep the kettle boiling, because a lot of interesting steam is produced. And we also miss out on so much by just moving towards those fixed, set views and opinions.

Where do you think that attitude comes from for you, that commitment or perspective?

Oh, definitely from my upbringing. My parents arrived in these islands in the late 1950s, early 1960s, coming from Antigua in the West Indies. They were both brought up in a very anglicised way. They respected institutions, established authorities. My mother, at least, was a genuine professing Christian – probably the most professing Christian I've ever encountered – and my father, by habits. But I think this comes from, again, partly from my father, who always made a point of exposing us to as broad a range of opinions and tastes as possible. I mean, we would have, for example, musically, all sorts of . . . the quite disreputable reggae tunes from the 1960s and 1970s being played, and at the same time, you know, Handel, Tchaikovsky and Jim Reeves. Do you know, we'd buy the *Observer* on a Sunday, but we'd also get the *News of the World*, so I was trained literally in enjoying that breadth of opinion, you know? The notion that there aren't any . . . what do they call it nowadays? Guilty pleasures. Everything can be used and enjoyed, and should be.

And you believe in the value of being exposed to that diversity?

Absolutely. We are missing out, literally. People are culturally deprived. Not to talk about anyone's dietary habits, but speaking as a carnivore, I'd say one is culturally deprived if you don't enjoy the odd Greggs now and again. The idea of excluding oneself from pleasures, even just to say that, 'No, that's not my cup of tea.' Again, that whole idea of having fixed positions . . . Why?

Why do you think that's important? I mean, exposing yourself to this diversity, going broad. Are you in that just for the experience of it, or is there an outcome to all of that?

Both, really. Obviously, I enjoy the variety of things in a really visceral way – it's important to me. But on the other hand, you can get insights into other people's values, and what compels them. Part of my practice as well is occasionally writing fiction. So I'm also interested in that. Trying to get into the minds of, say, someone who is trading in human lives in the late eighteenth century – I think it's important. We can't just come to absolute conclusions; you can't come to any connection to them without having some sort of feel of their world, or trying to imagine their world. Ultimately, I think that's where we all sort of come together, or can do – in the world of the imagination.

That's bringing us back to that desire to connect with, and understand, other people, the same as through history, but now you're talking about [doing so] through imagination and experience. Is that a value for you, to connect with others?

Absolutely. I'd say not just for me, I'd say for us all as mammals. We have the ability – I'd say, without pushing it too far, the enhanced ability – to cultivate empathy. And art goes a long way towards that, from the most basic shared jokes in a bus queue, to enjoying great pieces of music, wonderful paintings, and – particularly for me – fiction, and sharing those most personal insights through that. So just to enhance empathy, and develop empathy. Art is always the enemy in an authoritarian state. It must be controlled. It must be policed.

What do you get out of empathising with a slaver, though? Is it that you just get a broader understanding of people generally? Or are there actually some things about the mindset of a slaver that you want to understand for some reason?

Yes, there are. Now we're having this particular conversation, I'm interested in the mind of a slaver or somebody who trades in human lives, to the same degree that I'm interested in someone who, for example, believes in the concept of chosen people, the elect, the damned, eternal torture. For me, it's part of the same. It's something which I don't immediately identify with, hence my curiosity about it [. . .] But I think it's important to try and get some sort of hold or grip on who we are actually dealing with. Because those of us particularly who are either centre [or] centre left – basic-ally, those of us who are not far right – have this massive gap in our comprehension of neurodiversity: our realisation and under-standing of depravity, what we would call depravity, which for many people is the norm. Hence my fascination with extremists. My fascination, particularly, with that period of enslavement: how people can situate themselves within it without making excuses about it. How extreme right-wing Christians can create a comfort zone for themselves within the most depraved belief systems and anti-human belief systems. And I think that's very important, because it helps us to arm ourselves against their pretty weak arguments; it helps us to argue and see where they're coming from.

So you want to understand them to counter them.

Yes, they have to be countered. Without having those tools or developing those tools, we are always on the back foot. As I think the non-far-right is, currently, very much on the back foot. Because we have come to this body of opinions, which assumes that progress is natural and good, and that having human unity, fellowship and understanding is the end goal, which, broadly, I accept. But that position significantly downplays the role of depravity; I keep going back to that word. It's alien to most of our ways of life.

So, where do you think these habits of depravity in other people come from? Just the natural outcome of something, or has something gone wrong in society? Or are there conditions that you could change?

I do believe that, to a significant degree, a lot of it is generated through identification, over-identification, with established traditional authorities, unquestioning following of pre-set tenets and notions of humanity, which, to a degree, have sort of run their course. But it's the unquestioning aspect which I think is at the core of it, because, suddenly, one finds oneself of value; you are someone of value. You are, as I said, one of the elect, one of the chosen, one of the master race, one of the upper classes, and anything which threatens that – which is a lot, nowadays – anything which threatens that must be attacked, and will be attacked reflexively. Because that is where you are fixed, and where you see your family extending. And it affects people of all status, as you know: 'Little boy, you're a man. Little man, you're a king.' So it's that battle for status and meaning. And many people just take it off the shelf from the society in which they're born unquestioningly, and that's the key.

And your answer is empathy, imagination, human solidarity?

And questioning, always.

Where does this come from then, this commitment to questioning? Your parents, you say, exposed you – whether it was deliberate or just because they were like that – to a diversity of opinions and experiences and cultures and art and so on. What about this habit of questioning? Is this something that comes from your upbringing?

Yes, it does. Because the question of religion clearly reared its head. It's something that I entertained or tolerated until I was about thirteen. And my dad, who I'd say was the lesser believer, he offered us the option that, 'If you don't feel that you need to go to church any more, then you don't have to.' And of course, I leapt at the opportunity, because I was already a very serious reader, a dangerously serious reader, to an unhinged level for a young person. You know, I delved into the Bible, and I'd read about women being turned into pillars of salt, and all sorts of disgraceful activities. Murderous, genocidal, racist, sexist, homophobic, horrible, horrible, horrible activities that were condoned, including slavery, by the creator of the universe, and I was thinking. I can't really co-sign this, not with any good conscience. So yeah, that's where it comes from. Because I've spent a lot of time just interrogating texts and traditions, particularly, as they had been imparted to my ancestors in the Caribbean. And how that all came about, I found of great interest to me – or concern, rather.

So your criticism, then, of these stories was a moral one?

Yes, like the story of Noah's Ark – morally, it's totally disgusting. You know, drowning the entire population of the world apart from eight people and a couple of million animals. I mean, the argument wasn't about morality. It was about belief. It was about faith and about obedience. And, as an obedient person, you have that sanction to extend that authority into the world.

Are you a disobedient person?

Good question. I'd like to think so. I think I am, in my own way.

Because you've criticised a number of times, in what you've said, tradition, inertia, obedience.

Definitely opposed to those three. I have to be, as well, simply to exist. I don't have that comfort zone in that triangle.

You're outside of that.

Wilfully.

Natalie Haynes on Classics for all and the perspective of women

July, 2020

Natalie Haynes is a writer and broadcaster known for her bestselling novels and non-fiction which revive Classical stories for contemporary audiences. Her BBC Radio 4 programme *Natalie Haynes Stands Up for the Classics* has had nine series to date.

Latin isn't a particularly difficult language. It's much easier than French, which everybody had to study for decades in this country. It's easier than German. It's maybe not easier than Spanish, but you never have to speak it, so if you're naturally shy, which many British people are, it's a really safe bet, because you can just sort of sit there and take some time with it and not get embarrassed and blush. Yet, somehow, generations of people have been made to feel that they aren't good enough for Latin, and they get to the point where they retire from a perfectly reasonable working existence, and then they think, *Okay, now's my time*. The number of people who have retired and are then doing A levels in Latin or in Greek, or a degree! I had mail a few years ago from a woman who started Latin when she retired and then Greek in her seventies, which is a hard language. It is hard. Then she was doing a PhD in her eighties, because she'd waited her whole life.

Fantastic.

Classics will wait for you. We're the ones who've limited it to an elite because it's now pretty well only taught in private schools. Not only are there some amazing state schools really pushing the boundaries in order to be able to still teach Latin – and, very occasionally, even Greek – but for the most part, it's something like seven per cent of children who are taught in private schools who have access to Latin or Greek at school. We've limited it to an elite, and then we've hurled rocks at it because it's elitist – but Latin didn't do anything wrong!

I was very lucky; I got to study Classics at school with a brilliant teacher. I know most people don't have that. I have dedicated ten years of my life to taking Classics everywhere I can, to taking it all over the world where the opportunity has come up, to taking it to state schools. Sometimes I'm talking to audiences who already have access to these things, and lots of times I'm going up to a state school to visit. There's one incredible school that I try and visit once a year, where the teachers taught themselves Latin so they could teach the kids, and then they taught themselves Greek. And you think, *Well, if they can be bothered to do that, I can be bothered to go and visit their school and talk to their kids.* It just always feels like such a treat. I had a Facebook memory come up this week, which I really like. It always reminds me of things that I forgot, because I did them in such a rush. I think it was two years ago; it was the end of their summer term, and their reward for going to after-school Greek class ... Their teachers, either that year or the year before, sat the GCSE at the same time as the kids did. They were literally a week ahead. I can still hardly talk about it without crying, but their reward for being so brilliant and working so hard was to go to the British Museum, and I would talk to them about anything they liked: any Greek pot, any statue, as much nudity, as much violence, as much lasciviousness as we could find.

You've talked about it being a joy to study, and that's one of the reasons why you want to spread it. Why else have you chosen to spend your time promoting Classics?

It seems to me just awful that this part of our communal history, our collective history, is withheld from such an enormous percentage of students as they go through the school system.

So that's another reason, because it's part of our history.

It is part of our history. Scotland, for example, where Scottish Latinism was an enormous thing. At one point, about a quarter of Scottish history was being written in Latin. How mad is that? I made a documentary about it a few years ago for Radio 4, so unless it's changed since then, I don't think you can now learn Latin in any state school in Scotland. At the time, you certainly couldn't, because that was the peg for the programme. That isn't just our collective ancient history you're being cut off from, this is your own – by Classicist standards – *recent* history that you're being cut off from, and that's not good enough. It's not acceptable to say, 'Oh, well, you don't need to know about that,' because kids in private schools will learn about that, and they're the natural ruling class. I'm sorry, I have a problem with that. I don't think it's okay.

David Aaronovitch very brilliantly once pointed out at a debate we were doing about whether or not you should study Latin, that if all schools had Latin available to them, then private schools will start teaching hieroglyphs. They always need a reason to make people pay the money. It's like, 'We have to offer something that regular schools don't, otherwise why would anyone pay?' And, of course, he's right – and yet, I don't feel as strongly. Partly because I can't read hieroglyphs – so, my loss, and that's something I would have to fix first before I felt as passionately about it. But I feel like this stuff belongs to us all. This is our collective history, our philosophical history, our political history.

That's definitely my experience. I was the first in my family to go to university. I studied Classics at school, at an independent school, not because I was from a middle-class background, or because my mum had any money, but because I was whisked there by the government's assisted place scheme that ran in the eighties for poor children. If that hadn't happened to me, that one little moment, I would not have all the things in my head about the Roman world, about the Greek world, that have helped me make sense of my life. It's in my experience of everything. There's such a resource there for making meaning and making sense out of your life when you've got the Classical thinkers with you on your journey through life, and everyone should have that.

I feel exactly the same way. The idea of being without them would, I feel, be like losing a sense. I genuinely don't know how I would move through the world without that constant companionship of it, I suppose. I've made a habit – I didn't particularly intend to, it's just gone that way – of trying to democratise access to Classics, because I care about things like the effects of Aristotle's *Poetics* on soap opera. And people are like, 'Well, wait, soap opera, are you sure?' Yes, I'm absolutely sure. Does that mean it's not in *The Wire*? It's also in *The Wire*, but it's still in *EastEnders*, and that's just how it is. So, I feel like there's a sort of sense that this subject is limited to an elite, and then we're sort of given to understand that it's in their territory, and then it's only their stuff that it applies to – and that's just not true, and it's never been true. Right from the very start of – to pick a vastly contentious example – when the Parthenon frieze was brought to London, there were mass-produced copies of it, which people could buy incredibly cheaply. Across the country, they sold in enormous quantities.

One of the things I love about that is that it's something which has been going on since at least Roman times. For the Romans, they were buying mass-produced lamps of Zeus and Leda. We have found them at Pompeii. Mass-produced Classical art for the masses has existed since Classical art was new. It wasn't always just for an elite – and these huge buildings, the Parthenon itself, and the marbles which remain in Athens so that we can see them in their context, these weren't designed to be locked away, hidden away. They were designed to be displayed for everyone to see. This was a huge temple. We might not believe in the same gods, we might not believe in any gods at all, but the civic importance of these buildings and of these stories is undeniable. It still seems to me appalling to suggest that somehow this stuff should be limited to people who can afford to pay for it. How did that happen? The closest parallel between Greek tragedy and soap opera is that they're free to access, or relatively free to access. This stuff was originally part of your democratic civic engagement. You went to the theatre for the festival of Dionysus, with three Greek tragedies and then a satyr play across three separate days, and you didn't pay, because it was paid for by your rich fellow citizens who paid instead of income tax. This was part of being a person. Within enormous limitations, of course. Only Athenian citizens are allowed at some of these festivals – that means men, probably not women. We know that foreigners were allowed at some festivals, because Aristophanes was prosecuted for having been rude about the city in front of foreigners, but the citizenry of Athens was extremely limited. Still, though, it meant that you didn't need to be rich to go.

Well, this isn't the Classical Association podcast but the Humanists UK podcast, so we might have to . . .

Wait – what?!

Moving on to another theme – it's such a big feature of your work that 'theme' seems to be too small a word for it – which is the place and position and unique experiences of women. I think it's fair to say that you have, in recent books, been closing ever further inwards on women.

This makes it sound like I'm in disguise, and I've infiltrated.

There's a Greek comedy to be had here.

I think Aristophanes already did it.

There's nothing new. But it's true, isn't it? Especially most recently; there's not a single male narrator in A Thousand Ships.

There are male characters, but all the stories are told from women's perspectives.

And then there's another book about women on the way?

Pandora's Jar, but that's non-fiction. It's about ten women in Greek myth, looking at how those stories have been distorted, essentially, through time. For example, Pandora, to the Greeks is the ur-woman. There are no women before Pandora, and on ancient visual artefacts, she's only ever shown in the process of being created or having just been created. She was never shown with any kind of receptacle of any sort. But Pandora is almost never referenced now without reference to the idea of the box and the thing that you open that's full of terrible things. If you go back to Hesiod, to Aesop and to other sources, we can see that the jar isn't even hers; it's given to her by Hermes. It's clearly come from Zeus, who's had her created. Sometimes she opens the jar, sometimes it is opened, and sometimes her husband Epimetheus opens it (in Aesop, he does). Sometimes, the jar has good things in it and not bad things. The only thing which is consistent in every version of the story is that Hope (or Expectation, because it's not necessarily positive) is saved in the jar. But even that is contentious, because is that a good thing – she's kept hope safe for us – or is it a bad thing – all these terrible things are in the world, and we don't even have hope because that's in the freaking jar, and we don't have a go on it? It's an incredibly complicated story that has no 'right' version and yet, through time, what happens is she becomes Eve. She becomes entirely merged with the idea, and there are paintings where she's described as either Eve or Pandora. They have literally merged into one woman, and so she just becomes a pretty girl who opens a box and causes the downfall of man. Boo. Hiss.

This is your point, is it? To make us look at how women have been represented.

Look at how women have been represented. Sometimes it's ancient misogyny in action. Hesiod is not a super-fan of women, although he hates his brother at least as much. (His version of Pandora, of course, is all about a bad brother and a bad lady.

Excuse me, Dr Freud. I have a time-travel job for you.) Generally, these stories have often had women at their centre in the ancient world. When Euripides wrote about the Trojan War, we have eight, I think, of his tragedies surviving to us today which focused on the Trojan War. One of them, *Orestes*, has a man as the title character; seven of them have women as the title characters. I can do this, hang on: *Andromache*, *Hecuba*, *Helen*, *Iphigenia in Aulis*, *Iphigenia Among the Taurians*, *Electra* and *The Trojan Women*. Seven out of eight of his Trojan War plays focus on women, so when people say, 'Isn't it anachronistic, putting women at the centre of the Trojan War?' I think definitely you should call Euripides and tell him that. I was convinced when I wrote *The Children of Jocasta* that the story of Oedipus would stand up to being told from his wife's perspective, from Jocasta's perspective and, indeed, [from that of] their daughter, Ismene. Not least because there are so many different versions of it in the ancient world, which people just don't know. The version that's in Sophocles is the version which prevails.

It does make you think. I don't know if I felt this just because I'm really immersed in the stories and that culture, or whether it was just because I was reading it as a man – although, I hope, a relatively sensitive man . . .

So sensitive.

Thank you. But nonetheless a man. And it was really difficult to get my head around The Children of Jocasta. *It felt like a new story. It felt weird. I did a lot of thinking about that book, from that point of view. I thought, Am I so unaware of a woman's perspective that*

*reading a story that I know so well, from a woman's perspective, seems
so new and different? It makes you think.*

That's always the goal, isn't it? To take a story and illuminate it.
The thing is, that's been happening for as long as the story has
existed. It's just that what's happened over time is we've tended
to prefer one version, and the other versions get lost – and Jocasta
is a great example. So, in Sophocles, in *Oedipus Tyrannus*, she has
one hundred and twenty lines. We don't think about her very
much. But she solves the puzzle of who is who and who's married
to whom before Oedipus does. We're told all the way through the
play how clever he is, and yet she works it out before he does. I'm
just saying. Tell me again, who's the clever one in this marriage?
It never seems to come up, but in Euripides' version of her, in *The
Phoenician Women*, we get a completely different version. She has
this incredible monologue where she talks about the pain of losing
her child, and it's like, *How did we kind of miss that out before?* In
the story that we get in Homer – that's the earliest version of the
Jocasta story – she's called Epicaste in the *Odyssey*, we only have ten
lines and the story is pretty much fifty-fifty focused on them both.
Somehow, what happens is the Sophocles version is so mighty –
and it is an incredible play – that it just pulverises everything before
it, and we sort of lose track of the others.

Sometimes, I think there's a conscious effort to prefer or
prioritise men's narratives, and sometimes I think it just sort of
happens by accident. I mean, you probably see almost as many
productions of *Medea*, but I would guess, *Oedipus* maybe more,
because, horribly, it has a more contemporary feel, and so it's
still performed over and over again, and never seems to become
dated. I think when we think about Greek tragedy, we think
about Oedipus. Maybe also because Freud thought Oedipus was
important, but Freud was totally focused on the male experience

to such an extent that, magnificently, he could look at the decapitation of Medusa and see it as a fear of castration. Dude, it's literally not about you. What is wrong with you?

Sometimes a gorgon is just a gorgon.

Yes. I have long argued that the world would be enormously improved if everybody looked into a mirror once a day and said, 'It's not always about you,' and then simply carried on with their day, having just remembered that for a second.

That's a pretty big belief.

I really think it, because, quite often, it's really tempting to centre ourselves. Of course, we all want to be the hero of our own biopic, the centre of the narrative, but most of the time, most people aren't trying to antagonise you; they're not even thinking about you. They're not ignoring you, either, because that would still be thinking about you. Everyone is fighting their own miniature battles every day, and they don't have the bandwidth to make it all about you, because you're not the only person in the world. So, yes, it's not all about you: I would cheerfully go with that as a life belief.

Dan Snow on history, progress and luck

October, 2020

Dan Snow is a historian, broadcaster, and television presenter. Known as the 'History Guy', he brings history to life through TV, podcasts, and online content.

You've dedicated your working life – so far, at least – to history and the popularising of history. Why is that?

I come from a culture and a family of oral historians. We didn't watch TV at my grandma's house when we were kids. She was my Welsh nain, and she'd tell us stories about the past, particularly about her family – largely made up, I hasten to add – about how we descended from King Arthur. She'd tell us about them, and she'd give us a very rosy picture of her grandfather, or taid in Welsh, David Lloyd George, without some of the slightly more interesting and important character flaws and traits that I've come to know as I've read proper history. Anyway, she and my mum and dad, in our family, talked about history a lot, basically, and they also did a lot of broadcasting. My mum and dad were both journalists, so we were just told a lot of stories. We went to a lot of historical sites. I spent my entire childhood traipsing around bloody battlefields and abbeys, and eventually you just get Stockholm Syndrome. And this is how intergenerational trauma works. I now inflict that upon my children.

It's a pretty positive sort of trauma to suffer.

I hope so, although there's some days . . . We were in Ireland the other day on our third or fourth castle day, and it was torrential rain, and I'd made everyone get out of the car, and my four-year-old – as we came over the horizon to another castle – shouted, 'Oh, no, it's another smashed house!'

That's what history is. One smashed house after another.

I'd never thought of them as smashed houses, but she's absolutely right. And then, of course, pure luck, huge privilege. I got spotted doing the Oxford-Cambridge Boat Race and got asked to do some stuff at the BBC. My dad was a journalist, we would do stuff together; absolutely extraordinary luck at that moment. I found out I absolutely loved it. I just couldn't think of a thing I'd rather do, which is, tell extraordinary stories from the past, try to make them relevant and interesting. I love the intersection of history and contemporary politics and ideas. Why do people do the things they do? What is going on with Trump, Brexit, responses to the climate crisis, whatever it might be? How history helps us to understand our own experience, what we're going through. I'm not sophisticated enough to be one of those people that thinks that history has to be talked about and studied on its own terms, in complete isolation from the present.

So it's luck, to be given the opportunity, and then an enormous enthusiasm and passion for it once that's happened. I'm very lucky, I still absolutely love it. I love meeting people of integrity. I love meeting great historians, and I love synthesising their remarks and arguments and thoughts and broadcasting them.

So, explaining our own experience and events about us. Is that the most important thing [. . .] about history that you're trying to convey to others?

I think so. I think with a commercial hat on, I wouldn't be able to make a living if I didn't also realise that some stories are just epic and worth telling. Alexander the Great's conquest; the Persian Empire; Marie Curie's Nobel Prizes. Some things are just completely fascinating, and people want to hear those stories. They actually prefer reading or listening to that non-fiction, because they want to know about the siege of Vienna in the seventeenth century, and the gigantic cavalry charge that inspired Tolkien to write his cavalry charges in *Lord of the Rings*. Some people just enjoy that, and I think there's nothing wrong with that. I think that's a wonderful, diverting, inspiring pastime.

For me, deep down, my heart will always lie in the liminal space between politics and history. I think particularly as, post-9/11, post-2008, history has come back to bite us in the ass. You and I are old enough that we remember in the 1990s, there was a very powerful sense that history was a bit lacking in its impact and relevance, because we'd moved into a very different place post-communist, Francis Fukuyama, a world where the big questions had been sort of settled. China was beginning to open up. Russia was a proto-democracy of sorts, it looked like at that point. It was thought, actually, that studying the great power politics of the nineteenth century was sort of irrelevant. Well, it turns out that history has come back with an absolute vengeance, and we're dealing with democratic breakdown in the US, we're dealing with schism within the UK, and within the UK's relationship with transnational organisations like the EU, the breaking of international law. These are old and weighty and very familiar questions to historians. I almost can't believe that we're even talking about some of them. I mean, the idea that we've been discussing Trump and his attitude towards the defeat following the [2020] election is something I never thought I'd see in my lifetime. If there was ever a warning from history, if there was ever an appeal to study history, to interrogate the past to understand better, we're living through it now.

I think, especially those of us who were young in the nineties, we thought – maybe because we were young, and we were coming into maturity at the same time – we thought that just as we were entering this sort of brave new world, so was everyone, and this was the endpoint of lots of events. And that, like you say, didn't turn out to be the case. Obviously, this is an important thing about history to you. Do you think that it is something that is generally lacking in public awareness?

Well, actually, that's a great question. Just briefly, you and I – obviously we were very young in 1990, almost incognisant of what was going on, but I look back, and I left school the year that Friends Reunited started. The social internet literally happened the year I left school. Well, the year I left school, no one had heard of the internet. The year I arrived at university, everyone was like, 'Oh, there might be something on the internet, let's do some emailing.' So it coincided. It would be like being a French person coming of age in 1789. I mean, how mad. My world view must be so weird. Anyways, there's lots of history around, obviously. I mean, Boris Johnson gave a speech a few days ago (as we're recording this in October of 2020) which was riddled with history, all about Drake and Raleigh, and he was referring to offshore wind, wind generation, and he couldn't resist getting a dig in about [how] wind is what made the British Empire great, look at Drake and Nelson and Raleigh. We don't even need to rehearse the Brexit 'standing alone, 1940, Battle of Britain' parallels. I think history infused the Brexit vote. I think history infuses the debate around Scottish independence. Alex Salmond timed the vote to coincide with the seven-hundredth anniversary of the Battle of Bannockburn. I see it everywhere. Maybe, of course, that's my bias.

You're saying it's their beliefs about history that shape them.

I think so. If you look at the States, the partisanship, I think Vietnam is hugely important. Not just on the left, but if you look at the growth of a right-wing media environment ecosystem in the States, if you look at the beginnings of people starting to regard the other party as fundamentally un-American and a danger to the Republic – specialists will pick me up on this, but there's a sense of [it] growing out of Vietnam through Nixon's removal from office, forced resignation, [a sense] that you start to take partisan identity depending on what you think of those episodes, of those things. I think, in the UK, the way we talk about things like Empire, Northern Ireland, the Second World War, have shaped our political compasses.

What you're saying is true, I guess, for better or for worse – but do you think it is for better or for worse? Do you think that it'd be better if we could press restart? Famously, this country that we've both grown up and live in hasn't very often pressed restart, or at least has pretended that it never has. Whereas there are other countries that have, like Germany for example, built themselves up from zero to constitutional republic. Do you think that it's a good thing that history or beliefs about history infuse our life in this country in that way, or a bad thing?

I've got Edmund Burke here on my shoulder.

Brush him off!

What's so fascinating about Britain and the UK is that it really is one of the longest uninterrupted political entities on the planet, I think I'm right in saying. The British government is a good person to lend to, because since the 1690s, the British government has always paid its debts. Obviously on one level, that kind of continuity means that there's been no foreign invasion, gigantic upheavals in terms of violent revolution, civil war (with the important possible exception of Ireland a century ago), pogroms, of the type we've seen in the US, Germany, France, Japan, Russia, China – terrifying episodes. Clearly, the downside of it is that we have been lured into a sense of smug self-satisfaction. We occasionally think, like the old nineteenth-century expression, that God is an Englishman. We have a sense that we are a sort of providential race because everything's gone 'quite well' for us in the last three hundred years, and therefore we haven't been as self-critical as we might be – and we have missed the opportunity for reform, a reset. Sometimes crisis can bring opportunity.

But gentle, incremental change can have a lot going for it. We can also be too blasé about the achievements of our largely non-violent evolution. However there are downsides as well. I think that it would be nice to grapple with a problem like the House of Lords, our electoral system, where power should lie, our system of local, regional, federal power, and the established

Church, for example – it would be good to have a crack at. The problem is when you try and fix the roof when it's sunny, everyone thinks you're weird. You're some sort of strange, odd eccentric going, 'While everything's good, let's have a good old spring clean in terms of our legislature.' That, wrongly I think, is seen as a strange thing to do.

Have you ever felt any of that complacency or smugness, that feeling of your own sort of culture being a providential one, like in your youth? It seems that you still feel a little bit of exceptionalism because of what you've said about the bloodless or less violent history of the formation of Britain. Did you feel this exceptionalism yourself? Is it something you're growing out of?

I think I grew up with a very traditional historiographical tradition. My dad read me *Our Island Story* from cover to cover. I definitely had a kind of Whiggish view of history. I was very proud of that British tradition, and the projection of this kind of splendid progression as nations around were falling into turbulence and chaos. I am British, I am from the traditional elite, where my ancestors are admirals and doctors and surgeons and generals and politicians who've all done really well out of it. I'm a wealthy white guy that grew up in a nice house in London, as a result of obviously hard-working parents, but also enormous inherited privilege. I do think it's very difficult for me to separate that. I hope I'm able to. I hope I'm able to try and acknowledge that and then think about the good things that have derived from that. I'm really glad that we didn't suffer a crushing civil war in the hot summer of 1911, or when the aristocracy looked like they were going to put up a last-ditch effort against creeping democratisation – that could have been our kind of 1917 moment.

I'm glad that didn't happen. At the same time, I understand that by that not happening, compromises were reached, for example around the aristocratic House of Lords, that would remain loose ends. So yeah, I'm a work in progress. For example, the hopelessness of Brexit, the shortcomings in our Covid response have shaken my definitely inherited assumptions that the British state is pretty effective.

Do you think you'll continue to reconsider this? This is a dynamic process, and you're coming to terms all the time with different aspects of this, I take it?

Yeah. Institutional failures around Brexit and institutional failure around Covid have definitely, in the last couple of years, taken the sheen off my innate admiration for and confidence in the British system of government – which is not perfect, but it's been around for a while, and has endured a lot. It's a system of government that got us through financial crises, got us through foreign wars, and got us through emerging social movements that could have been hugely destabilising.

When you're talking about Britain in the past, even three or four hundred years ago, you're saying 'we', you're saying 'our', you're saying 'us'.

Yes.

I mean, you and I weren't alive then, of course, so obviously you don't mean literally us, you mean people in these islands who've lived here.

So you feel a continuity in that sense, with this particular society and nation obviously?

Do you know what? I do, Andrew, and that's very unusual. Usually, I'm very good at not saying 'we' and 'us'. It's embarrassing if you present television programmes or podcasts and go, 'Then we captured the bridge . . .'

I think it's revealing, isn't it?

I think it's revealing in this conversation, because we're talking about my relationship with it, and I think that's right. I'm trying to get the spotlight off my own prejudices, but I find American historical community historiography completely fascinating. I really do find, in America – that is, still even within the academy, which is decried as being sort of liberal bias and everything – I find them extraordinarily patriotic. I find those giant presidential biographies that come out every year by Ron Chernow and other people; I find the assumption in those books is that American history is a progress towards a more perfect union. I just find those amazing – but, of course, I'm guilty of it too.

Do you believe in progress, do you think? I resonate completely with what you said about when you were younger having a Whiggish view, and I'm not from any sort of elite background. My ancestors aren't doctors and admirals, they're coal miners and farm labourers, even in the last generation. But I had an elite education, of course, and so I grew up also with that Whiggish sense of progress. And if you study the eighteenth century, as we both did, then that's inculcated even further in you. I think I still have some residual feeling of a progress narrative in my mind, even now. It's not so much about Britain, it's more about our species in the world, and so on. Do you still believe in progress?

I do, but events, dear boy, are making it harder. The short version, which is the Steven Pinker version, is that in terms of our data, we are living in a radically improved world. We do, however, have the kind of issue of gigantic, advanced malaise in the Global North: obesity, mental health problems. I think as we saw gigantic numbers of people coming out of poverty in the nineties, following reforms in India and China in particular, but elsewhere, Vietnam, I think we were all just so excited about access to clean water and declining maternal mortality, and those are incredibly exciting. We now know those have come at a cost of potentially irreversible and catastrophic climate damage, which is a nightmare. I mean, it gives me literal nightmares. But our ability to live in vast numbers, feed ourselves and, on the whole, die peacefully in our beds whilst having elongated our lives through science and medicine – I find that an inspiring story. So I think the development story is a very exciting one, but I'm still an optimist on that front. I still believe that we can get it. I still believe that the world that I thought we'd have achieved by the time I was about twenty-five, we'll probably get there by the time we're about ninety-five.

Not only is it still possible, it will happen?

I think so. The decarbonising of our economy is really exciting. It's too slow, but I have to believe we can do this. I also believe, in terms of that mental health and obesity crisis – and, indeed, the social media crisis, I think we've created it, and I believe we've probably got the tools to overcome it.

Well, has the study of history taught you that that's a reasonable thing to expect?

I think it's plausible, isn't it? We're on a wild ride. There has been this insane period of explosive science and engineering that, from about 1680, saw us within three hundred years reaching the moon. Or with a longer view, you can go back to the domestication of animals, or cereal farming, or the creation of bronze. Actually, that's really the amazing one. So, for two hundred thousand years, humans knocked about eating berries and wandering around, and then, in the space of fifteen thousand years, we build all this. So we are on an explosive trajectory, and we may destroy our planet, and that first person that smelted copper and tin together to make bronze inadvertently took us down this path. We may also create the tools to create a liveable planet and sustain it. I still believe we will.

It's worth the risk. I think the last fifteen thousand years have been worth the risk.

Bronze is useful. I have no solutions, and I often have very little consistency, because no one is happier than me when I'm walking barefoot in the forest, eating berries with my children. I do it as much as possible. But also, no one's happier than me when I'm listening to Beyoncé in a comfortable room with the central heating on.

Or on a flight going somewhere amazing.

And able to access the sum total of humankind's literary and artistic output from a device that's in my hand. I can see it both ways.

Well, you want both of those things – that's not inconsistent, necessarily. I think that's a very humanist idea that you've expressed, this idea that we can, at the same time as being in touch with our fundamental nature, also give free rein to the possibilities that human technology and inventiveness have created, and enjoy those too. This is an integrated life, it's not necessarily a bipolar one.

You are like those people in the US that when Trump says something crazy, they take a few hours and come up with factual justification for it. One of my favourite podcasts is called *The Intellectual Zamboni*. You know those machines, they go on the ice when it's all scuffed up and sort of smooth it? That's what you are for me. Thank you very much.

That's a pleasure. We've talked about the study of history and a little bit about progress. I'm just wondering if there's any specific period that you've studied that you think has had a profound effect on shaping your beliefs and your ideas. Is there a particular time and place that you go back to, or looking back on, that you think has really shaped your own world view?

Well, again, my world view changes quite radically, as you've seen from this call already. If we'd been having this conversation ten years ago, I would not have been talking about democratic collapse, I would not talk about climate collapse probably as much, I would not have been as interested in nationalism, which felt dormant. Look at the ten years we've had. Also, you know, my age. The bits of history that I'm inspired by, appalled by, repulsed by, have changed dramatically. When I was in my twenties, I found the eighteenth century so fascinating: the crucible of the modern world, the development of the Industrial Revolution, of the Scientific Revolution. You've got Mary Wollstonecraft, feminists, Republicans in America – the first time in human history that a group of people (albeit an affluent coterie of white males) sat down and thought, *How should we govern ourselves, and what are we going to do?*, and tried to use precepts of reason to sit down and think about it. They made terrible errors, of course, but I found that incredibly exciting, and it felt like a world that I recognised, and a world full of possibility and optimism. Now, funnily enough, the history that I'm finding speaks to me more of the culpability and stupidity of politicians, of leaders. I'm sitting on the ground telling sad stories of kings who've died.

So now I find leadership fascinating, and I find myself thinking, *Is our whole human concept of a leader incredibly primitive? How do we find ourselves again and again subordinated to people like Donald Trump, Erdogan, Modi? Why do we lean towards charismatic leadership rather than say, a committee? Why do we have this desire? Why do we want a nice Joe Biden who can go out and say, 'I believe in America,' or, 'I believe in all our tomorrows. Young people are the future.' Why do we have that?* So I'm really interested in that, and I'm interested in fake news, propaganda, obviously, and I'm trying to go back and think about why we think that democracy is the best system, and to reconnect with what was driving those reformers and those thinkers, and to rediscover some of that passion to think about how we can renew democracy and renew the ideas around liberal democracy at a time when they're under threat. So yeah, the history that I'm reading and thinking about changes a lot.

You say you're inspired by the Enlightenment; are you talking about resurrecting that spirit?

I think I'm interested in reconnecting with why, for example, men and women risked their lives to vote, to extend the franchise. If you look at civil rights activists in the African American community in 1920s, they were not utopian; they were talking about local elections, they were talking about censuses, they were talking about electoral rolls. I think we need to kind of reconnect with that sense that we can improve a democracy from within it: what needs to be done, what housekeeping, what can be improved, how do we administer justice?

I want to ask you a more personal question. You said earlier on that you're conscious of being lucky, and I inferred – or maybe you implied – that that was luck by way of economic circumstances and background. Is that something that is important to you? The consciousness of your own good fortune and maybe luck as a factor in life?

Yeah. I think about it more and more as probably the swagger of my younger years defogs and things get a bit clearer. I think I was tempted to think, like that lovely expression about George Bush – he was born on third base and thought he hit a triple. I think that you don't know any better; I think I was not hugely observant. Funnily enough, having my own kids has reinforced that because I just look at them, particularly during the lockdown home-schooling, I just was aware on a daily basis that these kids are really lucky. They've got a mum and a dad with rewarding but not hugely time-consuming jobs, who are able to spend a long time with our three children reading, writing, learning. So sure enough, the kids do well at school. Not because of any natural bounty they've got, none of them are Camus. They haven't birthed fully formed like Athena from the head of Zeus. There are geniuses in our society, there are those who are likely to have flourished anywhere, anytime – but I ain't one of them, and my kids aren't, because they struggled with reading until I read with them for two hours every day, and now they're good at reading.

So I am really aware of luck. I'm also aware of luck in history. I think we are getting a bit better at seeing a contingency now. I think some historians used to quite like the idea of great men, the idea of people bending history, shaping the fate of the world by their own ambition – Alexander the Great, Napoleon. Increasingly I see luck. Alexander the Great was lucky not to have his head staved in at the Battle of the Granicus. The first thing he did when he invaded Persia was almost get killed; [he was] millimetres away from being killed. Napoleon was badly wounded in his first serious battle. Lenin was stupendously lucky. I see more of that now: I see contingency. I started a podcast that's now got millions of streams. I think that was basically luck. It was the right time, right place. It just caught a wave, really. I've backed that up and worked hard to bolster that luck, but, my goodness, I do think this journey that we're on is pretty fragile.

Sandi Toksvig on thoughtfulness and equality

August, 2023

Sandi Toksvig is a Danish-British broadcaster, writer, comedian and political activist. She's known for hosting *QI* and *The Great British Bake Off*. Her work spans radio, television, and advocacy for LGBTQ+ rights and gender equality.

When we both attended the World Humanist Congress recently at Copenhagen, you said that you had quite a few important values from your father, who was Denmark's foreign correspondent. So I thought we might start there. Tell us a little about him and about what he taught you.

Well, I liked that you say he was Denmark's foreign correspondent, because it means that you understand he was *the* foreign correspondent – we only had the one!

Is that actually true?

It's actually true. It was the 1960s. I'll give you an idea: my father worked for Danish television, but it was still known as Danish radio, because they weren't entirely sure that the whole thing with pictures was going to work out. He became a television correspondent for the radio, which is quietly pleasing, I think. My dad was incredibly well read. He didn't go to university, because it just was not an option. But he was, despite his lack of formal education, the cleverest person I think I've ever met: very thoughtful, incredibly well read. He taught me lots of silly things. Amongst which – [and] I have always agreed – [was] 'Never trust a man in a ready-made bow tie.' If you can't tie a bow tie, then don't bother with the whole thing. I think it's just ridiculous. He taught me that one martini is not enough, and three is too many.

That's an important value.

I think so. He taught me, as far as facts are concerned, to make sure that you had three sources for every single thing that you wanted to thoroughly believe in. He was a brilliant foreign cor- respondent, but he was absolutely painstaking in his research. And sometimes it was sort of remarkable. I remember when he was doing the live commentary for Denmark for Prince Charles and Princess Diana's wedding. He was very determined to find any Danish connection whatsoever that he could. He managed to discover – and I remember the glee with which he told us – that Kiri Te Kanawa, the opera singer who sang at the wedding, was wearing earrings made by a Danish jeweller.

I love that he bothered. He's trying to make a connection with the audience, he's trying to make them feel somehow involved in this great big, international occasion. He was determined that I understood that lots of people said things because it benefited them, and it wasn't necessarily the truth. That was particularly true of politics, if you imagine that I was in the United States with my dad covering the news during the Watergate era and so on. You can imagine that truth was a slippery beast – even then.

Very sadly, he would be horrified [to learn] it has become even more slippery.

And do you have that now, then: a love of truth?

I do. Although I increasingly find it incredibly difficult to narrow down. What is your truth and my truth are incredibly different. Even if you and I had exactly the same experience – we did, we both went to the Humanist Congress in Copenhagen – I imagine we have a very different view of even the same moment of what happened. What would be nice – in an ideal world, what would happen is that we would appreciate that those views are different; we would sit down, and we would try and find a common ground in them. What's happening more and more, particularly if you look at, for example, politics in the United States, is that people are becoming increasingly polarised. If you don't agree one hundred per cent [that] what I say is the truth, then you are my enemy. That is not a way forward for anybody.

What's the opposite of that? If that's what you don't want – that clash or that polarisation – what's the opposite? Is it acceptance of diversity? Is it tolerance? Is it more active than that?

I think it is more active than that. I think it's a thoughtfulness. I think it's an active pursuit of trying to understand what it's like to walk in another person's shoes. It's trying to understand why their mindset might be like that. What I find intolerable – and I am an impatient person – is when somebody says something that they blatantly know not to be the truth. Again, sticking with the United States, Donald Trump saying that he won the election – there's just madness there. Lately, more and more when people make statements, I just think, *Seriously, do you actually believe that? The trouble is, I don't even think you actually believe that, and yet, you're putting it out as a truth.*

You said a moment ago that you're impatient. Is that a good thing as well as a bad thing? Do you think that that has virtues in it?

I get a lot done.

It's a sort of dynamism, is it? Are you intolerant of sitting about?

Yes, I'm always doing something. I can't watch television without making something. I'm always multitasking. So, my favourite thing would be, for example, to have lots of friends around for chat, but I'm cooking at the same time. Something's happening. The person who just lays about, that doesn't work for me.

Do you know where that comes from?

I don't know where it comes from . . . Well, maybe I do . . . When I was in my early twenties, between my second and my third year of university, I was extremely unwell and very nearly died. I think it left me with a desire to make the most of every single day that I have. It's a very sobering thing to have happened to you. I think it's probably left me with an enormous dynamic to grab life by the throat.

When you were talking about what your father was like a moment ago, you talked about his love of truth, but you also talked about his desire to connect, to engage. I get the sense that that's something that you believe in too?

Absolutely. I trained initially as a human rights lawyer, and I have a great friend, the brilliant Helena Kennedy, and she is a wonderful human rights lawyer. I sometimes say to her, 'I think I made a mistake, Helena, and I should have pursued that path.' And she says, 'Sandi, you can do more for human rights with a well-placed joke, probably, than a well-placed case.' I mean, she's kidding, but . . .

Culture matters.

Yes, I do think culture matters. I've done one-woman shows where I'm not just trying to make people laugh, I'm trying to make them think.

And connection is as important as engagement?

Yes, I think so. I think you try and find the thing in the audience that makes you think, *Well, maybe this is the way in – to say the thing that I want to say.* So I do make very strong feminist points when I'm speaking, but I try and do it in a gentle way. I try and do it in a way that makes everybody laugh. There's no point in just appealing to the feminists in the audience. What you want is the guy in the audience whose partner made him come, and who doesn't want to be there – you want to get him on side.

Did you draw any moral lessons or other things that informed your world view now from your mum?

Yes. She's a talented woman whose talents were never allowed to be properly expressed. And she has dealt with that stoically. Weirdly, the lesson that I learned from that is maybe don't. Maybe get more angry, maybe become more furious. But it wasn't the time. It was the sixties and seventies. It literally wasn't the time. If you think about – we've just had the women's football – women were banned from football until 1971. The idea that my mother could have stood up and fought more is not fair on her. She literally couldn't. But I think it probably gave me more fight to watch her not get up and do things. I think a lot of my ... perhaps it's unfair, because my dad was out in the world, but a lot of my moral views and ethical views come from my father, probably more than anywhere. I once said to him, 'What will you do, Dad, if you die, and you are hauled before God and asked why you did not believe?'

And he said, 'I shall look him in the eye and say, "Sir, you gave me insufficient evidence."'

So he was quite a fan of a humanist approach to life as well then? I didn't know that.

Absolutely. In Denmark, when I was a child, it was a matter of law that everybody belonged to the state church. I don't know if this has changed, but it was as a child. If you wanted to leave the state church, which basically meant you no longer wished any portion of your taxes to go towards supporting the church, you actually had to have a private member's bill passed in Parliament – it's a small country – to say that you wished to leave the church. That's quite a palaver, isn't it? That's quite a lot of faff. He did that. And it was a nightmare when we wanted to get him buried.

You reap what you sow!

This is where fame triumphs over faith, because he is buried in the church of his choosing, because we had to put him somewhere.

You received your own education at the hands of nuns. I suppose that can't have left you unaffected, one way or another. How did it change you?

They would talk all the time about love, and were actually amongst the meanest group of people I've ever met in my entire life. They were just not nice. I knew that as a child. I first went to school at the age of four because I was a bit annoying at home; I was desperate to get on. My mother would take me to school on the back of her bicycle. And if you were late, the punishment was to sit on these very dark stairs that led up to the nuns' sleeping quarters in this very old building. It was very dark and quite frightening, and I was only four. I remember saying to Mother Bernadette – never forgotten – 'I don't know why I'm being punished. Surely my mother should sit in the dark, because I'm on the back of the bicycle and I can't decide when we get here. It's not up to me to decide when we get here.'

But it didn't have any effect on you religiously?

It did. We used to be taken into the chapel. It was large, it had very high ceilings ... I was a small child in a sailor's uniform – what did I know? – but it seemed enormous to me. We would watch the novices, the young nuns, swearing their ... I don't know what they were doing, swearing their allegiance to God. They would have to lie on the floor, face down, with their arms out and across, and – I don't know – kiss the hem of the mother superior's dress or something. I was really taken by this very dramatic moment. They would be singing and it seemed rather an extraordinary moment. So I took to going, on my break times, to lie on the floor in the chapel with my arms out, because God will ... surely, there'll be something, there'll be lightning. I was taken with the idea of a Lamb of God. I thought this would be a rather marvellous thing. I did this for several weeks, and I never heard a word. So I remember getting up ... It was actually a very pivotal moment, because I was genuine. My belief that something amazing was going to happen was genuine. And I got up, and I looked up at the big, massive cross – one of those ones that was really unpleasant, a lot of blood and a very gory depiction of execution. It was very unpleasant. And I just looked up. And I just thought it was very silly. And I left, and I remember talking to my father about crucifixion.

You said at the congress that you thought that love originally sat at the heart of at least most religions and philosophies – at the point when they were first promulgated, the original purpose of them. Do you think that love really is such an enormous motivating factor, and is it in your life?

It certainly is in my life. There's no question about it. Love and passion are probably my driving forces. But I do think, if you study religious texts, I do think at their core, there is love. I think of all the depictions of Jesus. This is not a man who goes about saying, 'You're a bad person.'

No, he's not a nun is he?

He does get cross with a fig tree. But haven't we all? I do think at the core of Islam, at the core of Judaism, at the core of Christianity, love ought to be the driving force. Too often, unfortunately, it is forgotten, as people endlessly interpret and reinterpret words. [It's] one of the problems with text of any kind; if you look at the problems with the American Constitution, and people analysing the Second Amendment, they've analysed it into something that was never meant. I think that you can find the same in any text that human beings have ever created: that we will find the thing we're looking for. So you could, in the old days, for example, say slavery is fine, because of the story of the curse of Ham – which is one of my favourite stories – [but] you forget that, what ought to be at the core, is that we're all equal, that there is love. If people could maybe just seek the initial imperatives of writing those things down, the initial thing was that they were loved by God – isn't that the main driving thing? And that from that ought to radiate all kinds of love, but instead it's used to vilify people, and to make some groups of people feel superior to others, as I think the LGBT community will attest to at the moment.

I think that's a good last thing to come on to, blending as it does love and equality, and imagining yourself in other people's shoes, and everything else. This is something that is rising in salience, at least for you at the present time.

I was very upset. The main takeaway from the synod seemed to be to reaffirm the position of LGBT people as not fully equal members of the Church of England family. So here's the thing: he's entitled to believe that; he's entitled to say it, he's entitled to put forward that view. Where I feel enraged is that he's also entitled, along with twenty-five other Church of England bishops, to sit in the House of Lords and pass laws. When same-sex marriage was voted upon, the bishops turned up and they all voted against. That's not okay. So, of course, I will defend to the death your right to say things that I don't agree with. But I will not agree that in a democracy, you then get to vote my life out of the picture. So that is what spurred me on recently. I find it very odd. It's one of those things that just slightly baffles me, that a religious person says, 'We're all created by God, but some of you were created not so well.' Does he have off days? I don't know how it works. Unless some of us are not okay. I remember in 1994, I was due to host a big event for the Save the Children Fund. I'd done lots of stuff for them before and been an ambassador for them before, and I came out in 1994. And they dropped me as an ambassador. And there was a sort of sense of, 'Let's save the children, but not all of them. Let's not save everybody.' And it's that notion in particularly evangelical religion, that it's a pick and mix. We can have some people who will be okay, and some people who will not.

And you worry about the general atmosphere in the world now?

Very much. I think if you look at some of the candidates for president, DeSantis is running on an openly anti-gay platform. It's become a sort of touchstone of how Republican you are, how conservative you are. One of the ways to do it is to pick a minority group and have a go at them. It's happened over and over in the past: it happens to migrants, it happens to all kinds of ethnic minorities, and the LGBT group is in the firing line for sure at the moment. Homophobic hate crime is on the rise in the UK. All I can do is keep standing up, and keep saying, 'I'm here, and I won't pick and choose who gets to be loved. That's not all right.'

Kate Pickett on society and equality

June, 2022

> Kate Pickett is an epidemiologist known for her work
> on the societal benefits of greater equality. She is the
> co-author of *The Spirit Level* and her research has
> influenced public health policies and debates on social
> justice worldwide.

Equality is not just the subject of my academic work. I think it
is an underpinning value in my life.

How do you think that that came to be the case for you?

All children are brought up, I suppose, being told that fairness
is a really important value, and the complaint that 'It's not fair'
is very characteristic of small children. And almost always, you
know, you'll get parents saying, 'Well, you must share,' treating
fairness as though it's something really important. And then, as
you get a bit older, you start to hear from adults, things like, life's
not fair. You can't expect things to be fair,' and it's a bit of a con-
tradiction. There are messages to little children, and then what
people get told as they get a bit older. But, in my upbringing, fairness was important. My parents were Labour voters, consciously
left-wing. And so those egalitarian principles, I think, were

always there. And then, as I grew up, I suppose it was a growing awareness of how hierarchy and privilege act in the world, and feeling that those things were not right. And probably it really crystallised for me when I went to university, because I went to a comprehensive school, I came from a very middle-class family. My parents came from working-class backgrounds, but through their jobs and education, we became a middle-class family. And then I went to Cambridge, where I suddenly encountered an entirely different world of privilege and class that made me think about those things much more consciously than I had before.

You saw this different class of people, this different way of being, and it triggered personal thoughts or social thoughts?

Both, I think. I think it was clear to me that there was a great deal of what I would characterise as unfairness in the whole schooling system and admission system. There we were, at this prestigious university that offers really excellent education – and it truly does – and people's access to that was being shaped by things that were not to do with their work ethic, or performance, or intelligence, or anything of that sort. It was shaped by what school they went to, and therefore by how much money their parents had, and all of that felt wrong. So I felt conscious that there were people missing from that context, that there were people who could have benefited from that, and who should have been there, in a way, and who were not there. That was to do with family incomes, to do with social class, to do with ethnicity, to do with the schools they went to. And instead of being inclusive, this was being provided to a very narrow group of people. And that didn't feel right. But I also felt quite sorry, I think, for a lot of the really posh people, because I thought they'd got no idea about the real world or how the other half live. And I think they'd led quite sheltered lives and had quite narrow perspectives.

You weren't envious of them.

No, I wasn't envious of them. They'd got to this amazing place, but they'd come there with quite a narrow outlook on life. I think for some of them, going to university certainly widened that. But I think that our entire system of schooling segregates us from one another in ways that are harmful to levels of trust within society and how we understand one another.

I asked about equality, and in what you've said, you've focused on fairness – is this the same thing? I suppose fairness doesn't lead naturally to equality, does it? Or ...?

No – I mean, they're closely related, but they're not exactly the same. Fairness, you think of it as a moral value, whereas equality is much more practical, isn't it? It's to do with what we have access to: what we do, or do not, have. And that can be material things, such as equality of income, but it can also be more ephemeral things, like equality in the face of the law. So they're not the same, but they are related.

So if fairness is a moral value, then are you saying that equality is something to work towards? It's a sort of aspiration for society?

Yes, I think so. I'm always quite impressed by the way Quakers talk about it, they have a testimony towards equality. I think that's the way I think about it as well. People get a bit bent out of shape when they talk about equality, saying things like: 'We can never have equality, and can never truly be equal, it's utopian.' And to a certain extent, that's true, but we can have *more* equality. And we can work towards reducing inequality gaps in various aspects. So we can think about working towards reducing gender pay gaps, for example, and that's improving equality. And even if we don't get to exactly the same level, then we're still making progress. So that idea of complete equivalence, that utopian idea that makes people say, 'Oh, it's nonsense, and you can't have it' – I'm just not interested in that argument, really, because we can always do better. And a lot of the things that anti-egalitarians talk about when they're talking about equality as utopian, I think they're not understanding properly. So they talk a lot about, 'We all have different sorts of capabilities and talents,' not recognising that what we measure as talent is itself quite often shaped by inequalities. They think of life, society, as a sort of meritocracy where the super intelligent should be rewarded much more highly. And I don't think that we actually have such huge differences in things like natural intelligence. And what we see as measured intelligence is shaped by the kinds of things I was talking about earlier: by schools, by expectations, by family background. And anyway, I'm not so sure that we should have a situation where people who do particular kinds of tasks get valued so much more than people who do other kinds of tasks, when all of those different tasks are really important for the functioning of a decent society.

The work that you became most famous for, The Spirit Level, *examines that society-level picture in terms of the impact of equality, both on those who have more, as well as [on] those who have less. Tell us a little bit about that, because I think it reflects your own personal priorities and what you believe, and what you think about.*

In *The Spirit Level*, what Richard Wilkinson and I were showing was that societies that have greater levels of income inequality – a bigger gap between the incomes of the rich and the poor – perform worse on a whole range of different health and social outcomes. That includes everything from physical and mental health and things like obesity, to what we might think of as human capital development – how well kids do in school, social mobility, teenage pregnancy rates – but also things to do with social cohesion, like trust, levels of violence, and imprisonment. And a society that does worse on one does worse on all of them. And they're all significantly related to inequality. And the differences are really big. The differences are stark: eightfold differences between more or less equal countries in rates of teenage pregnancy; twelvefold differences in levels of imprisonment, three- to fourfold in mental illness. That's because these aren't just effects that affect the poor; the whole population is tending to do less well. So if you or I, as well-educated, middle-class, probably decently paid individuals, were to live in a more equal society, even our life expectancy would, on average, be higher, and our children would be less likely to drop out of school. Those were the findings.

What drove us to do it? It's an interesting question. It is coming out of a strong tradition in public health to look at the social determinants of health broadly, and to understand the social context that shapes health. Among the key findings in social epidemiology over the past few decades has been the importance of two things. One is relative social position: how you're doing relative to others. So that it's not just your income that matters, but where that places you in a ranking, and how you feel about that. And then also social connectivity: your relation-ships to other people and the quality of those connections. And so an emphasis on the psychosocial determinants of health and wellbeing had become quite strong. All we were doing showing that in more unequal societies, all of that stuff becomes more important. The inequality heightens the importance, the salience, of those social comparisons, those ranking factors. It's as if the social ladder – because all societies have a social ladder – has become steeper and the rungs further apart, and that has conse-quences for all of those different outcomes.

And was it a surprise to you, as it certainly must have been a surprise to the readers of your work, that among the victims of inequality were the better-off?

Yes, I think that is a surprise to people. I think that's something that probably dawned on us fairly gradually. There were some early – I'm talking about the 1990s – analyses that other people had done that were starting to suggest that. One I remember very clearly was comparing infant mortality rates in England and Wales with Sweden. And seeing that at all levels of social class, across the social gradient, those death rates were higher in England and Wales than they were in Sweden. We were seeing a deficit associated with being from England and Wales, even among the top social classes. And I think that evidence is just getting stronger and stronger. But then when you invoke that psychosocial explanation – that it is to do with how we feel we rank in society, where we feel we're placed, how we feel other people view us – it's more understandable why somebody who's not at the top, but near the top, might still be disadvantaged by not being at the very top. Whereas if you were thinking about health and other outcomes, just in terms of material things like income itself, why would you have a difference near the top? Those people have got sufficient resources. So the psychosocial pathways and explanations helped to clarify why those social gradients exist, and why those of us even near the top, do less well than if we're at the very, very top, and do less well than we would in a more equal society.

When we wrote *The Spirit Level*, inequality was not a matter of public discourse. It wasn't on the political agenda. It wasn't on the policy agenda. People didn't talk about it. That's changed. Now, I don't think you would find a mainstream political party willing to say that inequality was not important. And you see an acknowledgement of the problem of inequality at multiple levels. So we see it at the international level, the OECD [Organisation for Economic Cooperation and Development] is very focused on it, the World Bank talks about it, the International Monetary Fund talks about it. The World Economic Forum, at one point, had it at the top of their list of future problems – problems that are likely to affect economic growth and development in the future. So, a real shift at that level, as well as a real shift in discourse in our national politics, if not action; and, indeed, discussion at local level too. So I think there has been a real growing understanding of the problem. And that is a necessary first step, I suppose, in us seeing policy and political change to reduce inequality.

In the UK, we've got the government's 'Levelling Up' agenda. So we have rhetoric that is right, in this space, about trying to reduce regional and other inequalities. We've got the language there and an expressed intent. Now we have to wait and see what gets put in place to try and achieve that.

That's interesting, isn't it, because the proponents of that particular policy, of course, went a little bit out of their way to stress how it wasn't about reducing inequality, per se, because they didn't want to reduce the gap by bringing people at the top down; they wanted to reduce the gap by bringing the people at the bottom up, but allowing people at the top to still get even higher and higher.

Yes, and that's a fundamental misconception, I think, really, on the political right. That the only thing that needs attention is what's going on at the bottom. Certainly, what's going on at the bottom is important. We do need to see increases in people's employment and stability, and increases in people's incomes and protections of their employment and income rights, and attention paid to the cost-of-living crisis, and all of that. But because inequality itself is a problem, not just poverty, then we really do need to think about how we tackle the top – and there we can start to think about top incomes, but even more important is thinking about assets and wealth.

How hopeful do you feel on a global level? If you think of two babies born today, there's a baby born today that will die tomorrow, and then there's a baby born today that might live to 150 in incredible comfort, and have some of the greatest levels of human happiness and fulfilment ever known to our species. Those two babies have both been born today, but they have those different destinies simply because of their fortune or lack of it. Isn't that global context a really dark context in which to be aspiring to reduce inequality today? Doesn't it make you pessimistic about the chances of doing it?

No.

Is that because you're a hopeful person?

I think it's because I'm a hopeful person, and I just function better with an optimistic outlook. We are talking about huge challenges. And we're talking about the need for long-term action and shifts, and this won't change overnight. But I suppose there's four things that give me hope.

The first is that our level of inequality isn't just a static thing. It's not just that we in the UK have always been an unequal country, and there's nothing we can do to fix it. Or [that] another country over there – America, say – has always been unequal, and there's nothing they can do about it. One does see changes in inequality in societies over time that are shaped by government policy, and by other aspects of social change. So change can happen. That's a hopeful thing, because it means we're not stuck with some rigid things that can't move. We used to be as equal as Sweden is today. There's no reason why we can't be again. Our top tax rates used to be ninety per cent – there's no reason why they couldn't be again. So that's one thing that gives me hope: that there's always potential for change.

The second is that young people give me hope. If we look at the voting patterns of young people, the voting preferences, what they say about what matters to them, I think that gives me hope for the future. We had our Brexit referendum in the UK and it went one way, but only by a very small margin. And people calculated that if that vote had taken place just a few months later, or a year later, the result would have been different simply because of demographic shifts. The older people who were more likely to vote that we should leave had died, and more young people who were more likely to think that we should remain had reached the age of eighteen. So demographic change really matters. I do think that young people today give me hope in their social attitudes to all kinds of things, and greater equality is one of them.

The third thing is the hope that the drastic challenges that we're facing within the environment, including the climate change emergency, will shift our attention towards what needs to change in the social and economic world to address those problems, and that that might actually shape what we do.

The fourth reason is that, if we look back at other social changes, where people have been given legal rights, or there's been social change in the acceptance of different social groups – feminism and the gay rights movement, and those sorts of things – change has been quite rapid. None of those changes came about because people in power decided to extend the franchise or extend rights or support people; change came about from grassroots movements, from pressure for change, and then politics at the top shifted in alignment with those grassroots movements. So I think we can see large amounts of social change in a short time.

Leo Igwe on optimism and fighting superstition

July, 2020

Leo Igwe is a Nigerian human rights activist and
founder of the Humanist Association of Nigeria. He
has faced numerous lawsuits and attacks in opposition
to his activism to protect children from human rights
violations caused by 'witchcraft' accusations and his
promotion of humanism more generally.

I was raised a Catholic, and I was sent to Catholic seminaries and
I was training to be a priest. But, in the course of that training,
I had issues with religion and the religious world view, and it is
those issues – doubts about religious teachings, questionable religious rituals that are sometimes very harmful, not just to adults,
but also to children – that drove me to start thinking about an
alternative. As I was growing up, I was made to understand that
there was no alternative to religion. Just find a way to be religious,
period. Even if you are doubting, just pray harder so that that
will go away! So, you keep struggling on with the whole idea
of religion.

While I was there, I just felt, 'Why is there no alternative?' and
in the course of my reading, I read about humanism as a philosophy. It was presented in a way that suggested it's a corrupt way
of life, a corrupt way of looking at the world. They, of course, try
to present the religious view as the perfect way, so however you

try to look for alternatives, you just eventually have to return to religion, but I was deeply dissatisfied with the religious outlook. That made me decide to explore an alternative, and instead of dedicating my life to serving God, let me dedicate my life to serving humanity. I think it was when I made that switch that everything made sense in terms of humanism.

You said that one of the things that started you off in this direction was the feeling that harm was being caused to people. Was that the most important thing to you?

Yes, of course, it was very important to me because, like I said, I confronted situations where innocent people were branded witches or wizards, or they were branded as involved in some occult activities, or they were branded as possessed. Sometimes sick people, people who have some health issues, they are tortured or maltreated because they are believed to be possessed. In other words, the devil or the demons have tried to relocate to a person's body, operating from there. As a result of that, he's being tortured. These are ordinary people who deserve care, who need to be taken care of, but they're now maltreated, and it's because it is believed that their health problem is actually a sign of the devil's possession. I found this very unsatisfactory, and that is why I kept on exploring the rational alternative – and, of course, the compassion that goes with a rational approach to life.

So, it's both sides. You weren't satisfied with the explanation, you thought it wasn't right. But that really began for you with compassion for the suffering that you were seeing and wanting to avoid that harm.

Yes, because that religious interpretation of the world, the religious interpretation of hard problems, is not benign. Some people were saying that it was benign superstition, and I say, well, maybe when you sit somewhere, you're in the comfort of your bedroom, you might think that this is benign, but when you see how this interferes with people's lives, especially vulnerable people, elderly people, people who are very sick, you will know that superstition is not as benign as you people might think. It can really motivate people to commit atrocities with impunity. There is this idea that when they do it, they have done the right thing, and they don't care about the law, they don't care about any human decency, they don't care about human rights. Now, it is that impunity that goes with religious interpretation, or magical interpretation, supernatural interpretation of our day-to-day problems that I really found disgusting, and that attracted me to the naturalistic, the rationalist view of life, and, like I said, the compassion that comes when you apply rational interpretation to situations people ordinarily attribute to what you could call irrational or supernatural entities or agencies.

In what you were just saying, you addressed a sort of imaginary person and said, 'You know, from your position of comfort, maybe you can just see superstition as harmless, but actually it's causing all these problems.' Who were you addressing then? Were you talking to people who don't take this topic as seriously as you think they should? Were you talking to people outside of Nigeria? Who are you disputing with?

I am talking to so many people. There are some people who have this impression that there are benign superstitions. These are sometimes people who live in the West and who are not so close to the harshness of reality – the reality of situations we have where superstition is used to abuse, to maim, to destroy the lives and property of people. Sometimes the people in Africa who try to brand those who challenge religion-based abuses, superstition-based abuses, as extremists or fundamentalists. In other words, who try to undermine the very important, fundamental campaign trying to address the evil, the destruction, the savagery that is unleashed in situations where people are consumed by religious extremist ideas and superstitious beliefs. So, they try to create the impression that some of these superstitions are not as harmful as you present them.

Something that is irrational, you might say it's comforting – some people say 'comforting superstitions' – but when this intersects with solutions to problems like ailments, explaining misfortune, now you can see that comforting superstitions are not as comforting as people present them as being. They are poisonous, they are destructive and they drain the compassion from human hearts. Human beings are capable of very kind acts. They are also capable of very cruel acts. Where religion comes in and superstition comes in, it has a way of draining their compassion and then unleashing unimaginable cruelty from a human being who ordinarily would have been very caring.

I was interested in a TED Talk that you gave a few years ago, where you expressed your very strong belief in the potential of human beings to make change. You said that that had been inspired in part by your own parents. I'm assuming that they were Catholics if you were raised in a Catholic environment. So how did you come to have this belief in the transformative possibilities of human agency, either from them or more generally?

The thing is, I was inspired by their lives. I was inspired by the efforts they made to train us, to expose us to life – but, of course, I am not guided and dictated by their own world view. I want to make that distinction. My parents were born traditional African religionists, but in the course of trying to get education, they got converted to Christianity, and then they became Catholics. Of course, when I was born, I was born into a Catholic family, and they tried to bring me up the Catholic way. I used to tell them – and I used to tell other people – my parents made a switch based on the circumstances of their own time and their own understanding of so many issues. I also have to make my own switch based on my own understanding, and the issues, and how I try to look at the world. They changed, they made that change, which is very important. It is important that [. . .] they made the change based on what they thought was right or true or moral, as the case may be, and it is important that this process continues. What we have as the situation today in some parts of Nigeria is that when you are born into Islam, you are told you cannot change, you cannot leave, because it is apostasy and it is a crime. If they don't go after you legally, they go after you through social sanctions, as we are seeing in the case of one of our colleagues, Mubarak [later sentenced to twenty-four years in prison].

Despite all the religions, my parents worked hard; they believed in hard work. This is one of the things I drew from. While they prayed, I know that there was this belief in hard work, in making efforts, in trying and in not just resigning yourself to the world as it is, but striving to see how you can change the world to be as you would like it to be. That was why they gave us education that they'd never had, and [why] they made us explore opportunities that they'd never had. So we are where we are today because of that adventurous spirit, that explorative tendency, that idea to look across the board in terms of their own religious orientation, their own cultural understanding, their own ambitions and careers, and all that. We stood on their shoulders and we can now see higher and we can now see better. This is an inspiration I drew from them, and that is why there's a need for us to keep encouraging such a world where coming generations could change their beliefs based on the realities of the time. They should not be persecuted; they should not be imprisoned or jailed for expressing ideas freely just like today. I used to tell my parents that the world I'm living in today is different from the world you lived in. How can we have that in terms of future generations if we don't allow them to explore new ideas, new understanding and new possibilities? So, I drew that inspiration as I was growing up from them, in terms of hard work, and the ability to look at the world and try hard to change it and make it suit my own idea of how life should be and how the world should be.

That sense of progress, that sense of ever-expanding horizons and standing on the shoulders of those that went before us to make that progress – is that something that you have high hopes for in Nigeria today?

When it comes to hope and Nigeria, I'm always very cautious, because sometimes my country moves two steps forward, three steps backward. They keep moving back and forth, back and forth. I still have this impregnable sense of optimism. Yes. That no matter what happens, in spite of all the dark difficulties and challenges, I still think that Nigeria will make progress – but, of course, there will be a cost. There will be prices to pay, as we are seeing today. It has always been the case. When I was studying in Germany, they were telling me about the Thirty Years' War. I was imagining thirty years. Remove thirty years from my life now. I'll be left with about twenty. Okay, so I can imagine thirty years of war. What are people fighting for? How big is the scale of destruction? Look at the World Wars. Look at all the tragic situations human beings have come through. Look at the Rwandan genocide. What I'm saying is this: even in a dark and destructive situation – killings, fighting, imprisoning somebody just because a person made a comment on Facebook, something that sounds very outrageous, killing somebody because the person said something critical of your faith – I still have the sense that that arc of human history bends towards justice, towards progress. Just like you see the second hand; it shakes as it moves, but it keeps moving towards that progress. That is the way I look at it.

Even though it appears that things are very bad, and people might want to despair and say, 'How can Nigeria make ease with all this mess around? How can Africans make it with this situation and all their problems?', there is still this feeling I have that at the end of the day, like the second hand, it keeps moving and shaking towards progress, towards betterment, towards development. That is what I have seen, even in my own short life.

Let me give you an example, drawing from our professional humanism, as you mentioned initially. In the 1990s, when I started the Nigerian Humanist Movement, we used to write letters and it used to take three months before we got a reply to one letter. So when you write a letter, you just go on holiday; you just forget it, you know, because it has to take a while before you get feedback. But what is it like today? Today, it takes a second. Sometimes I write a letter, and before I could check my inbox again, the reply is already waiting for me. You can see that. Imagine something that takes three months now taking you a second. Is that not progress? It is, and this is what gives me optimism. There is some hope.

I am inspired by this sense of hope – not the sense of hope of something that will materialise when I'm dead. I'm talking about a sense of hope for something that will materialise here and now. Yes, the technology, the scientific discoveries, they are not equally distributed – fine! But it is all a result of human ingenuity over the course of time, the medicine we have. So there is this quest to keep hoping, to keep striving, to keep trying, to keep creating and recreating. It's all about innovation; it's all about that sense that I told you I got from my parents, when you look at the world and say, 'Okay, it is not perfect. How do I make it better? How do I alter the situation? How do I satisfy this need?' And in the course of time, somebody draws fulfilment from it. By being inventive and innovative, you make available something that was limited to a few people. So that is why, although there are those who promote division, there are those who also draw from their ingenuity to knock down those fences – as we saw in Germany, where they got people in the East and West, people deprived and those people who had abundance, to meet together, to join, to embrace. This is what gives me hope, even amidst all the inequality, division and despair.

Siân Berry on a Green view of the human being

February, 2021

Siân Berry is a politician and environmental activist. She is a leading figure in the Green Party, having served as its co-leader and is the current MP for Brighton Pavilion. She is the author of several non-fiction books helping readers to become more environmentally friendly.

The last time we saw each other in real life, we were both speaking at a humanist conference on the climate crisis in Iceland. You said something that really stayed with me. You said that your environmentalism was about human beings having the chance to still live abundantly, live with abundance. I thought that was really interesting, because a lot of people have this idea, quite often, of the Green movement, that it's a bit down on people, it's about living less and doing less. That's not your approach?

No, and I deliberately chose that theme because I think we can achieve abundance for everybody. When you talk about equality, people often think that means levelling down. You find a lot of the people who are currently doing very well think that means you're coming for them, you're coming for their stuff. Actually, we are talking about building up a society where everybody gets to be fulfilled – and fulfilled in ways that really matter to them.

Stuff isn't really my priority. I've got policies for the London elections where I'm trying to make reducing 'stuff turnover' happen. So I'm saying things to businesses like, 'We need to reduce the turnover of the economy in terms of resources,' to reduce the amount of stuff – but the reason we want to do that is so that we can have a society where everybody can flourish, so that we can do things like have businesses where we're repairing things at a much more local level, where people can genuinely go to somewhere that's part of their community to get that stuff repaired to make it last longer. That, in turn, generates more jobs, and we can create a society where people do know each other, where there's fellowship and community and all kinds of things like that. To me, that's what abundance is all about, as well as abundance of things like freedom and opportunity and things that really people want in their lives. They don't want more stuff, they don't want to be fearful of losing the stuff they already have. People want to have that unlimited opportunity to get by, to feel that society has a belief in them.

That's one of the things that I feel in my work with youth services, for example. With lots of young people, the thing that makes a difference to them when they get a good youth worker or a good youth centre that gives them something to do is this feeling that society is investing in them because they see them as someone to be promoted and supported. That gives people so much joy, and the feeling that somebody believes in them – particularly, that society as a whole believes in them. A lot of that gets pulled away from young people in today's world. I think this is one of those really important things. It's about applying that kind of mindset, instead of letting other people frame your philosophy and your values as Greens as something that involves less. I don't like that at all. Instead, what could we *have*? How could we do this better? How could we make everything work well?

What is distinctively Green about that?

If you want to characterise something about the Greens, it's about how we look to the future. We want to make sure that everything is growing in its value. We're thinking about future generations, not just in terms of whether or not they've got a habitable planet to live on, which is obviously a very motivating factor for a lot of Greens, but also whether or not they will have a good life, whether or not they will have something better than what we've got today. All those things motivate us as well. It's all to do with thinking a bit further forward into the future, and thinking about building something better.

What is sustainability as a value to you?

It's a very simple concept of things being able to be sustained into the future, that things can go on, that we're not winding things down. The sense that we're running out of things is a worry for a lot of people. The idea that we can have a circular economy or a society where we're making things better each time things go round, that is sustainability. It's about things that carry on into the future. There's obviously a risk side to that, but also an opportunity and development side.

Is that an optimistic view?

Yes! Because think about what we could have. Think about the ways in which, for example, I have way more opportunities than my ancestors, the people in my past. That's a good thing. That's a really optimistic thing. The idea that we wouldn't be passing down the same advantages, the same progress to people, is wrong. So I think, yes, it's definitely an optimistic thing that we're trying to build something better in the future. I think so.

Why would it be wrong? A lot of people don't live their lives with a view to the future and with a view to passing better things on.

I guess what I'm getting at there is not to be too egotistical as a generation. I just said that I've got loads more opportunities than my grandparents. I could be tempted, and we as a generation could be tempted, to think that we're the optimal people, and we'll reap the rewards of our predecessors and use everything up, and leave nothing to people who come after. That seems to me to be a very selfish thing to do. I think I'm thinking about the duty you owe to keep things as they were, and to not leave your mark on the world, on society or on the planet in a way that leaves scars or difficulties for people in the future. I think that's a moral question, isn't it?

Well, you're investing in future people, and that's not something that everyone naturally thinks about. They can think about people who are alive today and our interactions with them and our obligations to each other, but you're saying something different. It's future people that don't yet exist, and our moral obligation is to them. I wonder what it was that first made you think that way. When did you first start caring about those people that don't exist yet?

I did, very consciously, decide to examine my own values and my own philosophy when I was in my early twenties, and some of it came out of science. The fact that I was aware of climate change being a threat. I was also, earlier in my life, aware of things like the rainforests and the ozone holes; the damage we were doing to the planet became something very clear to me. I started to think then about the damage we were doing, and what the problem might be. I think when you start to then go and read your philosophy, and get your Bertrand Russell out, you do end up taking quite a long view; if that's your starting point of the history of humanity and the possible damage that we're doing to the planet, then you do take a very long view, and you're going to take that same sort of view into the future as well. I'm trying to think if there's anyone that I actually read [who] said you must think about future generations. It's a very strong part of Green philosophy, and I think the core values and philosophical basis, which are the things I read and that helped me decide to become a Green, they do talk about that in a way that's very clear. They talk about every person, including future generations, having a right to basic material security, for example – that's Green policy.

You're implying that it's quite radical to say that policy formation should be led by the spirit of enquiry. If you're right, is it tribalism in politics or oppositionalism in politics that you think is the barrier to that?

Exactly that. If somebody is proposing to hold an inquiry into what went wrong [with government responses to Covid-19], and to do it properly so that we learn as we go along, in our oppositional two-party system, the other side can only react to that, it seems, in ways that are either saying, 'You're questioning my judgement by trying to have an inquiry into it,' or 'You're blaming me for it.' People then see the other side as being unnecessarily political about an issue. Nobody's admitting that none of us really knew what to do initially – it was not obvious. No one is saying that we're all learning, that obviously, we were going to make mistakes, but we need to examine those mistakes and learn from them in an honest way. That just isn't coming through at all. It's going to be absolutely politicised. This question of how we learn from this and that isn't going to be right; that isn't a scientific way of approaching it.

You've been a critic of oppositional politics, but it's not the case that one can just follow a scientific trail and then the answer will be at the end of it, obvious for all to see. There are values that shape our approaches, and different values are available, and we have to choose some values to be the ones that inform our joint approach as a society. If it's not through political opposition that we'd decide what those values should be, what would you replace that with in politics?

I think political debate is really important, and debating those values is exactly what politics is all about. I think a system where all the power is concentrated in one place and then all transferred to another place is very, very unhealthy. I think we need to have more cooperative politics so that debates don't just take place at election time, and then someone wins, and then they're right about everything for the next four years. I think we need something that's a lot more cooperative, where nobody wins all the power, where there's always going to have to be cooperation between the people who win on a continual basis, so that when each issue arises, there is a debate. I'm obviously a Remain supporter, I wanted to stay in the European Union, but having lost that initial referendum, it was really hard to spend those four years watching, at every step of the way, things going wrong. Even if you accept that the goal is to exit the EU in an orderly way and maintain as many benefits as possible, you weren't allowed to say that things were going badly because the answer was always, 'Well, you lost, so shut up now.' That is unhelpful. That is extremely unhelpful politics. That is actually the way that our current electoral system is set up: to select a government that will have a majority and be able to tell the other side to shut up for four years. It is not healthy at all. I think every issue ought to be debated in a way that doesn't happen.

Through a lot of what you've said, there are two themes running. On the one hand, you're very strongly in favour of human development, which implies the personal development of the individual, because they're the person who will be empowered, who will be living abundantly and all the rest of it. You're also making arguments that are quite strongly about whole populations. Where does that balance between the individual and the community lie for you?

One of the causes I personally get involved in quite a lot is freedom, human rights, free speech and anti-authoritarianism. I think I'll never get away from that. There are some debates within the Greens that I just don't support. They're not in our policies. But some people have said, for example, that there should be a committee that can veto democratic decisions. I just think, *Hang on a minute, that's getting a little bit authoritarian. Who chooses the experts who are going to be in this committee?* That is where I've started to draw the line.

With things like facial recognition, new ideas that pose a threat to people's individual freedoms and individual rights, I'll always come down on the side of individual rights when it comes to that. The police are pushing ahead with facial recognition on the grounds of public safety. I'm not convinced... That technology has so much potential to impact your freedom of movement, your freedom of association, your freedom of expression – so many human rights that are engaged by the idea of having databases of images of where you've been and knowledge of what you've done. It would take so much to convince me that that was a good technology to be using. I'm so much in favour of essentially banning it, as a real threat to all kinds of things. It's very worrying.

It sounds like when it comes to it and there's a judgement to be made, or these two things are in tension, you tilt towards the individual.

I tilt towards that because, in the end, what are we human for? What is being a human if it's not to be a free individual? We can't always subsume ourselves into the common good. But given that, the point is to give individuals the democratic responsibility for guardianship. So you'd hope that by debate, by argument, by good democratic structures, that the free human individuals who can all vote on these things would come to the right decision – and if they don't, that is their responsibility. I think it's important that we have responsibility, we have the ability to make mistakes. That is an important freedom too.

Mike Little on an open-source world

September, 2021

> Mike Little is the co-creator of the widely used website building tool, WordPress. As an open-source project, WordPress has since been developed by a huge worldwide community and today powers more than 40% of the web.

You're best known for the development of WordPress, so I think just for those who are not completely up to speed on every aspect of technology to do with the internet, you might tell us a little bit, first of all, about what WordPress is.

WordPress is a piece of open-source software that allows you to easily create a website – or fairly easily [. . .] It's been going for, in internet terms, a really long time. Eighteen years now. One of the key things that we set out to do when we first created WordPress was to, as we phrased it, democratise publishing. The idea being that it made it easy for someone who was not very technical (originally, you needed a little bit of technology but not too much) to have a voice on the web, to very simply create a website or blog at the time, and share their thoughts with the world, to set up a business site, all kinds of things. It's grown incredibly. To cover some statistics, more than forty per cent of the top ten million websites use WordPress in some way.

Anyone who's made a website has probably used WordPress, and everyone who's listening has been on a website made with WordPress. That's pretty much certain, isn't it?

Almost certain.

So it's that pervasive. And of course, what we're really interested in on this podcast are the values behind that. Already in what you've said, there's some exciting ground to cover, because you talked about giving people a voice, and you've talked about democracy. Were those two things important to you as you developed this platform?

They were. Originally, back in the early 2000s, as I decided to look into this blogging thing that people were getting into, there were a few different pieces of software that you could use at the time. Having looked at them, the one that I chose was one that was called b2. So, before WordPress, there was a thing called b2. One of the reasons that I chose it was that it was open-source – and that's something that I've been passionate about since the late eighties, before the term 'open-source' existed, but the concept of free and open software where you could actually see the source code and know how it worked. That was fundamental to the decision that I made to go with b2, as it was at the time. Probably a year or so after I started using it, the guy who was responsible for that software disappeared off the net. There were a few people using that software at the time, maybe about a thousand people, something like that, and one of the users, who I'd interacted with on the support forums for the software, wrote a blog post using b2, and he called it 'The blogging software dilemma'. And he just talked about the fact that he'd looked through these various different pieces of software, he'd decided on b2, the guy responsible for it had disappeared off the net, and he said, basically, that because it was open-source, he could take that, fix the bugs that we knew were in it, and carry on enhancing it. If he got run over by a bus, someone else could take over. I responded to that blog post with a simple comment that basically said, 'Matt, if you're interested in forking b2' – forking is that process of taking that open-source software – 'count me in.' That comment on a blog post started the project that eventually became WordPress, and the key fundamental to it was that open-source nature of it, that openness, that allowed us to take the existing code and make changes to it and distribute it to other people.

What do you think it was that made you feel so strongly about that? About the desirability of people having ready access to this?

I guess my real passion for open-source software, for free software, started in the eighties, when I first came across the concept of the GNU software, which was started by a chap called Richard Stallman. He started it because when he was at university learning to code, the computers that were in the universities at the time were very much about research and enhancing the students' ways of working. It was early, and at the time, most of the money in computers, as they were, was all about the hardware. The software was kind of just something that came with it to enable it to be used. In particular, as a university might upgrade their hardware, they would have their local people modify the software to work with the new hardware. This was just a fairly standard way of behaving. Then these computer companies started realising that they could make money out of the software as well, and started putting restrictions on it. Richard Stallman and a few others were really cheesed off with this. They'd got used to this idea of being able to just modify the software to make it control the hardware better or differently, and suddenly they weren't allowed to do that.

That was the spark for him, and he eventually created the General Public Licence, which is described as a copyright hack. It's a legal hack whereby you use the standard Geneva Convention copyright laws to license the software that you create to the world. Then you use the licensing laws. You grant the world a licence to use the software in whatever way they want, allowing them to modify the software. You give them the source code, so that they can do that, and they are able to share the software with their neighbours and whoever they want, and are also able to share those modifications. The key thing is that the almost sole restriction is that you cannot then restrict anyone else's rights whom you give it to. So when you benefit from it and make something that's better from it, you can pass it on, but you can't restrict someone else's rights to do the same. Crucially, there's not any mention of money in these rights and restrictions. It's quite fine to sell this software that you've obtained for free and enhanced, but then you can't restrict anybody else's right to do the same, or to give it away for free.

So it's almost a cooperative evolution of a product?

It is absolutely, which is what's really odd in this technical world that we live in.

So this whole open-source philosophy is extremely important to you. Are there applications of it other than in software?

One great example from last year was that someone open-sourced a ventilator design that allowed people to create ventilators for something like $400 worth of off-the-shelf parts versus the $20,000 that they normally cost. Not as sophisticated, but at the time, they could help save lives. People are open-sourcing prosthetic designs so that people in poorer countries can get prosthetic limbs, and so on. The whole idea is incredible. One of the interesting things about one of the definitions of the open-source licences in particular is one that describes itself as free as in freedom, not free as in beer. In actual fact, microbreweries have been open-sourcing beer recipes. BrewDog actually open-source all their beer recipes as well, which I think is a clever play on that concept.

And they don't see that as being in conflict with their commercial interests at all?

I think the reality is that most people aren't going to homebrew their beer, and they'd rather have it done for them and just have the pleasure of drinking it. But some people will. I guess they just see that as a good thing. To be honest, software's a little bit the same. Some people are not interested in learning how to program and learning how to run a piece of open-source software on their computer. They'd rather just get something off the shelf, or buy something and download it and have it work for them. It's the same thing. I love the fact that the concept of making money from it but also sharing it with the world is fine, and the two can coexist.

When you think about your own motivations to get involved in that, would you say it was more about your own support for freedom – as in your freedom to operate in this way on the internet – or was it more altruistic?

I think it was more the altruistic side of it, because it just really gelled with me that this was the right way to behave. Once software has been written, it costs a negligible amount to copy it and reproduce it, and so, technically, nobody's losing anything. If it's reproduced and given away for free, you don't lose anything from it. Sure, people want to earn money from writing software, and that's fine. That's why, in particular, this licence doesn't mention money, and allows people to sell their software and so on. But the fact that perhaps people who can't afford it still get to use that software – it just always seemed the right thing to do for me. I just really gelled with this, the idea of benefiting society. At the time, it was relatively new, being applied to that kind of technology.

The whole idea has been around for a long time. Science is the example that a lot of people think of: the whole idea of sharing your results, sharing your research, so that future scientists can benefit from that and enhance science for the greater good. A really classic, home-based idea is recipes. When you share a recipe for something with somebody, you've kind of given it away for free, and they might enhance it and change it. Maybe they didn't have salt that day, so they put something else in it, and then they share that with their family, and it goes on, and different versions of it get spread around. That's just a concept that nobody would worry about, even though there are recipe books, and there are famous TV chefs and all the rest of it. That basic concept of sharing the recipe, the ingredients, to make something good – I think people regard that as perfectly normal. Software, at the end of the day, is a set of instructions to a machine on how to do something; it's a recipe to make a machine do something. And that idea of being able to share it and enhance it, it's very similar.

It sounds like you think that there's a fundamental difference between this cooperative sharing, developing for the benefit of others and passing it on, and the approach of marketing something, holding it firmly to yourself for the benefit of yourself and your own profitability. It also sounds as though you think that those two things can coexist. Is that right?

Yeah, I think that's key. They can coexist. I know that we live in a capitalist society, in mostly a capitalist world, and we can't get away from that right now. Maybe in the far future, things might change, but right now that's how we operate. That's how we have to earn money to put food on the table and a roof over our heads, and so on. But when you create an artificial scarcity, that starts to feel morally wrong – in particular, when you do so purely in order to make money. If you think about an artist creating paintings, for example, that's automatically scarce: a single painting. Even if they might do a different version of the same one. When you are manufacturing goods and you create those artificial scarcities, whether that's through reducing the number that you create, pulling the price out of the reach of the majority, or, as is the normal case, just not letting anyone else create the same thing that you've done through so-called intellectual property laws, it feels morally wrong to me.

So you're begrudgingly willing to allow these two models to coexist, but you do think actually that the other is unjust?

I do. Yeah. The history of the copyright laws is quite interesting. The original copyright laws, my understanding is that they were granted for, I think it was seven years initially, and this was only for books at the time – the idea being that an author should benefit from their creation for seven years, and after that the rest of the world should benefit. Anybody should be able to reproduce the book, and everybody can benefit from the value of that book – which, initially, were mostly non-fiction books. So people would benefit from them because they were about learning things, and so on. That has changed over the years to the horrendous state that we're in now, driven by Disney amongst others, where copyright now exists for seventy-five years after the death of the author. It's just crazy to me, because it is restricting the value of that creation being shared with the world for purely financial reasons. That's the issue. I don't mind that people have to recover the cost of manufacture. I don't mind that people want to gain some advantage from their creativity, from their prowess, the skill that they have. It's when it goes to an extreme, when you restrict people's access to things almost in perpetuity, as some companies would like to do – that's where it feels unjust. To me, it feels that you're sacrificing the world for your own personal benefit, and that's hard for me to reconcile.

Alf Dubs on human rights

February, 2024

Alf Dubs is a Labour Party peer and former MP, best known for his championing of the rights of child refugees, and in particular, his work on the Dubs Amendment. He was born in Prague in 1932 and arrived in Britain on the Kindertransport in 1939, having fled the Nazis.

When you look back on your life, what do you think the values that have motivated you have been, particularly in your work in standing up for child refugees, which is one of the things you've been best known for?

I suppose, a sense of wanting to support the underdog, a sense of social justice, human rights. And of course, in my case, having come as an unaccompanied child refugee to Britain, it would not be surprising if I was more emotionally involved with the cause of refugees, particularly child refugees, than I would otherwise have been. I don't think one needs to have that sort of background to argue the case, but it does help me because of the emotional involvement.

How much do you remember of the time when you came to Britain as a young child? Is it something that's still very vivid to you?

Bits of it are. I can remember the day the Germans occupied Prague in 1939. I can remember we had to take the picture of the Czech president out of our school books. My father left, as he was Jewish; my mother wasn't. And my mother tried to get permission to leave and was refused. And she got me on a Kindertransport. And I can still see the scene late at night: Prague station, anxious parents saying goodbye to their kids, possibly for the last time. Off the train went: two days, hard wooden seats, but as a six-year-old, one doesn't mind that. We reached the Dutch border, and the older ones cheered now we were out of reach of the Nazis. I just knew it was something significant, but didn't understand quite what was going on.

You're right that a person shouldn't have to have been a refugee in order to empathise with refugees, but that experience must have been one of the most important things that gives you that emotional connection, that empathy with people in those situations today.

I suppose so. But as it's been with me since the age of six, I've never really analysed it in detail to see what effect it did have. But yes, of course, it would be absurd for me to deny the emotional involvement, and therefore the effect it's had on me and my attitudes. I've always had a bit of a struggle to sort out my sense of identity, which I've done now. I didn't talk about my background; the media picked it up. I neither boasted about my background, nor did I deny it. It's one of the facts of life. But it has been helpful in the politics of the issue more recently.

Moving away from the politics of the particular issue, what other impact or role did those experiences have on the development of your values? It's a big rupture in the life of a child.

I suppose it is. But we were a secular family in Prague, so it wasn't that big a change when I came to Britain. I went through all the business of school, and so on, and I didn't have the strength to say, 'No, I don't want to be part of this.' So I just let it happen, wash over me. It wasn't until I left school and became an undergraduate that I really set out to question all this religious stuff and felt there'd been too much of it at school, and it hadn't really been necessary. And it certainly hadn't been helpful. What I took from that, I don't know.

Well, what I've noticed is that you're not a humanist who's very anti-religious; you're quite a tolerant person with other people's beliefs.

Well, I think so, because I'm not a militant atheist. That's why I'm a humanist. I take what is helpful from other people's beliefs, and use it. I think that works quite well. Sometimes I'm pretty scathing in my own mind – and sometimes publicly – about religions and the harm they do, and the misogyny and all that. I don't find what they do is often very helpful. Sometimes, they can be okay: that's normally where we agree on our relations with our fellow human beings and that we need to show compassion and the humane attitude. And there, of course, we can see eye to eye. But then I see eye to eye with all people who think that.

Was there a moment in your life, whether at school or in later education or political life, when human rights became a particularly important concept to you?

I think they always were, from the point when I became conscious of these things. In other words, they almost went automatically. I suppose, my mother was once turned down for a job – difficult circumstances for her, because my father was long dead. And she was struggling in Britain without very much English at the beginning. She applied for a job. And she heard somebody on the interview panel say, 'We're not giving a job to that bloody foreigner.' I think I began to realise that there was a lot of discrimination, a lot of difficulty. And I suppose I thought through that, and decided that being a humanist was the right thing for me, and human rights loomed as a large part of that. And of course, from an early age, I was passionately interested in politics, and I decided very quickly to try and understand why what had happened to me had happened. I was aware that evil men had done terrible things in politics. But maybe politics could also be used to redress the balance. So I became interested in politics as a vehicle for achieving decent values.

And what would you say your particular interests were when you were a Member of Parliament?

I was interested in refugees and immigration; I was interested in human rights. I was interested in penal reform, and what we're doing about the awful things happening in our prisons.

Penal reform is an issue that no one has talked about here before. And it's interesting, because a lot of humanists have got a background in it, but no one's actually mentioned it before here as a particular interest. How did you come to be particularly interested in the conditions for prisoners?

I had Wandsworth prison in my first constituency. So I went around the prison, and I began to learn quite a lot about penal affairs. I was on the Home Affairs Select Committee, and we looked at prisons there as well. I began visiting a number of prisons. And all of this builds up, and I became very interested in what a lousy regime we had in our prisons. I even went to see Cook County Jail in Chicago once. In that way, I learned an awful lot about our prisons, talking to the prisoners. More recently, I'm afraid refugees have overtaken that. But I still think it's a crucial issue. And we don't handle it at all well in this country.

If you were Prisons Minister tomorrow, what reforms would you be introducing?

Well, there's so many. First of all, we send far too many people to jail anyway. We have too large a proportion of our population in jail, compared to virtually every other European country. In the Netherlands, for example, I understand that they even have empty prison places, because they managed to reform so much. It's not just the prison system, it's the overall criminal justice system that gets people into jail. I'd like to see us look at that. I would like to see different regimes in jail, much more positive ones, for work, and so on. I once visited Wormwood Scrubs, and there were three young men lying down in their bunks. They were given an hour outside every day, and for the rest of the time, they were just lying on their bunks. And I thought, *This must fester.* Almost everybody who goes to jail in Britain is going to come out again. But we don't work in our prisons in such a way that they become better human beings before they do. So we should treat them differently in prison – not softly, but differently, as a way of developing them for their future life in the community. And we shouldn't send so many people to prison; we send far too many. There's no point in sending people for very short sentences – that does nothing at all. And I think we should only send people who are a serious danger to society.

So you think prison really has those two functions: one to keep people who are a danger to society from society, and the other to help them have better lives when they leave, to improve their own situation?

I think so. There has to be an element of punishment about prison because society demands it. And some of the things that are happening by way of physical assaults on people and murder, they're awful, and people have to be punished. But I think we should look at it more in terms of, 'How do we move forward?' and, 'How do we ensure that we are the safest society when people come out?'

It doesn't sound like you personally believe in punishment.

Well, look, there has to be an element of it – society demands it. We wouldn't achieve the other reforms unless there was an element of punishment. Otherwise, we'd have the newspapers saying we don't care about the effect on people who are knifed and murdered and have acid thrown in their faces. We mustn't be in that position. We will never achieve any reform that way. So there has to be an element where society punishes the severe wrongdoers.

How far are you conscious in your political life and the arguments you make of the need to be pragmatic? You've just said, for example, society might want to punish wrongdoers. How many times have you found yourself doing that in your political life: squaring off what you'd like to see as the ideal with what's achievable? Is it hard to do?

Well, I hope I'm not a compromiser to the point where all my principles go out of the window. That is a danger. Let me talk to you about refugees. There's a need to get public opinion on our side. And by that, I mean that we need people to understand better what was happening to refugees who come to this country, what was happening to them in Afghanistan, or Syria, or in the Horn of Africa ... the terrible things that were happening to them. For example, I quote a Syrian boy who said to me his father had been blown up in front of him by a bomb in Damascus. Terrible experiences, these people have gone through. The more we understand why it is they sought safety in this country, the more we will be supportive of their wish to be here.

Are there people who just refuse to empathise with others? Have you come across people like that in your work?

Well, I have a bit, yes, of course. Sometimes I get quite abusive emails, and stuff on Twitter, and so on, because people are not to be persuaded. I've had threats, I've had people say, 'It's a pity you survived the Holocaust,' and stuff like that. I've had much worse! But on the other hand, women in public life get it much worse than men in public life, and Black women in public life get it worse than any others. So, in that sense, I probably don't get nearly as much as [is] possible. But when there was a bomb on the underground, I was told it [was] all my fault, because the person had come from another country as a refugee. On the other hand, I think some of these people are a bit sick. Some of these people must be very unhappy souls. And the trouble is, the electronic media have given them a chance to express themselves in a way in which we couldn't do easily before. I don't believe I can influence all these people; I don't believe I have such effective powers of persuasion, but one has to try.

But there's also a middle ground of people who are open to arguments, are open to facts and ideas. I think they're the ones we have to concentrate on in terms of the public discourse on the more difficult issues. You know, stuff like assisted dying: there are some passionate opponents of assisted dying. I believe very much that assisted dying is a humane, sensible way forward, with all the safeguards that are necessary. And we've got those built into the thinking around assisted dying. There are people I can't persuade. I've talked to people and they just will not budge.

You alluded earlier to your time in Northern Ireland, and I thought we'd come to that, because not only has it been a source of some of the best jokes I've heard you tell – which is not what this podcast is about – but I think it was a real experience, as well, of seeing first-hand the difficulties of negotiation and discussion, and the long tail of religious conflict in particular. But did that time in Northern Ireland have any other effects on your beliefs and values?

I think it had a profound effect. It was a great privilege to be there. But it was a privilege to be there at a time when we had a peace process in mind. We had a peace process we were working towards. To be there as a junior minister, as I was, when the only job was to contain the violence must have been a very unhappy experience. But while we were there, there was a positive sense that we were going to move forward with a peace process. And secondly, our policy was to get on with all of them. I think in Britain, a villain is a villain, but in Northern Ireland, even the villains are charming. We made a determined effort to get on with them all. People always used to say to me, 'What do you think of us in Northern Ireland?' It's that sense of national self-confidence – a lack of self-confidence. I said – it sounds a bit clichéd, but I said – 'If you're always as nice to each other as you are to me, no problem.' But what I found disturbing to see first-hand is that, of course, people of the different backgrounds didn't mix at all. Sometimes they never met and had a cup of tea with anybody else.

Anyway, there were significant things happening. But what it did teach me was that it is possible, even when there is tremendous antagonism, to bring groups and communities together. It's possible. And it's well worth doing, because the rewards are enormous, in terms of peace, a decent life for people in Northern Ireland, which was certainly not there for them during the Troubles. So I think that matters. And I think it matters that we have to talk to people, and we have to persevere in the process of negotiation. We have to persevere in the process of understanding what they're about. And realising that if we put out a hand of solidarity, in terms of what the community is about, that can be helpful. I think if we can argue that it is best for them all to try and get on with each other – not in those terms, of course, but in the sense of achieving a context where people can cooperate, or people can work together for the same ends – that can be very positive. So it was a really a very powerful experience for me, being in Northern Ireland. And today's news of the Stormont assembly coming back again, that an agreement has been reached, I think that's a very encouraging thing, because I wouldn't want to see all that effort in the past go to waste. And while there's no functioning government in Northern Ireland, then the danger is that the men of violence – and usually it is men – can seek comfort from that and we don't want to give them that.

This idea of peace and justice through dialogue and cooperation, that sounds like it's influenced almost every corner of your life, every part of your politics.

I suppose it has really, put that way. Nobody's put it to me quite in those terms before. Thank you. I feel I'm lying on the psychiatrist's couch! What other ways forward are there? I look with horror at what's happening in Israel and in Gaza, and I think, *We've got to have a way forward, we can't just allow this situation to go on, with the tragedy, the loss of life, you know, thousands of people being murdered, killed. We can't let this go on. There's got to be a better way forward.* I think the whole world, for too long, has put the Middle East into the 'too difficult' box. And we've all failed, and it's our fault that we failed.

Where do these values come from? You've got a very coherent, robust set of attitudes. Did they come from your mother, from your community, from your political upbringing? Because you've been involved in Labour politics for a very long time, many decades. Did they shape you from an early age, Labour politics?

I think so, yes. I think Labour politics did, and also the camaraderie that goes with being in a political party that believes we can work for a better world. A camaraderie that comes from believing that the enormous inequalities in our society are unacceptable, that we'd be a much better society if we had more equality, and not such large differences. If we didn't have people who are really very badly suffering, real poverty, people who can't feed their kids, can't keep the homes warm – this is terrible. And from that, I believe that politics can be a power for good, and can achieve things. I'm not saying everything about the Labour Party is good. I'm a critic of some of it, of course. I wouldn't be in it if I wasn't also critical. But certainly, it's helped me. It's helped me to have a good sense of my fellow human beings, and have a good sense of what society I'd like to help to achieve.

Were there any particular political heroes you had when you were younger and starting out in politics?

I was passionately interested in politics when I was younger. When I saw the 1945 election – I was living in Manchester then, following all the details of that. Can I just tell you a little story? My mum took me to a boarding house near Blackpool. And it was the 1945 election results, and because the armed forces had to have their vote sent from the Far East, they didn't start counting until the morning. So the first results would come out at midday.

And the people in the boarding house said – there was no television, of course – that the BBC were going to broadcast from the town square what the early election results were as they were coming in. So I went there and I heard the results, and I went back. And they said, 'Well, what is it?' And I said, very proudly, something like 'Labour, one hundred and forty; Conservatives, thirty.' And I heard a voice say, 'Oh, my God, it's the end of England.' And I thought to myself, *Well, if that's what they think, I don't agree with them.* Attlee, Bevan – I admired them.

I was in the hospital the day the health service began. I was in Stockport Infirmary – and in those days, when the consultant came around, the consultants were like gods, and you didn't speak to them unless they spoke to you first. And the whole entourage was there – consultant, hospital matron, doctors – and they looked at me and walked by, and I said, 'Excuse me, I've got a question to ask.' And they spun out – 'What is it?' And I said, 'Are we having a party?' And they said, 'What for?' I said, 'Well, the hospital's ours today.' And there was a look of disapproval on one or two faces. And off they went. And the adults at the other end of the ward said, 'Hey, Alf, what's going on?'

I explained, this was a fantastic day, the hospital was ours. And I was very proud, in fact, to have been ill in the NHS on the day it all began.